To Dan
X. P.B.!!
Every blessing.

Stuart Bell

FLOWING STREAMS

STUART BRISCOE

FLOWING STREAMS

Journeys of a

Life Well Lived

ZONDERVAN

ZONDERVAN.com/
AUTHORTRACKER
follow your favorite authors

Flowing Streams
Copyright © 2008 by Stuart Briscoe

Requests for information should be addressed to:
Zondervan, *Grand Rapids, Michigan* 49530

Library of Congress Cataloging-in-Publication Data

Briscoe, D. Stuart.
        Flowing streams : journeys of a life well-lived / Stuart Briscoe.
            p. cm.
        Includes bibliographical references.
        ISBN 978-0-310-27719-4 (hardcover, jacketed)
        1. Briscoe, D. Stuart. 2. Clergy—Wisconsin—Brookfield—Biography. I. Title.
    BX4827.B65A3 2008
    280'.4092—dc22
    [B]
                                                                                2008009419

Published in association with the literary agency of Alive Communications, Inc., 7680 Goddard Street, Suite 200, Colorado Springs, CO 80920. www.alivecommunications.com

Interior design by Ben Fetterley

Printed in the United States of America

08 09 10 11 12 13 14 15 16 17 18 19 20 • 19 18 17 16 15 14 13 12 11 10 9 8 7 6 5 4 3 2 1

DEDICATED

to those who have gone before
with cherished memories,

to those who stand with me today
with greatest gratitude,

and to those coming on behind
with best wishes and every blessing.

CONTENTS

PREFACE

Let's face it: age sneaks up behind you in early years, catches up with you in midlife, and then rushes ahead in later life until it steps into eternity. So it is that with each succeeding birthday I ask myself and anyone else within earshot, "How can someone as young as I am be as old as this?" But as I was born in 1930 and have made relentless progress ever since at the rate of 365 days per annum, I have arrived at my late seventies. Some call this stage "the golden years" and others, less charitably, "borrowed time." But now, lest I continue to live in denial of my advancing — advanced? — years, I have been invited by my friends at Zondervan to write my "memoirs." This is as sure a sign of aging as the now frequently asked question, "What would you have done differently?"

I freely admit that until Zondervan suggested such a venture, the thought had never occurred to me. This was probably because I don't regard myself as being old enough for that sort of thing. And while I do occasionally lapse into "good old days" ways of thinking and have been known to use in conversations with my grandchildren such mind-numbing expressions as "when I was your age," my orientation is nevertheless more prospective than retrospective. Be that as it may, I received strong encouragement from my wife and family, and they at least promised to read my efforts. Also, various friends and colleagues assured me that over the years I had experienced a lot and learned a little, some of which might prove helpful and encouraging to other people in later days.

It is now more than forty years since I was introduced to the late Pat Zondervan in Grand Rapids. He said he liked the talk I had just given and wanted to publish it. I was astounded and agreed. He subsequently produced my first three books, and my writing career took off. So I am no stranger to the challenges and delights of authoring books, responding to editors, meeting deadlines, and receiving rejection slips, overstocks, and out-of-print notices. Oh yes, and royalties! But writing about myself posed a new set of problems. Who would read my memoirs? And why should they? How accurate would my recollections be since I had never kept a journal? Would I be able to portray others kindly and accurately? Would their memories coincide with mine where their lives and mine intersected? And considering that many of the people who form parts of my story live in troubled, difficult, and sometimes dangerous areas of the world, how could I tell their stories without making life more hazardous for them? Despite these concerns I set to work.

I knew immediately that I wanted to call the book *Flowing Streams*. Like many a river that has a number of sources, the imagery behind my story has at least three origins. First is a saying from the late Major Ian Thomas, who profoundly influenced my life over a sixty-year period. He constantly and consistently enunciated the principle "A flowing stream cuts its own channel." He stressed the unique capabilities of each individual to live a significant life and the need to allow and encourage the development of this life in the same way each river cuts its own course. So he gave oversight and freedom, he expressed confidence and trust, and he engendered devotion and loyalty. His view of humanity in this regard contributed hugely to my own development and to the way I have exercised my responsibilities in marriage, family, business, and ministry these many years.

Second, since boyhood I have loved Alfred Lord Tennyson's poem "The Brook." It tells the story of a tiny rivulet that has its birth among the wild, remote "haunts of coot and her[o]n." Burbling and gurgling, it makes its unheralded way down hillsides and through valleys until it winds quietly through towns and villages and pleasant meadows. Periods of calmness alternate with seasons of full flow until it "joins the brimming river," and as time passes it realises that "men may come and men may go, but I go on for ever." In my early days I resonated with the little river that like me started out in unknown territory among the moors and hills of northern England where coots and herons abounded. Surprisingly, however, my life began to course through towns and villages and big cities until I found myself joining the brimming river of the wide, wide world. Eventually it dawned on me that my life, like everyone else's, was intended to have eternal significance, and in the divine economy there was a sense in which it should "go on for ever." The format of this book follows this outline and frequently quotes from the poem.

Third, the words of the Lord Jesus on the great feast day in the temple of Jerusalem have thrilled my heart for many decades. "Whoever believes in me, as the Scripture has said, streams of living water will flow from within him." And John the evangelist helpfully added, "By this he meant the Spirit, whom those who believed in him were later to receive" (John 7:38–39).

This universal promise of outflowing life in the Spirit to all who believe first gripped me in my late teens. It still excites me, for it speaks to me of boundless depths of power and grace, of lively progress and impact springing from deep within and spilling out and over into the lives of those living within an ever-increasing sphere of influence. It brings to mind pictures of a life that brings encouragement and refreshment, fruitfulness and bounty attributable only to the mysterious work of the Holy Spirit. This image, this vision, has informed my life in business, in the military, and in athletic endeavours; as husband, father, and grandfather; and as evangelist, pastor, trainer, and encourager. For where we are at any given moment is relatively unimportant. What really matters is that our lives are like a river and the Spirit lives in us to provide the impetus and power, the grace and energy and life-transforming dynamic to make an eternal difference wherever we are whenever we are there. Like flowing streams.

Many of the people who appear in these pages are no longer with us, and my sincere hope is that I have reflected accurately on our interaction and portrayed them honourably. Others scattered around the world have been most helpful in corresponding and encouraging while at the same time confirming, correcting, and supplementing my recollections. Special thanks to Rick Christian and Beth Jusino at Alive Communications, whose personal friendship and encouragement are matched only by their skill and expertise in all matters related to Christian publishing. Their contribution to this book has been immeasurable.

Paul Engle at Zondervan is an old friend whom I met forty years ago on one of my first visits to the United States. We have stayed in touch ever since, and it was he who sowed the seed of an idea for the book and nurtured it through the publishing process with quiet encouragement. And of course the editorial skills and warm enthusiasm for the project of Christine Anderson and Jim Ruark have been greatly helpful and deeply appreciated. They have unerringly steered this old-timer through the tangled thickets of PC language and patiently led this transplanted Brit through the puzzling maze of American English and the real kind. The fact that they all understand and appreciate—tolerate?—British humour was a bonus and a blessing too.

I express my great gratitude for the help and support of ministry colleagues on every continent. And of course to my wife, Jill, our three children and their spouses, and our thirteen grandchildren, I once again say, "Thank you for allowing your flowing streams to intersect mine, producing a life rich and full of blessing. This life and its brief account would not have happened without you."

And thanks be to God for his unfailing mercies.

PART I

SPRINGS AND OTHER SOURCES

If life is like a river, formative influences are like springs. They seep imperceptibly, unmistakably into the earliest beginnings of life's stream — and never leave. Born as I was in the days of the Great Depression, I still watch my pennies. Raised as I was during the dark days of World War II, I learned devotion to duty by seeing it lived out by brave men and women. I was educated prematurely in the harsher side of life as sirens wailed and bombs rained down too close for comfort. And introduced as I was to a life of faith as the firstborn of a couple of devoted believers, it is no surprise that eternal, spiritual issues found their way into my thinking in early days. In addition to the influence of physical environment, social realities, home life, and parents, the streams of many remarkable people flowed into mine, carving out the channels, dredging the depths, and strengthening the banks. And there is little doubt in my mind that I am today in large part what they were in days gone by. Allow me to introduce them to you.

CHAPTER I

THE TIN CHAPEL

A flowing stream cuts its own channel.

—Major Ian Thomas

"You love prostitutes, don't you? I know you do. I can tell!"

She stood in the crowded church foyer, no more than five feet tall. Her fur-collared coat was a somber black, her matching hat firmly placed on gray hair, her umbrella grasped in kid-gloved hands. The elderly woman was probably in her early eighties, but she fixed me with a bright eye and spoke clearly in a voice that penetrated the after-church conversations happening around us.

She had approached me with determination, her umbrella pecking the hardwood floor, after I preached in her staid Baptist church on the outskirts of Belfast in Northern Ireland.

"You need to be our new pastor," she announced without preamble. Apparently my sermon had met with her approval, which I gathered was more than could be said for the existing resident pastor.

When I pointed out the reverend gentleman already in service to her community, she replied with force. "He's no good, and if you will come, we'll get rid of him!"

Embarrassed, I looked at the people surrounding me. They showed no signs of having heard her pronouncement, although given her volume, I assumed they were either all deaf or they chose to ignore her. I breathed a silent prayer for the unsuspecting incumbent.

"They don't like me in this church," she added, noting my glance around the room. To reinforce the point, she poked me in the ribs with her umbrella.

"I'm sure they love you," I responded guardedly, wincing.

"No they don't." She dug the umbrella into me again to reinforce her point. "You see, I work among the prostitutes in this town. Dear girls. I bring them to church, and these stuffy people don't like it. If the girls sit in the same pew, they move away. But I bring them anyway, and they don't like that either. Or me!" Her pale, creased face developed a flush of pink.

I hurriedly revised my initial evaluation of the woman, who reminded me of a feisty blackbird somehow. This was an extraordinary woman.

She went on. "I know you wouldn't be like that. You love prostitutes, don't you? I know you do. I can tell!"

Not wishing to go down that road, I didn't answer.

The umbrella was once again forcefully applied, and she said, "Don't you see? We need a pastor who understands that there's a world to reach. We need someone to shake us out of our complacency. Our lethargy. Sitting here in our pews, looking down our noses at other people. You understand that, don't you? You must come and be our pastor. I'll see that we get rid of the one we've got if you'll come!"

The church foyer had emptied rapidly. We were left alone, except for the church warden—or whatever Baptists call the man who holds the keys and switches off the lights. The gentleman stood by the door, discreetly rattling his keys to remind us that his lunch was ready for him and that he was ready for his lunch. It was time to go.

The conversation had to end, but I had no idea how to beat a dignified retreat. So I said formally, "I'm terribly sorry, but I really cannot entertain the possibility of being your pastor, and as I have another appointment, I must reluctantly bid you farewell." I hoped the extra-polite and slightly anachronistic tone would help me withdraw with grace and avoid any further ministrations from the umbrella.

Instead, I could see that the woman was startled. Seeking to soften the moment, I added, "By the way, you didn't tell me your name." I genuinely wanted to know; I liked this little woman. Tact was clearly not her forte, church politics obviously not her calling. But the vision in her eyes, the fire in her heart, and the determination with which she approached life at an age when most of her contemporaries, if not dead, were well on their way to glory or elsewhere appealed to me immensely.

She replied, "My name is Miss Stuart Watt."

I forgot the rattling keys. "Are you Miss Eva Stuart Watt?"

"No," she replied, "I'm dear Eva's sister. Eva passed away."

"Are you the sister who traveled with Eva through the Belgian Congo?"

"Oh yes," she replied, her eyes taking on a faraway look. Her mind was back in the days of pioneer jungle missionary activity, when she and her sister—in fact, the entire Stuart Watt family—had reached the pygmies of the equatorial jungle with the gospel. "Oh yes. They were wonderful days. But how did you know about my sister and me?"

"Let me tell you a story." I tried to ignore the rattling keys and the impatient bearer of them, since my own heart was beating loudly enough to drown him out. "I heard about a man who was reading a book titled *In the Heart of Savagedom*, which tells the story of you and your sister, Eva Stuart Watt."

"Yes," she interrupted eagerly. "It tells some of the stories of our ministry in the Congo."

"This man," I went on, "was reading the book aloud to his wife, who was about to deliver their firstborn child. He was so excited about your story and so moved by your courage and devotion that he said to his wife, 'If this baby is a boy, his name is Stuart.' Apparently it never occurred to him that the baby might turn out to be female, deserving to be named Eva."

"How nice," she replied politely but with little enthusiasm.

I explained further. "I was that baby. My name is Stuart. My father named me after you and your sister—the Stuart Watt family."

It took a moment to register, but then she positively shouted, "Then you'll have to be our pastor, won't you?"

The rattling keys grew silent. The venerable oak panels of the foyer absorbed the tiny woman's words. Her face shone. The lion heart in the blackbird body beat a little faster. She knew. In her mind I was the man of the hour.

But not in my mind.

Reluctantly, I left the woman still adamantly convinced of my calling. I stepped outside the church and into the biting Belfast wind blowing off the grey waters of the ocean. The bracing air was familiar, the nose-numbing cold perfectly normal.

I had been born on the other side of this Irish Sea in a small town called Millom, Cumberland, in the north of England. John Wesley described the town as "a habitation of thieves and robbers" and advised travelers to avoid it. But my newlywed parents, Stanley and Mary, ignored the advice if they were aware of it, bought a small grocery business, and moved to Millom in the late 1920s, in the Depression years. It was here that my father, struggling in his first business venture and worried about his pregnant wife, came across a tattered copy of *In the Heart of Savagedom*, read it, and shared it with my mother. Her heart, like his, was touched, and I was named Stuart in admiration of Eva Stuart Watt and her disconsolate sister I had just left in the church.

My parents were devoted disciples of Jesus. They believed there was a world to win for Christ, and they never gave up trying, though their influence did not stray much farther than the promontory on which Millom stood. But their vision was much greater. "Stuart" to them spoke of missions and jungles and people without God. In their minds my name was a reminder that courage was needed, that commitment was necessary, that sacrifice was normative, that service was lifestyle, and that life was earnest. And they passed on that vision to me in a name.

"What's in a name?" Shakespeare famously asked.

I reply, "More than I can ever say!"

I, prenamed and, I'm told, eagerly awaited, made my entrance into the world one cold November afternoon in 1930. It was Armistice Day, the annual day of remembrance of those who had died in World War I. A parade of veterans marched past our house as I made my entrance into the world. The town band was playing a rousing tune to welcome me, my mother used to say.

The march was jaunty, but England was in the depths of a Depression. We were still recovering from the madness of World War I, and war clouds were already gathering again over Europe. I was born in a dark, dangerous place — perhaps not too unlike the world today. But I was born to godly parents, and that made all the difference.

The city of Millom had one ugly landmark — the slag heaps from the ironworks that provided most of the town's jobs — and one beautiful point — St. George's Anglican Church, which stood on a minor hill in the center of the town. It boasted a slender spire that pointed heavenward and a peal of bells that merrily — and unevenly — summoned the faithful to prayer. A sweeping driveway led from Millom's Victorian market square through imposing gates. Mature beeches, sycamores, and elms supervised the weekly gathering of people and prevented me from getting a better look at the heavy church doors. Sunday by Sunday, during my intensely impressionable "growing up" years, I walked past the church gate with my family, looking longingly at the driveway leading to I-knew-not-what. I only knew that we didn't go there, and that alone made it unbearably attractive to my boyish heart. What secrets did the people who went there know? What mysterious rites were performed under that imposing spire? The people walking up the driveway looked ordinary enough, but they weren't carrying Bibles as we were, and the women were not wearing hats as they were supposed to.

I never went to St. George's, because my parents belonged to what everybody called the Tin Chapel. It wasn't a "proper" church, because it boasted no spire, sounded no bells, and stood on a small unkempt piece of ground without benefit of imposing driveway. It was made of tin — or rather, corrugated iron painted a faded green — and it smelled of dust and damp and was downright depressing. That was the Tin Chapel.

In the minds of the few in town who acknowledged it, the Tin Chapel was a little odd, and the people who went there were regarded as equally odd. The "flock" who gathered in the Tin Chapel did not believe in professional ministers or pastors, and so they were led by my father, a grocer by trade. He was a good man of profound convictions that revealed themselves in deep devotion, energetic involvement, and a tendency to be rigid and inflexible. He knew what he believed, and he stuck with it.

Unfortunately, I was stuck, too, and I wanted out. I didn't want to be odd. I wanted to go to a proper church. And yet deep down, I respected his faith—a faith I had embraced and made my own with childlike trust and some childish notions. I recognised, and admired, my father's faithfulness—how he would load up a small tent on his grocer's bicycle, ride to a nearby village, and hold evangelistic meetings. Very few people came, but I went along and gave out the hymnbooks, sat on the front row, and mingled my boyish soprano with his loud tenor in a desperate attempt to get the handful of curious villagers to sing. I listened as well as I could to the familiar stories he told in a forceful voice. People sat in stolid silence and left without saying a word. Occasionally they offered a limp handshake with averted gaze while failing to respond to my dad's eager, "Do please come again." But he kept at it.

On occasion a visiting preacher would come to the Tin Chapel and suggest that we hold an "open-air meeting." The words sent a chill through my whole being, because I knew it meant that we—the little flock—would stand in a circle outside a pub and sing a couple of hymns without the benefit of musical instruments, and then the visiting preacher and my father would shout—preach—as loudly as possible at the closed pub door.

On one occasion a man hurrying into the pub paused briefly to hear us sing:

Are you washed in the blood?
In the soul cleansing blood of the Lamb?
Are your garments spotless, are they white as snow ...

He retorted, "Can't you see I'm wearing my blue suit? Of course it isn't as white as snow! Are you blind or stupid?" And with a derisive wave, he disappeared, laughing, into the pub. I wished I, too, could disappear. Anywhere would do. I was tall for my age, but on these occasions I would have settled, if not for invisibility, certainly for something less noticeable. My slicked-back hair and my well-pressed suit and carefully knotted tie—we "dressed up" in those days for church; in fact, we talked about our "Sunday best"—made me even more conspicuous among my contemporaries who, when they saw me standing in our little circle, made no attempt to hide their amusement while I made unavailing attempts to cover my embarrassment.

So I learned the hard way about belief, conviction, faithfulness, standing alone, service, and hard work. I knew these were admirable qualities—however, I wasn't interested in embracing them just yet. Years later I read a quote from Augustine, the bishop of Hippo, who confessed, "Give me chastity—and constancy—but not yet." Never would I think of myself and Augustine in the same sentence, but I entertained similar sentiments. I knew the way I ought to go, but I was reluctant to go there yet.

My shame was compounded by the apostle Paul's statement, "I am not ashamed of the gospel," and I became ashamed of being ashamed. My faith was real, but there was little joy in it.

So I went to the Tin Chapel without enthusiasm, and I went to school with a similarly deficient attitude. Each afternoon I delivered groceries on a bicycle with a strong metal carrier over the front wheel. Occasionally I received a tip, frequently a "Thank you, Stuart." And whenever I could, I roamed the hills—fells, we called them—where coots and herons nested and blueberries grew in profusion. I was given remarkable freedom to roam and explore a region ideally suited to inquisitive, energetic boys—a blessing and privilege I did not always acknowledge or appreciate.

My grandfather, David Henry Wardle, was my hero. I barely knew him as a child, but I heard stories that made him seem very close. On one occasion he was summoned to his father's study, where he found not only his irate father but an equally irate neighbour. The neighbour accused young David Henry of throwing a brick through his window. My grandfather vehemently denied the charge, but as the manner was in those days, his father believed the neighbour and told David Henry he would be punished twice—once for the misdemeanor and once for lying about it. The boy protested but was warned to say no more. His father ceremoniously removed his belt, and to the satisfaction of the neighbour and the discomfort of the boy, administered the punishment. When it was over, David Henry again said, "Father, I told you I didn't do it." He was dismissed, and he immediately went to the neighbour's house, selected a brick, and threw it through the window. He assumed, I suppose, that having been punished for what he had not done, he might as well enjoy doing it belatedly. David Henry was my hero, I think, because I never would have dared to do such a thing.

Our sleepy small-town life ended in my tenth year when the Germans invaded Europe. Hundreds of young men from around the empire—the British still had one in those days—were sent to a nearby Royal Air Force station to be trained as pilots and navigators. From Rhodesia, South Africa, New Zealand, Australia, Canada, and India they came. Dozens were believers, and they found their way to our house and the Tin Chapel.

Almost overnight the little assembly was not so little or so old or so dispiritingly inward-looking. I walked past St. George's on Sunday mornings with a group of young men in smart uniforms, carrying Bibles just like me. The locals began to look at us with incredulity rather than amusement. Kids at school gathered around, not to kid me about the Tin Chapel, but to ask about the airmen. Who were they? How did I know them? Why did they come to my house? And why did they go to the Tin Chapel?

Suddenly the center of attention, I stuck out my chest and told them what I had learned from my new heroes about New Zealand sheep farms and Canadian prairies and Rhodesian copper mines and South African gold and Australian beaches. I bragged on the exploits of those who, their training completed, joined Bomber Command and flew Lancasters and Halifaxes over Germany, those who had won medals and those who lost their lives.

But beyond the hero worship, I discovered normal young men from around the world who thought my parents were wonderful, who loved my home as a safe haven, and who thought the Tin Chapel was a sanctuary. Not only that, most of them played rugby.

My dad dismissed rugby in particular and sports in general as "worldliness." When I developed into one of the better players on my school team, I came home after bruising games to face hearty disapproval at best and verbal condemnation at worst. But the airmen influenced my dad, forcing him to revise his understanding of "worldliness." Some of the soldiers were—whisper it softly—Anglicans and Methodists, yet they were real believers! It was an eye-opening discovery for me as a child, and I daresay for my father as an adult.

The airmen became my friends and confidants. I shared my fears and frustrations and asked far too many questions. They, in turn, taught me it was okay to ask questions and normal to worry about what friends think. These grown men had resisted and even resented some of the disciplines imposed upon them in their adolescence. They showed me a dimension of spiritual life that refused to major on what we couldn't and didn't do and instead introduced me to loud laughter, practical joking, and unabashed talking about faith—a joie de vivre I had never seen before—all in the face of impending danger and possible untimely death in a blazing crash in enemy territory. These young men left home and country to come to the aid of the Old Country in her hour of deep need—never knowing they were really coming to aid a young British boy, as well.

During the war, my mother ran the grocery by herself, as my father had been drafted into the National Fire Service. He was a "noncombatant" as a registered conscientious objector, but he risked his life every night during the air raids, when the first wave of bombers dropped incendiary bombs that would start fires and light the targets for the second bombing wave. The firemen would rush in to douse the flames, knowing they were right in the bull's-eye of the bombardiers above. In other parts of the city, noncombatants were stationed on searchlight duty—they didn't carry arms, but they could aim the lights for those who did. Unfortunately, the piercing rays made inviting targets for bombers, and German rear gunners could aim with devastating accuracy. Searchlight men were sitting ducks.

My mother cared for us two boys — my brother Bernard was four years younger — and for the dozens of young men from around the world who found a home away from home in our kitchen. She fed them — I don't know how, for food was strictly rationed. She listened to them, advised them, prayed for them, shared their heartaches, and corresponded with their parents, wives, and sweethearts back home.

My mother came to faith in her late teens. She was a beautiful young woman who was deeply discouraged because she wanted to train as a nurse, but her Victorian father told her "a daughter's place is in the kitchen helping her mother." A wise church elder put the matter into perspective for her, showing her that Scripture tells us, "Whatsoever ye do, do it heartily, as to the Lord, and not unto men" (Colossians 3:23 KJV). So she decided that even if all she could do was clean shoes, she would clean them as if Jesus was going to wear them. Everything was done "as unto the Lord." Half measures were not tolerated, halfheartedness was anathema. People today would probably call my mother "driven" — a not totally complimentary designation. I think she was driven — by a magnificent obsession — and I mean that as an intentional heartfelt compliment.

Among the air force blue there was one khaki army uniform in our home. Captain H. S. May, a career soldier in the Royal Artillery, wore slacks pressed with knife-sharp creases, boots, and a Sam Browne belt polished to high intensity. Unlike the airmen who, on completing their training, moved on to fly with Bomber Command, Captain May was permanently stationed in our neighbourhood. He became a fixture in our home and a stanchion in my life.

His regular greeting was, "What's your best thought today, Stuart, my boy?" Intimidating though the question was at first, I began to realise he was being perfectly natural; he had a lot of "best thoughts," and thought everybody else should have them too. The captain was genuinely interested in me and wanted to know what I was thinking. He listened intently to my fumbling responses, asked leading questions, explored with me my ideas, and encouraged me to think, to speak, and to find my feet in a dangerous world.

One night, after the heart-stopping wail of the air-raid siren warned that the Luftwaffe was on its way to the nearby shipyards again, he took me to the third story of our home. Incendiary bombs showered down, and the night sky blazed with the light of a hundred fires. We knew what to expect next — a second wave of bombers dropping high explosives on the lighted target, a huge aircraft carrier being built for the Royal Navy and nearing completion. The Luftwaffe knew it was there and were intent on sinking it in the shipyard. It wasn't the first time they had come bombing. Over the course of the war, the shipyard a few miles from my house produced three aircraft carriers—the *Indomitable*, the *Illustrious*, and the *Indefatigable*. Each ship was repeatedly targeted while it was being built; none of the ships was ever hit, but the town was flattened.

In the darkness we watched the probing beams of the searchlights, the tracer shells shooting skyward like strings of burning sausages and the bright bursts of shells exploding in the night sky. Occasionally the sky was lit by a midair explosion of a direct hit on a circling Junker or a Heinkel, and we watched as the plane disintegrated into wreckage that cartwheeled and corkscrewed in a fiery spiral into the inferno below. The flash of exploding bombs was followed seconds later by the thump of the explosion, the rattling of the windows, and the shaking of the building. And the most unnerving sound in the midst of such chaos was the relentless, incongruous, dissonant chiming of our grandfather clock agitated by the constant explosive tremors.

My artillery-veteran guardian was unperturbed as we stood in the darkness. He took out his watch and timed the interval between flash and thump, explaining how light travels quicker than sound and showing me how to work out the exact distance between where the bombs were landing and where we were standing. Then with a smile he reminded me of safety in the midst of danger—a lesson he reinforced by pointing to the text my mother had hung on the wall: "Thou wilt keep him in perfect peace, whose mind is stayed on thee" (Isaiah 26:3 KJV).

The captain had the happy knack of being "at peace" with his Lord, himself, his life, his circumstances, and his neighbours—all the time. Boys need heroes—and this army captain was certainly mine. My day brightened when he entered the room, and I was sad whenever he left. He brought what the apostle Paul, as I learned later, called "the aroma of Christ."

These were the earliest source waters for my stream—the earliest influences on my life.

CHAPTER 2

TRIBUTARIES

I come from haunts of coot and hern,
I make a sudden sally,
And sparkle out among the fern
To bicker down a valley.

—Alfred Lord Tennyson, "The Brook"

Like Tennyson's "brook," my life for a number of years did little more than "bicker down a valley," but then the pace increased rapidly. In those far-off days, the thirties and forties, England had an iniquitous educational system that required eleven-year-olds to spend a single Saturday morning taking an examination imaginatively named "The 11 Plus Exam." The significance of this pressure-packed exercise was that it determined the professional future of the young people involved. If you passed, you gained entrance to a school designed to prepare you for university and the professions. If you failed, you were destined to attend school until you were sixteen and then find a job somewhere. My parents, aware of this, decided I should take the examination "for practice" when I was ten years of age, which I obediently did. I also did what was not intended—I passed!

At the tender age of ten, proudly and self-consciously clad in my green blazer and matching cap with silver piping and emblazoned with M.S.S., I trudged along with the eleven-year-olds to the imposing buildings of the Millom Secondary School. To my deep shame, they all wore long pants, but my mother, who "liked boys with big knees," insisted I wear short pants, presumably to show off my mammoth joints, which served only to compound my feelings of overwhelming insecurity. Finding my way to a large classroom full of boisterous youngsters, I slunk hastily into a corner seat on the back row as far from the action as possible. Then the headmaster, who bore a remarkable likeness to Joseph Stalin, marched into the room, welcomed us, and announced that the school had admitted three too many students. I was heartily relieved to hear that news and assumed I would be allowed to return to the familiar surroundings of my little junior school. But the headmaster went on, "So we decided to take the top three students from the county and place them in the 2nd Form." To my amazement and horror, I was one of the three, and so I dragged my ten-year-old body into a class full of seemingly huge twelve-year-olds and began the rocky journey of my secondary education.

Understandably, I was totally intimidated by my school environment. The situation was exacerbated when a classmate discovered that I attended the Tin Chapel, which they all recognised as a place frequented by people who were not "Church of England" and therefore weird. At the same time, my teacher asked me in front of the class, "Briscoe, what is a nonconformist? You should know."

As I had no idea, I said so. She then asked, "Well, what are you?"

Lamely, I responded, "I don't know," much to the collective amusement of my classmates, all of whom knew they were "C of E," which in most cases meant only that they were regular attendees every Easter and Christmas.

Sensing what was coming next, I squirmed in my seat as she asked, "Don't you attend the Tin Chapel?" I admitted that I did, and she triumphantly said, "You're a member of the Brethren then, aren't you?"

Strictly speaking, I was not a member, as the Brethren did not believe in membership; and anyway, I had not arrived at the ill-defined age when I could "break bread," but wild horses would not have dragged that out of me at that moment, so I answered in the affirmative.

"Then you are a nonconformist," she stated. This was news to me and a source of untold delight to the whole class who then did what twelve- and thirteen-year-olds do best — they held me up to ridicule for weeks to come. As you can imagine, this did nothing for my "self-image" — something I had never heard of; in fact, I didn't know I had one until I came to America many years later.

When I poured out my woes to my father at home that evening, he said, "Oh yes. That teacher is a difficult lady. She used to shop here, but she owes me a lot of money, and I have refused to serve her until she starts to pay off her debts." That didn't help one little bit. It seemed to me she "had it in for me" for no fault of my own. I concluded that life was not fair.

Looking back on those days, I am surprised my young faith was not shaken. I had no difficulty saying, if challenged, that I was a Christian, but I suffered intense embarrassment because, like most kids of that age, I hated the thought of being considered different. In the minds of my schoolmates, people who didn't go to the cinema, didn't play sports, didn't cuss, didn't drink or smoke, and didn't go to St. George's with its lovely spire were weird by definition.

I do, however, have fond memories of three of my teachers, unknowing tributaries all, and I have no doubt that the fact they taught my favorite subjects was not a coincidence. They poured into me freshness and delight. Miss Hobson was a red-faced, rotund, single woman who instilled in me a love for the English language. I was her only pupil during my final year in school, so I spent many tutorial-like sessions with her, ploughing through Chaucer, Wordsworth, and Shakespeare. She derived great delight in Chaucer's more ribald passages. "He really is rather naughty, isn't he?" she would say, shaking with laughter as I curled up with embarrassment. She told me on one occasion, "Briscoe, I do not like your writing style." But then with her customary chuckle and wobbling chins, she added, "But then the only other student I said that to was Norman Nicholson, and he now is the Lakeland poet, so you're in good company!"

"Spike" Siddle was a mild-mannered man with a dome of a bald head over which he carefully draped six surviving hairs that were clearly on the endangered species list. He taught me geography, a love for maps, and a fascination with the great rivers of the world and the lands through which they flowed and to which they brought life. Little did I—or he—know that in years to come I would either stand on the banks or sail on the waters of the Amazon, the Mississippi, the Rhine, the Danube, the Zambezi, the Nile, the Yangtze, the Ganges, the Mekong, and dozens of others.

And then there was a mysterious little man who tried to teach us music. Rumours circulated as soon as he arrived at our school. Surprising rumours. The story went around the classrooms like wildfire that our new music teacher was an ex-con—a former bank manager who misappropriated funds, went to jail, and came out and built a beautiful house overlooking the bank. Be that as it may, he taught me to sing and persuaded me to overcome chronic shyness enough to lead the whole school in singing Edward Elgar's rousing arrangement of old John O'Gaunt's dying words of praise for his beloved England:

> This royal throne of kings, this sceptr'd isle,
> This earth of majesty, this seat of Mars,
> This other Eden, demi paradise
> This fortress built by Nature for herself
> Against infection and the hand of war,
> This happy breed of men, this little world,
> This precious stone set in the silver sea . . .
> This blessed plot, this earth, this realm, this England.

> — *Richard II* 2.1.43 – 53

If the words sound a little over the top to modern ears, please remember that I was still a boy soprano and England was still at war with the threat of an unthinkable Nazi invasion of our "fortress built by Nature for herself."

The more I look back on my school days, the more I agree with whomever it was who said that education is a wonderful thing, but it's a shame to waste it on young people. Nevertheless, these three instructors managed to impart to me a love for words, a fascination for the world and its people, and a deep appreciation for music—all of which would figure largely in the life that was unfolding before me.

I survived the ups and downs of my school days, always the youngest in the class, always unsure, shy, and insecure. After six years I graduated with university entrance qualifications intact but with something less than affirmation from the headmaster, who wrote, "The youngest person ever to graduate from this school. No telling what he could have accomplished if he had worked!" I'm afraid the gentleman in question and I had not enjoyed the warmest of relations. No doubt the fact that I was two years ahead of my peers—through no fault of my own—and two years behind my class-mates and emotionally and socially immature, coupled with the fact that the headmaster was intensely disliked by all (he was eventually fired), led to my eager anticipation of the day when I could bid him a not-at-all-fond farewell. And he, no doubt, entertained similar sentiments toward me. But it was not to be, because I could not enter university for two more years, and in any case, my parents were not sure they wanted me to attend such a "worldly" place at any age and certainly not at sixteen.

So I went cap in hand to talk to "Old Joe"—the Stalin-look-alike headmaster—and asked him what I should do. He replied without any great enthusiasm that I had failed Latin "ignominiously" and should there-fore spend two years studying what I regarded as a dead language and which for six years had imposed a morbidly deadening effect on my brain. The thought filled me with dread, but I apparently had no alternative, so I returned reluctantly to reading the likes of "*Dum spiro spero*," which being interpreted means, "While I breathe I hope." But while I was breathing, I was facing the next two years with little hope. The one bright spot was rugby, which I played with some success, great joy, many bruises from opponents, and constant frowns from my parents.

It was during this potentially sterile period that yet another powerful influence flowed into my life with surprising vigor. Harry Green was his name. He was a large man with a florid face, a loud voice, an irrepressible enthusiasm for life, a highly developed sense of humour, and a vibrant faith life. He was also a high-ranking official with the District Bank. His wife, Dorothy, who handled this larger-than-life gentleman with great ease and managed a family of boisterous kids with considerable élan, welcomed me into their family, and in short order the Greens won my heart. Harry loved to tease his wife, but she was totally unfazed. On one occasion, after listening to him "grumbling" about something, she retorted, "Harry Green, you had the entire world to choose from, and you chose me. Now please be satisfied and be quiet!" Harry acknowledged defeat with a grin and changed the subject.

Harry Green took his natural enthusiasm to work with him every day and in no time at all painted such an attractive picture of banking as a career that I developed a keen interest in abandoning my stalled school experience and embarking on what I assumed would be my life's work. He explained to me that his position as a bank official in either a small town or a large city gave him a network of acquaintances and associates within which he could move freely as a convinced Christian, not preaching and posturing, but living vibrantly, winsomely, and convincingly. He reminded me, "God needs his men in the business world, Stuart, and I see you doing well there." So I stayed at school until the rugby season ended and then announced that I was forgetting about university and would enter the service of the District Bank. I applied, was accepted (Harry Green helped!), and was promptly transferred to another town. And so at seventeen I left home.

In the ancient market town of Kendal, reputedly the hometown of Catherine Parr, the only wife of Henry VIII to avoid a sticky end, I quickly settled into a busy routine of learning banking, initially by making tea. The manager, Mr. Jordan, was a pleasant, fussy little man who scuttled about the office flourishing a document and calling out, "Mr.... Er ... Mr.... Er ... Mr.... Er ... Mr.... Er," until he arrived safely at the desk of the person whose name he could not remember. The accountant, or second in command, and the person with whom the whole staff of twenty had to do, was a former major in the Royal Marines who demanded discipline and accuracy in everything we did. He ran a tight ship, possessed a short fuse, and was never in a mood to suffer fools gladly. Even senior men like Johnny Snowball and Reggie Dent trod very lightly around Cyril Brownlow.

One man who seemed perfectly at ease in all circumstances when others were decidedly uncomfortable—especially in the tense atmosphere in the office—was Bill Harrison. Bill had served as a rear gunner in Lancaster bombers with the Royal Air Force. He and his kind were known as "Tail End Charlies" and in that role had a life expectancy close to zero. He was a quiet, modest man, unassuming and kind—and a hero who had been awarded the Distinguished Flying Cross for his exploits over Nazi Germany. He was the sort of man you would want to have with you in a tight corner. He quickly became my big brother at work and took me aside to explain that some of the older men in the office were simply putting in time waiting for retirement and had been for many years. They were unchallenged, bored, and dissatisfied with their lot, as promotions had passed them by and the only thing they had to look forward to was walking away, drawing their pension, and growing roses. "You don't want that to happen to you," he said, "so this is what you need to do. You should volunteer to study for your associate membership of the Institute of Bankers. The bank will not help you with time off to study, but you'll finish up like those men if you don't work hard and study." He then made enquiries for me, and before a couple of weeks had elapsed, I was busy studying economics, foreign trade, accountancy, and other related subjects.

Ideally, I should have attended a local night school, but no suitable courses were being offered. The other alternative was to enroll in a correspondence course, which I did. The course required me to begin by filling out and submitting the first lesson. It turned out to be the last lesson as well. On reflection, I decided that doing the course that way was a waste of time, so I simply bought the textbooks and studied on my own. Bill Harrison unwittingly played a major role in my life, because he pushed me into a situation in which I had to do what school had never persuaded me to do—learn how to learn! Not long ago I read a quote from a famous person whose name I've forgotten: "An educated person is someone who has learned how to learn and never stopped learning." It was beginning to look as if I might get an education.

And I was about to learn how to learn a whole lot more than financial theory.

It happened like this. My parents were not at all happy that their immature seventeen-year-old was setting out in the big cold world. So they arranged for me to live with their acquaintances Neil and Annie Taylor who attended the local Brethren assembly—which I was delighted to discover did not meet in a tin chapel. I was even more delighted to find there were young people my age in the congregation, and I gladly joined in their activities. One night shortly after I arrived in Kendal, I was standing at the rear of the church after a youth meeting when a man named John Ward, whom I had never met, came up to me and asked, "How old are you?"

"Seventeen," I answered timidly.

"Ah, then it's time you were preaching!" he replied to my amazement.

I hastily remonstrated, "I can't preach."

But he quickly queried, "Have you ever tried?"

When I mumbled an embarrassed negative, he quickly added, "Then how do you know you can't do it?"

Incidentally, this question has stayed with me over the years—and I have asked it a thousand times, for I believe the world in general and the church in particular is filled with people who are happily convinced that they cannot do what they have never attempted. But more on that later.

To my horror, the persistent Mr. Ward then said, "You will preach next Tuesday to the youth group, and your subject is the church at Ephesus."

Now, you need to know that while I had sat in church for endless hours throughout my childhood and adolescence, I was, at that juncture, not aware that there was a church in Ephesus. And even if I had been aware of it, I doubt very much if its existence would have riveted my attention for more than a couple of minutes. So, for no other reason than I had a deep desire to hide my ignorance of the subject, I set about studying the church at Ephesus.

On the appointed day I stood before a small group of my peers, all of whom were looking at me with mingled awe and amusement. I took a deep breath to quiet my pounding heart, and when that failed, I buried my nose in my notes and launched into my first point. I had heard enough preaching, mainly from my father, to know that for some reason I needed three points, and I was pleased that I had found three. Unfortunately, however, the first time I dared to look at the clock, I discovered that my time had elapsed and two further points were staring at me from my notes waiting to be expounded. I know what I intended to say, but sadly I blurted out, "I'm terribly sorry, but I don't know how to stop." Whereupon a kindly gentleman who had crashed the youth meeting shouted from the back row, "Just shut up and sit down!" which I promptly did, assuming that my preaching career had come to an abrupt and merciful end.

I was wrong, however. The persistent Mr. Ward told me to return the following week to finish my talk on the church at Ephesus. Then, without consulting me, he enrolled me as a lay preacher on the Methodist circuit. This meant that I was required to mount my bicycle on Sunday afternoons, ride out to small Methodist chapels, and conduct services for the three or four stalwarts. Before I got to them, these admirable people had already milked their cows and fed their chickens, cooked and consumed a huge Sunday lunch, squeezed themselves into the Sunday suits in which they had been married many moons previously, and made their way to their familiar pews in their overheated places of worship. It was in those chapels that I first learned how to keep people awake while preaching a message. They were hardy, godly folks who encouraged me in my fumbling efforts by interspersing my remarks with loud shouts of "Amen," "Tha's right lad. You tell 'em." So I did!

I had been told, "Preaching is not complicated. You study your Bible, and then you tell people what it says and what it means. If you're any good at it, more and more people will ask you to do it, and if they do and you're free, the answer is yes." So I did as I was told, and soon I was driven not only to my textbooks on banking and foreign trade but to my Bible and commentaries and theological tomes. I discovered two things. One, I loved studying biblical truth more than economics; and two, I was discovering a gift I didn't know I had. My little brook was beginning to cut a channel. As gifting was coming to the surface, I was learning more about who I was and accordingly was discovering what I was created and redeemed to be. My life was taking shape. But I knew none of this at the time.

My busy life was rudely interrupted one day when I received a letter from the British government—a summons to report for military duty. After exhaustive physical tests, I was pronounced A1—I think that was rather good—and I was asked which service I would like to join. To my shame, I must admit that I had no idea, but I saw a young man resplendent in a magnificent uniform, and I volunteered to join whatever he was in. And that's how I became a Royal Marine!

Captain May, my childhood friend and hero, was delighted to hear that I was about to join the British armed forces; my mother was less enthusiastic. When she enquired about the marines, I admitted I knew very little about them, but I thought one started as a sub-marine and worked one's way up. That did not help at all. But the captain wished to pursue the subject, and he told me, "You must nail your colours to the mast. Right away!" As I had never heard the expression before, he explained that in the old days when a ship of the Royal Navy sailed into battle, the colours of the sovereign were hoisted to the top of the mast and remained there throughout the conflict unless they were defeated or surrendered. Then, of course, the colours were replaced either with the white flag of surrender or the colours of the conquering sovereign. But with that in mind, some naval captains would order the colours to be nailed to the mast so that defeat and surrender were shown to be out of the question; they would rather "go down with all flags flying."

"You must show your fellow marines right away whose you are and whom you serve, Stuart," my military hero explained forcefully. Too forcefully for my liking.

"Did you do that?" I asked timidly.

"Yes, I did," he replied. "The first night in the barrack room I knelt by my bed and prayed."

"What happened?" I ventured.

"They threw boots at me," he replied casually, as if this were an everyday occurrence.

"What did you do?" I queried, hardly daring to ask.

Looking at me as if the answer was so obvious he was surprised I should ask, he replied, "I cleaned them and returned them, of course!"

As far as I can remember, we didn't have mentors in those days. At least we didn't call them that, and I have no recollection of anyone ever saying to me that I needed a mentor, nor did it ever occur to me that I should ask for one. But without knowing that was what you called it, I was being molded, fashioned, discipled, spiritually formed, developed by the simple expedient of being in the company of godly men who loved the Lord and his church and wanted me to share that love too. They showed me how to do it by doing it before me and with me. It was perfectly normal and natural. There was nothing stereotyped or programmed. It was entirely un-self-conscious.

My parents and the young airmen never would have paraphrased the apostle Paul and said, "Follow me as I follow Christ." That would have sounded far too arrogant and self-serving in their ears. But they didn't need to. I saw enough in them to know the rightness of who they were, and although I struggled with some of the details, I wanted that kind of rightness in my life. Harry Green, who launched my banking career, would have been highly amused if I had called him a "mentor," but his life was contagious, his example compelling. Bill Harrison, who encouraged me to study at the Institute of Bankers, attended church with his family and said little about spiritual issues, but his impact on me was profound. He didn't need to say anything.

Life in the marines was a physical, moral, and spiritual testing ground. Playing rugby had introduced me to the world of hard knocks but had hardly prepared me for training at commando school. Some of it was brutal, all of it was stretching, but as our physical fitness levels increased, I learned much about endurance, perseverance, and the physiological and mental reserves that lie within, hidden and unused for most of our lives. I learned the difference between being tired and being exhausted and forever afterward knew how to differentiate between being mildly inconvenienced and being utterly at wits' end.

Morally, I was presented with opportunities to "go wrong" that previously had not only been unknown to me; most of them had in my case been unheard of. Many aspects of the lifestyle of my fellow marines were profane and perverse, and when they wanted me to join them, I was confronted with choices that were unavoidable and unmistakable. Wanting, like most young people, to be liked and accepted, I was presented for the first time with black-and-white options that required a decision to be either popular or faithful. At this point, Captain May came unbidden to the rescue. "Nail your colours to the mast, Stuart," resounded loud and clear in the echo chamber of memory, and by God's grace I did. It meant many lonely hours.

My rugby team, like most rugby teams, could not pass a pub on the way home from a game, so I sat in the bus alone for many hours, often nursing injuries. My parents, of course, thought I had no business being on the team, or on that bus, but I begged to differ, and as a result, I learned firsthand what it means to be "in the world" but not "of it." But more than anything, I learned from these tough men that despite their wayward ways, they occasionally demonstrated readily recognisable qualities that spoke of another side to their nature. This led me to a lot of heart searching on the enigma that is humanity. How could men who became violent and out of control in a heartbeat be capable of acts of kindness and generosity a few minutes later? And how could these men who thought nothing of ripping on me for my Christianity demonstrate unequivocally that, if push came to shove, they would put their lives on the line for me? How can men be so kind and cruel, so creative and so destructive, so grudging and so generous?

As time went by, these men—some of whom my parents would not have welcomed in our home—actually became my friends. Usually during a hangover, they would ask me about my lifestyle and my Christianity and occasionally wistfully talk about how they had gone to Sunday school for a year or two when they were kids. One of them even recited, "Consider the lilies of the field, how they grow; they toil not, neither do they spin. And yet I say unto you, That even Solomon in all his glory was not arrayed like one of these" (Matthew 6:28–29 KJV). But on enquiry he confessed he had no idea what it meant. He was a former boxing champion, raised in a rough neighbourhood, whose only means of communicating eloquently was with his fists. But he confided in me his nasty secret—he was afraid of the dark. This, as you can imagine, posed major problems for him on night exercises on the windswept barren moors of Dartmoor where Britain's major prison and marine training grounds appeared to be the only uses the authorities had found for this corner of England. On these occasions I looked after him as he stuck with me out in the wilds on moonless nights. Fortunately, it was I who walked into an electric fence in the pitch dark. If he had done it, I doubt we ever would have caught up with him again. But on cliff assaults as I dangled over Atlantic rollers breaking on the seaweed covered rocks a hundred feet below, there was no more welcome sight than his battered face grinning down at me as he held my rope. I was learning to relate to and then to befriend and then to love these hard men.

So I came out of the marines toughened in body (playing rugby in the Royal Marine Commandos will do that to you if you survive it), strengthened in spirit, and challenged in my understanding of humankind. The closer I got to these men, the more easily I recognised fragmented traces of the image of God among the tragic evidences of their fallenness—and saw them in myself, too, in startlingly vivid colours. In later years I learned theologically from Dr. J. I. Packer that total depravity does not mean that man (and woman) is at every point as bad as he can be; rather, he is at no point as good as he should be. He is not totally depraved (beyond redemption); he is depraved in his totality (every part of his being is twisted and warped and less than it ought to be). The marines had shown me this, but now I grasped it from a biblical point of view. I also came to believe deeply and practically that each person, however dissolute, is redeemable and should not be written off. The difference now was that I welcomed opportunities to reach out to and mingle with those whose lives differed wildly from that of a young bank clerk raised in a conservative Christian home. So conservative that my father had only recently taken a risk and brought a radio into the house and would never own a television.

My time in the marines did me a world of good. I became better equipped for life in general, more at ease in my dealings with people, more convinced of the validity of my faith, and more aware of the necessity to know how to share it where most needed. Some people learn their theology and its applications in the strangest places.

Little brooks become deeper and stronger through the quiet, almost imperceptible input of hidden springs and the more obvious contribution of tributaries. I had no shortage of either, although at that time I recognised none of them as such. Tributaries were flowing into my life on every side—and my little brook was deepening although I knew it not.

CHAPTER 3

STREAMS OF LIVING WATER

"Whoever believes in me, as the Scripture has said,
streams of living water will flow from within him."

—John 7:38

Dismissed from the marines two years later, just before my twenty-first birthday, I returned to Kendal to resume my banking career and to pick up where I had left off preaching in the small chapels. My parents, both of whom were struggling with health issues, and my brother, Bernard, who had grown out of recognition during my absence, had all moved to Kendal. On my return, I found my kid brother wearing my clothes and making it clear he had every intention of catching up with me and being my friend. He became more. With two other friends, he joined me in a gospel quartet, and we added our own music to my preaching around the hills and valleys of northern England.

A few miles south of Kendal was one of the stately homes of England. It had been built in the early 1800s for George Marton, a wealthy landowner who was also the lord lieutenant of Lancashire. A huge, imposing building, it stood in acres of rolling parkland dotted with mature beeches and syca-mores, overlooked by pine plantations and banks of brilliant rhododendrons. Stretching across the valley in front of the "manor house" were more than twenty-five farms that made up the Marton estate. Before World War II thirty servants were required to care for the five members of the resident family, but by war's end only one member of the family and few servants remained. Huge estate taxes had necessitated the division of the estate and the progressive sale of farms and land until eventually Capernwray Hall came up for sale.

A young British army officer with a distinguished war record named Major W. Ian Thomas was coming to the end of his military service, which had started six years earlier before the war was declared. He was busy making plans in Germany to return to civilian life, which, in his case, meant resum-ing a very effective evangelistic ministry. Convinced that he should open a youth centre in the northwest of England and learning that Capernwray Hall was for sale, he sent word to his wife to attend the auction and to bid up to a certain amount. The stated amount was agreed upon and contributed to by the Thomases and a small group of army officers who shared their vision. Mrs. Thomas bid as she was bidden, and to her mingled joy and panic, the bid was accepted and the Thomases and friends became proud owners of a formerly stately home. Having been occupied by a boys' school and subsequently by the army during the war years, the home needed a lot of work before it could once again be called stately.

The intention in acquiring the hall was to make it a place where young people from all over the British Isles could come together for Christian fellowship and teaching. But through an unusual set of circumstances, the first young people to arrive came from Germany, and soon the corridors of the grand old building reverberated with the "foreign" voices of young people, some of whom until recently had been enrolled in the Hitler Youth. Under the dynamic leadership of "the major," whom the German students soon learned to respect and admire, many of them came to faith in the Lord Jesus. Immediately they were taught that Christ was now resident in their hearts, that he was an expert "soul winner," and that they should therefore *expect* to win their friends to Christ. They were encouraged to return to their devastated homeland to spread the light of the gospel to their friends and families.

From this small beginning, many young Germans came to England — and came to Christ — and a wide door of opportunity had opened to reach young people who had gone through the trauma of war, had seen towns and villages destroyed, and had been subjected to the iniquitous regime of the Nazis. As a result, a burgeoning Fellowship of Torchbearers was formed. Although the ministry originated in England and spread into other nations under the English name "Torchbearers," it was known at first by the delightful tongue-twisting title given by those inspired German students: *Fackeltraeger Gemeinschaft*.

A couple of my friends and I, on hearing of these unusual happenings on our doorstep, went one evening to explore. We knocked on the solid, metal-studded oak door of the hall. No one answered, so we tentatively turned the heavy latch on the door, which opened with a resounding clang, and we walked through into an imposing hallway. A massive staircase greeted us, lit by a rainbow of colours filtered through a graceful stained-glass window. On hearing voices, we peered round a door into a large room in which a small group of young people was sitting in a circle around a roaring log fire, listening to a military-looking gentleman. When he saw us, he warmly greeted us and invited us to join the circle. Little did I realise that this encounter would change my life forever. I had met Major Thomas who, like Captain May, was destined to influence my life for good and for God. When streams converge the river deepens.

Immediately after the informal meeting, we were invited to have "tea and biscuits" served by a charming woman with a lilting Northern Ireland accent, Joan Thomas, the major's wife. Although I did not know it, this woman would become one of the most profound influences in the life of the wife I as yet had not met but who would cross my path years later not a dozen yards from where I stood at that moment.

I took my tea and biscuits from Mrs. Thomas, who warned me with a smile that I was in danger of dropping them. I assured her I was not in danger of doing any such thing and promptly did—all over everything. As they say, "You never get a second chance to make a first impression!"

She betrayed not the slightest trace of annoyance, briskly mopped up my mess, assured me all was well, and quickly produced more biscuits. I had caught my first glimpse of a gracious woman who, to this day, almost sixty years later, still serves tea and biscuits busily and cheerfully and projects with great grace and serenity an infectious spirituality that over the years has blessed countless young people and drawn them to Christ.

For the next few years, I was influenced more and more by the people and ministry of Capernwray. Mixing with young Europeans created in me the beginning of a world vision. Being able to argue with young Germans about the war (both we and they were lamentably ignorant of one another's experiences and perceptions) was stretching and illuminating. One day my friend Peter Wiegand, a very bright and articulate young man from Hamburg, complained to me about the British bombing of his city. I replied by telling him that the bombing of Hamburg was in retaliation for the devastation of Coventry. (He had never heard of Coventry.) For good measure I added, "Anyway, it wasn't the British, it was the Americans who bombed Hamburg." (I had no idea if this was true, but my British blood was coming to a boil!) Quick-witted Peter replied, "If that is true, then it was the Japanese not the Germans who bombed Coventry." Not for the first time, or the last, a young German got the better of me. We both laughed, I conceded the point, and our friendship thrived.

The social interaction with young Europeans was undoubtedly rich and rewarding, but it was the teaching of the Scriptures at Capernwray that made the most profound, far-reaching impact on my life.

From early days I had been introduced to a healthy orthodoxy, a reasonably sound evangelical grasp of gospel truth, and a desire to put it into practice in the context of the conservative lifestyle of my upbringing. But at Capernwray I was brought face-to-face with the fact that people who normally circulated outside the church's orbit were being thoroughly converted. They were the kind of people my church rarely would have contacted. In fact, it is doubtful if they would have considered trying to reach them with the gospel. I could not avoid noting the difference, and of course I had to ask myself the cause.

It was customary at Capernwray, before a speaker addressed a group, to thank the Lord "in advance for what he was going to do." To me that sounded rather preposterous and presumptuous. But they actually believed the promises of God—not in a technical sense, but in a sense of expectancy. More than that, there was an emphasis that was refreshing to someone born and brought up in the Brethren assemblies where there is a weekly "remembrance of the Lord in his own appointed manner" and the high point of the service is the literal breaking of the bread and drinking of the cup. This remembrance usually meant a solemn reflection on and reiteration of the betrayal, trial, humiliation, and crucifixion of the Lord and the blessings that accrue to us through his sacrifice. (And I must admit that some segments of the modern church are not always as meticulous in observing this regular remembrance as the Brethren were and are.)

At Capernwray we followed all these practices. But we didn't reflect on the dying of Jesus without it leading naturally to a powerful, thoroughly biblical emphasis on the resurrection of Jesus. And the emphasis went further and taught us that the risen Christ really was alive and had taken up residence in the hearts of the redeemed in order to carry on his ancient work in us and through us. So with great expectation that God would keep his promise to honour the proclamation of his Word and with the knowledge that Christ himself dwelt within us in the power of the resurrection through the Holy Spirit to take the Word home with power, who would not anticipate blessings to flow?

My dad was a gifted and earnest preacher. But he took my emphasis on expecting the preaching of the Word to bring forth fruit as a personal criticism of his own ministry, whereas he freely admitted nothing much ever seemed to happen. I tried to explain that it was not a criticism of his preaching but rather a challenge to look realistically at the kind of people he was reaching. In other words, he couldn't catch fish in a swimming pool—even if he was using the most orthodox worms!

The result of all this for me was a reevaluation of my life and ministry, such as it was at that time. I was well aware that Christ had left me instructions and outlined expectations and that he was sitting up in heaven praying for me, but learning that he was actually living within me to empower me was revolutionary. The often repeated principle "Christ himself is the dynamic of his own demands" served to liberate me from a focus on myself and my own best efforts and to refocus me on the indwelling Lord Jesus. It freed me from being overwhelmed by the enormity of the imperatives of discipleship and directed my thinking to the possibilities of Holy Spirit activity in and through my fragile obedience. Flowing streams.

Much of the tension I experienced with my father was my fault, because in my excitement of being introduced to a life of trusting Christ to be active in my life, I had given the impression that all I had to do was trust and not bother to obey. My father pointed this out to me. So I was faced with the need to balance a life of faith based on the promises of the all-sufficient Christ and a life of obedience required by the instructions of the sovereign Lord. The apostle Paul came to my rescue, telling the Colossians with delicate balance, "I labor, struggling with all his energy, which so powerfully works in me" (Colossians 1:29). Paul did the labor and engaged in the struggle out of obedience. Christ was the power, and he was mightily at work in Paul through faith. I would always struggle to obey but also would always have a full supply of grace to "nerve my faint endeavour." My responsibility to act was in no way negated by Christ's commitment to engage in divine activity. On the contrary, Christ's desire to work in and through his redeemed people demands that they become the vehicle of his moving as a sail full of wind requires the prow to bear the brunt of the waves and scythe through the water — rough and contrary though it may be.

Meanwhile, Cyril Brownlow had been promoted to manager of the bank in Bowness on Windermere — the idyllic little town in the Lake District where my father and grandfather were born. And I was transferred with him. Thus I was given bigger responsibilities in a smaller situation, and I began to work closely with a difficult man who, since I had served in the marines — as he had done with distinction — seemed to think positively of me. At least he was much more relaxed and approachable than he had been. He encouraged me in my banking studies and was intrigued when I told him I was going to preach a series of messages in the small chapel across the street from the bank. But not intrigued enough to come and listen.

However, to my astonishment, one of my customers did. Norman Whiteley arrived late, marched right up to the front row, put his feet up on the pulpit, and grinned up at me as if to say, "All right, you invited me to come. Here I am. Now what?" I must admit that I was distracted by his unexpected presence — he had a reputation in town as a high-living, convention-busting entrepreneur who waged continual battles with the local authorities. His mode of operation was to seek forgiveness rather than permission for all he did — an approach that rarely enthuses bureaucrats.

At the end of my talk, he got up and left without a word. Two days later he called me and said, "Come down to the office when you've finished work." So I duly reported to his mansion and its surrounding grounds, which he had turned into a huge, flourishing caravan park — trailer park — on the lake front. As I walked into his office, he said, "I've been trying to write and tell you what happened. But I don't know the words."

"What happened to whom, when?" I asked, bewildered.

With a touch of impatience, he added, "What happened the other night in the church. I did what you told me to do."

To my utter astonishment, Norman Whiteley, entrepreneur extraordinaire, had come to faith!

Never a man to let moss grow under his feet or anything else to impede his progress, when I tried to talk more to Norman about his newfound faith, he listened briefly and then said, "All right, this is what we're going to do. I've booked the town band for Sunday afternoon. I've sent out five hundred invitations to all my friends and business associates who never go near a church, and we're going to have a strawberries and cream and champagne garden party out there on the lake front, and you're going to tell everybody what you told me the other night." Norman did not believe in asking permission, and in this case neither did he intend to ask for forgiveness. It was all arranged as far as he was concerned—and I was on the spot.

Sunday afternoon was warmed by brilliant sunshine. Dressed in light, colourful summer wear, the people arrived in expensive cars and devoured strawberries and cream with great enthusiasm and downed champagne with even greater delight. The band played jaunty tunes as the people strolled around the freshly mown lawns among the towering cedars and well-dressed rose gardens, feeding the swans and trying to guess what Norman was "up to" this time. It was a picture of expensive elegance.

Eventually Norman called everybody to gather close to the band, which had just finished a lively rendition of "Another little drink won't do us any harm," and he announced that he had listened to me preach a few days earlier and thought everybody else needed to hear what I had to say. The people listened with varying degrees of bewilderment, thanked us politely, and made their escape. Norman Whiteley had "gone religious," and the whole town knew. But the big point of interest now was "Yeah, but how long will it last?"

I began to spend many hours with Norman, but conventional methods of "mentoring"—we called it "follow-up"—proved practically impossible. Yet somehow Norman grew in the faith, and in no time the whole town was buzzing with the news. The Norman river was cutting a large channel in a hurry.

Norman was generous to a fault. On one occasion he rounded up a group of "senior citizens"—Brits with characteristic lack of sensitivity call them "old-age pensioners"—hired a plane, flew them all down to Majorca in the Mediterranean, rented a complete floor of a hotel, and gave them the holiday of their lives. More controversially, he dedicated one of his slot machines—and its considerable profits—to missions. Some mission societies regarded these funds as "ill-gotten gain" and spoke of "filthy lucre" and wouldn't touch them, much to Norman's amazement. Others quickly chloroformed their compunctions.

Meanwhile, back at the bank, my relationship with my boss, the redoubtable Mr. Brownlow, took a dramatic—and traumatic—turn. One day he told me, "If Mrs. Jones asks for me, tell her I'm out."

I was surprised to hear he was going, so I said, "Oh, are you going out?"

"Of course not," he replied. "Just tell her I'm out."

"I can't do that if you're in," I stammered.

"You can if you know what's good for you," he replied aggressively. I had seen ominous signs of his temper a score of times before, and I knew what was coming.

"But you're asking me to lie for you," I countered, knowing full well I was getting in way over my head but not knowing what else to do. He became very angry, and I heard a little voice (it turned out to be mine) saying, "I think I've upset you, and I'm sorry. But if I lie for you, you'll know I'm a liar and will never be able to trust me again. But if I won't lie for you, you can assume I won't lie to you." This sounds much braver than it actually was. I was frankly terrified. He stormed out of the office and disappeared for an hour while I ran the bank on my own.

On his return he said, "I'm sorry. You're right. And if I have any say, you'll go to the top of this bank." I had no idea how to respond. What happened next was a totally new work experience with a new boss. I lived in a different world. A world in which mutual respect, mutual enjoyment, and mutual help became normative. Banking was looking promising, but preaching was a delight.

One day I ventured to my parents that I was considering asking the elders to "commend me to the ministry of evangelism." To my surprise and chagrin, they immediately dissuaded me from making any such move, but they agreed to seek the opinions of half a dozen reputable, respected men who knew me. To my added chagrin, the six men, without exception, agreed with my parents. One of the more vocal men asked me, "Are you being asked to do so much ministry that you do not have time to earn your living?"

"No," I replied, chastened.

"Then why should you expect someone else to work hard to do for you what you are perfectly capable of doing for yourself?"

That effectively blew a hole beneath my waterline, and I sank without a trace. I spent a confused night tossing and turning and wondering where I had got it wrong. And how was I to know if I had got it wrong? In fact, how was I supposed to discern God's will for my life? Of course, if I had belonged to another Christian communion, I probably would have been encouraged to attend Bible college and seminary, but such institutions did not, in those days, shine too brightly in the circles in which I rotated. In my opinion this was a somewhat understandable but grossly exaggerated reaction to the theological liberalism that was being exported from Germany into some segments of Britsh thinking

The very next morning, saddened and somewhat humiliated by what seemed a wholesale rejection, I went to work and was met by Mr. Brownlow. And he was smiling.

"Look what I've got," he said excitedly and gave me a letter from the chief inspector of the bank inviting me to go to head office in Manchester to be interviewed for a post on the inspection staff. I was being considered for what would be a plumb job for a young man of twenty-four or twenty-five. It was a post where I would be given the opportunity to move from the relative backwoods of the Lake District to the heady heights of the big city, and from the limited experience of a small branch to a base in head office and access to every branch in the bank.

Suddenly thoughts of "full-time ministry" disappeared from my mind and thoughts of "heading for the top" took over.

So a few days later I arrived at head office in Manchester where I was introduced to two conservatively dressed middle-aged gentlemen who greeted me with somber courtesy, called me "Mr. Briscoe," instead of the usual "Briscoe," complimented me on my career so far, asked about the marines, and enquired about my career objectives. When they moved on to hobbies, they nodded approvingly as I told them I sang first tenor in the famous Greenside choir—we had recently won a national title—but fortunately they did not ask me to audition. When, however, I told them about my preaching, they were taken aback. It was widely assumed in banking circles that officials did not take an active role in "religion or politics" as it might offend customers.

They recovered quickly from their surprise and began to pepper me with questions about youth, the burgeoning drug scene, the youth culture in general, and my experience with Germans in particular. After some time the chief inspector, Mr. Forsyth, a courteous, stately, fatherly gentleman, suddenly said, "Mr. Briscoe, it's a delight to meet a young man who knows what he believes and does something about it. We need more like you. If I were to offer you a place on my staff, would you be ready to take it in a couple of weeks?" The correct answer to that question, I knew, was "Oh yes. I can start today if you wish."

Taking a deep breath, I replied, "Sir, I'm sorry, but I'm booked up for nine months with preaching engagements, and I cannot break those commitments." That, I knew, would "cook my goose"—in fact, burn it to a cinder.

But he immediately replied, "Tell me when you'll come, and I promise not to send for you a day earlier." I got the job!

Walking away through head office, I recognised that in the space of a few days, God had shown me again that if he wishes, he will open doors and close them—and both are his means of getting us where he wants us to be. I was also sensing powerful inner workings beyond my control, certainly not of my making; yet unmistakably they were fashioning my life. They were like a river silently, powerfully cutting its own channel.

Mr. Forsyth, "the chief," called for me on the agreed date, and when I arrived after a few pleasantries, he said, "Let's go and do an inspection."

I panicked and blurted out, "Excuse me, sir, but what do I do?"

He smiled and said simply, "Mr. Briscoe, in this job you accept nothing and question everything."

During the next four years, I met not a few rogues and rascals in the bank's employ. Mr. Forsyth's words kept coming back like a song. And they never stopped singing in later years either. His principle was imperative in bank inspections, but it served to help me in developing insights in numerous ways. I applied it in thinking through what I believed. I had never questioned anything fundamental—I had accepted it at face value and barely thought it through. What previously had been simply accepted—"The Bible says it, I believe it, that settles it!"—was the favorite saying of the preachers I had listened to. But now I questioned—"The Bible says it, *this is what it means*, I believe it, that settles it"—so how did I find out what it meant?

Tradition came under the same microscope. I knew what we did but had no idea why we did it. Questioning rather than accepting made for uneasy moments, further awkward questions, occasional irritated answers, and gradual maturity. In coming years there were many times in counseling situations when I was required to listen to heated "he said, she said" altercations. I knew both could not be true, and I had learned not to believe all I was told. I had also learned how to be probing and quizzical, a counseling necessity—and I learned it in banking. But I still needed to pray for the unique spiritual gift of discernment.

Now, of course, a questioning attitude can lead you into the sinkhole of cynicism, but carefully applied it can save you from the pit of naivety.

I was assigned to a younger inspector named David Jones who was to be my constant workmate and immediate boss for the next two years. Word of my "religion" had clearly preceded me, so when we were introduced, Mr. Jones greeted me warmly and said, "You need to know right away that I am a god-fearing atheist."

Welcome to the real world of educated, sophisticated, skeptical, challenging secularism, Briscoe! Jones was never less than polite and courteous, and he never passed up a chance to take a sly dig at anything religious. For a man of his intelligence—and that was never in doubt—he had surprisingly raunchy tastes, and when we were away from home staying in hotels at the bank's expense, he would go his way and I would go mine. To say they were divergent is to grossly understate the very obvious. It was like long nights spent in a bus after rugby matches in the marines all over again—only more comfortable. Everybody's life is a flowing stream—where the stream flows is another matter.

In Manchester I lived in a state-of-the-art YMCA hostel named Montgomery House. On the day of my arrival, the desk clerk said, "Mr. Briscoe, we have a small chapel and we hold vespers each evening. Would you be willing to speak in our chapel this evening?" I agreed and went almost immediately to the small chapel to discover that "small" meant miniscule. But it was big enough for the three young men who came. I spoke to them and then went to my room to unpack only to see a note being slipped under my door. Picking it up, I read, "I listened to you tonight, and I live in the room next to you. Would you mind explaining to me more of what you talked about?" The note was signed "Keith Blackburn."

I forgot about unpacking, knocked on Keith's door, and discovered a young man eagerly seeking the Lord and more than ready to become his disciple. Within a matter of days, Keith introduced me to his school friend John Smallwood, who was also seeking the Lord but didn't seem to know it. His social graces were somewhat underdeveloped. Before entering my room, which he did constantly, he never bothered to knock. The door would fly open, he would march into my little abode, and stamp around the limited space shouting, "How could a whale swallow Jonah?" or "How could Elijah go to heaven in a fiery chariot?" Then, without pausing, he would march out, slamming the door behind him. I became quite accustomed to these fascinating interludes and was rarely required to respond to them. So I watched them in amused silence and proceeded with my studies. One night, however, I decided to change tactics. When, as expected, the door flew open and John marched in with his latest rhetorical question, I grabbed him, pushed him into a chair, and gave him a Bible and a pair of scissors.

Startled, he asked, "What are these for?"

"I want you to go back to your room, read the Bible—start with the Gospel According to St. John—and cut out all that you don't accept. When you've done it, then come back, and not before, and we'll discuss what's left."

"Why? I couldn't possibly cut a Bible to pieces," he replied.

"You've ripped on it with your tongue every day since I've met you. So why not make it final and just cut out the pieces you can't accept?"

"No," he said firmly, "I can't. I won't do it."

"Then stop treating it the way you do," I answered. "And don't forget that as you pick and choose which parts of the Bible are acceptable to you, all that is left will fit into the confines of your intellect; and with all due respect to your intelligence, my hunch is that we would be left with a God who doesn't amount to much at all. Take the Bible with you, start reading where I suggested with as open a mind as you possess, and ask God to reveal himself to you."

He left the room soberly, taking the Bible but declining the scissors. It was only a matter of a few days before the Lord opened his heart. (This week we received an email message from him—after more than forty years! He still ministers to young men.) And so began some of the most exhilarating, exciting days of my life as week by week young men from all over the world found the Saviour. We never held any public meetings. It was all personal evangelism based on concerted prayer, honest friendship, genuine care, thoughtful open discussion, and careful teaching of the Scriptures. It was a remarkable work of the Spirit. As Jesus had promised in John's gospel, the streams were flowing, the river was cutting its own channel.

I co-opted the help of a couple of friends, and together we put together teams from the young converts. As time went on, we discovered gifts of teaching and preaching among some of them. Keith eventually became an architect and a Methodist preacher. On one occasion he returned from an assignment and we eagerly waited to hear what had transpired. "Well," he said ruefully, "there were only three people there. One of them played the organ, and while I was preaching, one of them had an epileptic fit, the other man helped him outside, and I carried on talking to the organist. But after a few minutes, he said, 'It's not a bit of good, young fella, I'm stone deaf and can't hear a word you're saying.'" Keith was discovering that in ministry, like everything else, you win some and you lose some!

In Manchester I met yet another man who became a lifelong friend. His name was Val Grieve—so named because he was born on St. Valentine's Day. He was an Oxford-trained lawyer who during his student days had embraced Marxism with great enthusiasm and also had become captain of Oxford's chess team. At some point in his intellectual, spiritual, and philosophical pilgrimage, he had wandered into a small Pentecostal chapel in Italy and had been converted. The result was a very clear-thinking, highly intelligent, wonderfully articulate, fearless, tireless, highly regarded businessman whose passion was to reach as many people as possible with the good news of the gospel. He moved with equal ease among the intelligentsia, the wealthy, the down-and-outs, the religious, and the irreligious. And he was an Anglican!

Val was a confirmed bachelor until he met a girl whom I already knew. Sheila was a medical student at Manchester University. She was a lively, opinionated, outspoken, fun-loving, adventurous, straightforward, plainspoken young woman, impatient with cant or pomposity—the product of a small Lancashire town, and she could never have been mistaken for anything else. What you saw was what you got with Sheila. Val saw her and got her! Separate they were dynamite; together they were unstoppable. Nothing was beyond their vision, nobody beyond their reach. To be near them was to be blessed. They did you good.

It was through Val that I received a totally unexpected invitation to join an evangelistic team led by a well-known Anglican minister named J. R. W. Stott who was conducting a week's mission to Manchester University.

Val encouraged me to spend one of my two precious weeks of annual holiday working on the team, and such were his powers of persuasion that I approached my inspector to ask if I could be released for the week. He asked what I intended to do, and when I told him about the university mission, he seemed nonplussed but agreed. With considerable trepidation, I reported to the university and met the team. Most of them seemed to be Cambridge students or graduates. All conversed knowledgeably in the cultured accents of the wealthy private schools they had attended, and all I wanted to do was disappear into a corner and not open my mouth to divulge in the rounded accents of my native north of England that I hadn't studied theology, that I hadn't even attended university, and that Millom Secondary School was my alma mater. And I wasn't an Anglican!

I did, however, learn a lot that week. Iain Claire, a well-known Cambridge athlete, had been chosen to debate a philosophy student on the motion "This house believes religious conversion is the product of psychological manipulation," or something to that effect. His opponent arrived carrying an enormous pile of books all carefully marked with the references he wanted to use. The student then embarked on a long, tedious explanation of the psychological techniques purportedly used by religious people to further their ends. He discussed the philosophical teaching of the famous atheistic mathematician-philosopher Bertrand Russell and his arguments for atheism, and concluded triumphantly that Christianity was at worst a fraud and at best irrelevant.

Iain, who had been up most of the previous night talking and debating athletes and had struggled to stay awake during the first part of the debate was invited to respond. He was totally unfazed by the arguments of the other speaker, admitted cheerfully where he had a point, and conceded without hesitation what he could not refute. He pointed out that Bertrand Russell seemed to have a problem staying married, as his affairs were well documented, and suggested that perhaps he was looking for something called love and peace, which his philosophy could not provide. Moreover, he suggested that people who have no personal experience of Christ cannot possibly speak with authority on the reality of Christian conversion, because it is outside their realm of experience. But as he had been on both sides of the argument, he believed he was better equipped to say where truth lay. Then he sat down. Time for rebuttal was given, which the student took. Iain simply repeated an invitation to "taste and see that the Lord is good." The vote was taken, and Iain won. We were all kept there for a long time picking up the pieces of the debate, but my heart was singing.

I had seen firsthand the power of personal testimony, which cannot be refuted. Arguments can be refuted — personal experience cannot. I had witnessed the compelling power of a winsome, honest, good-humoured man speaking from his heart in contrast to dry, contentious, academic argumentation.

I had heard a clear presentation of the gospel in an environment in which many people would have pulled in their horns — and as promised it had proved once again to be "the power of God unto salvation."

And on a personal note, I had discovered that while I did not have the firepower of these sophisticated, educated, cultured brothers and sisters, I did have an "in" with north country people who attended the university. I could speak their language and relate to their environment. In fact, to my surprise, I was better suited for the task at hand than some of the more highly "qualified" people on the team. And that was a salutary reminder that I was God's man, I was not someone else, and he was alive in me to work out his purposes. Rather than be intimidated by invidious comparisons and overwhelmed by my inadequacies, I should be satisfied with the lot he had apportioned me and confident in who he is in me. The country preacher explained it best: "Be who you is, because if you ain't who you is, you is who you ain't." These were lessons I carefully stored away in my mind and heart — they would serve me well for decades to come.

Watching John Stott in action was an education; spending time with him, although limited, was a delight. Years later in Manila I reminded him of the mission in Manchester. He remembered it well. Not surprisingly, he had no recollection of me. But I will never forget hearing him preach with such grace and power to a hostile group of '60s students that he brought them to silent, reverent listening. And his mastery of "Question Time" was, to me, a thing of wonder. Standing alone on the bare platform in the huge commons packed with kids, many of whom were there with less than honourable intentions, he took all and any questions and responded without hesitation. He calmly replied to an angry young student who asked belligerently, "How can there be a God when there is so much evil in the world?" He said, as well as

I can remember, "My dear young friend, I have asked myself that question a thousand times but always coupled with another question of equal importance, namely, 'How can there not be a God when there is so much good in the world?' We cannot ask the one without the other, can we? But I will admit to you that I could not believe in a God of mercy if it were not for the fact that he came into our world of suffering and entered into it at the deepest level. Look at the cross, young man. He knows your suffering intimately, he knows your pain, and he loves you." Silence! Thoughts adroitly turned to the cross in a moment—perhaps for the first time ever.

But it was only for a moment, because soon another young student rose to challenge a basic Christian belief in much the same way the student in the debate had done. Mr. Stott listened carefully and then said, "Thank you for that. You have obviously done some careful thinking on the issue, and that is commendable. But may I respectfully point out that this is a question and answer time, and I think you will all agree that was more of a statement than a question. So could we perhaps have the next question?"

Mr. Stott did it all so courteously, so calmly, so firmly and winsomely that the student body burst into laughter and clapped their appreciation, and even the student who had suffered the "put down" grinned ruefully and took his seat. Hostility seeped out of the room. Soft answers do turn away wrath!

One day, years later, on a visit to Manchester, my friends Val and Sheila presented me with a print of a famous L. S. Lowery painting of old industrial Manchester. It captures perfectly the grime, the smoke, the damp air, and the oppressive fog as well as the monolithic mills and the people wrapped warmly against the chill, bent over against the winds. It is not a pretty picture, but on giving it to me, Val said, "Display this in a prominent place, and never forget your roots." That picture has hung in my study on both sides of the Atlantic ever since. I have not forgotten Manchester, and I never will, for there so many people flowed into my life. God used them to change me forever. But little did I dream of what lay around the next bend of the river.

CHAPTER 4

WHEN FLOWING
STREAMS MEET

Two are better than one,
because they have a good return for their work.

—Ecclesiastes 4:9

The water was pink beneath my feet. Not from an infusion of industrial waste upstream or a film crew's attempts to reproduce a bloody scene where valiant men battled on a strategic ford. No, I was staring at nothing more unusual than the reflection in slowly gliding water of the bridge on which I stood. Japanese-style, quaint, and painted pink. The sun was beginning to warm the cool air. Grey clouds tinged with rose and mauve were giving way to bright sky; fish hawks circled above silently and ominously; herons stood menacingly immobile, ready to spear unsuspecting fish within range; and in the reeds and weeds, carp in a feeding frenzy stirred the water like a hot spring boiling with volcanic activity. To my right was another bridge less colourful spanning another stream less tranquil. And downstream a few metres the silent pink stream and the turbulent white waters met and mingled, and both were changed. And the river, fuller and less turbulent, swifter and less silent, neither pink now nor white, flowed on. Changed. When flowing streams that cut their own channels converge, a new river is born, the banks are stretched, and new channels are formed.

Spring was in the air when I traveled north to Capernwray to spend Easter weekend 1957 with friends. Daffodils, my favorite flowers, trumpeted spring and spoke volumes to me of resurrection as they triumphantly burst through the unrelenting crust of the frostbitten earth to defy the odds and bloom in unmistakable glory. The fresh grass sparkled with early dew, lambs bounced around long-suffering ewes, stately trees wore new greenery, and the harsh winds blowing off the Irish Sea had finally moderated, allowing warmer breezes to banish the chill from our bones. My work required constant concentration over long hours, and meeting the growing needs of the new believers in Montgomery House was a challenge. I was ready for a break. The message of Easter, I knew, would be renewing and refreshing.

Many old friends were there, but one group of about twenty whom I had never seen before caught my attention. They were teenagers, and by the way they conducted themselves in the countryside, they looked as if they came from the city. Their speech banished all doubt—they spoke with the unmistakable nasal accents of Liverpool in Merseyside, the great port city that had originally made its money in the nefarious slave trade. But more recently Liverpool had gained the everlasting respect and gratitude of the British people as the port into which the convoys from America brought us our daily bread during World War II. Liverpool had paid a dreadful price for it at the hands of the Luftwaffe.

The "Wackers," as Liverpudlians are known, were clearly full of life—I never met one who wasn't—and they obviously needed a lot of handling. And surprisingly the person apparently charged with that task was a tall, slim, pretty girl in her very early twenties. She joined in all their games with an easy, natural athleticism, and she corralled them for the morning and evening Bible studies and hovered over them like a mother hen, finding the places in the unfamiliar Scriptures for them, explaining what was going on, and calmly correcting borderline behaviour. It was all very impressive to my casual eye. Well, maybe not very casual. Perhaps to my eagle eye? Did I say she was tall, slim, and pretty? Something was happening to me!

I contrived to catch her without her usual retinue of kids and suggested a game of table tennis. She played tennis for her college at Cambridge and easily transferred her skills on the grass court to the green table—with devastating effect. The kids came looking for her and stood around eyeing suspiciously the man who had dared to take "Miss" away from them for a few minutes. But I had seen enough of Jill Ryder at close quarters, if only for a few humiliating moments, to know I wanted to know her more. *But how to get rid of these kids?* I figured, rightly, that they may not be at their best early in the morning, so audaciously and not at all confidently, I suggested a walk—before breakfast. And to my amazement and delight, she said, "I'd love to!"

The next morning was chilly, but I barely noticed. There was a touch of rain in the air, but we didn't care. We walked and we talked. I asked about the kids. She told me they were mostly young believers whom she had reached through her professional teaching. They were part of a much larger group she was leading. There was a spontaneity about the spread of the good news she was describing, like another kind of Montgomery House event—another river was flowing. I was intrigued.

Unfortunately, the presence of her flock prevented any more personal time together, but as I was leaving Capernwray at the end of the weekend, I was able to tell her that my business required periodic visits to Liverpool and I would be happy to help her with her youth group if she would like that. She said, "Oh, that would be wonderful," and I wondered if it was the offer of help that she considered wonderful or if it could possibly be my being the helper that she regarded as wonderful. Time would tell. Let it be said that I genuinely wanted to help with the kids who had recently come to faith, but ulterior motives lurked not far beneath the surface. I could only hope she was clever enough to see them—and approve. And I hoped she would not find the motives inferior because ulterior.

The next time we met, I think she was a little uneasy about the chemistry we both knew existed between us, and she told me straightforwardly that she had recently made a commitment to the Lord that her life would be predicated on the ancient principle "As for me and my house, we will serve the LORD" (Joshua 24:15 KJV). She was at pains to tell me that in her mind this meant that any relationship she would enter into would necessarily require a joint commitment to a life of service. As Jill quoted the biblical verse, I could hardly believe my ears, because not long before, I had arrived at the identical conclusion and had solemnly made the same commitment. I told her I was only interested in a relationship that could blossom into a life of partnership in service, and that was the moment I think we both knew that the flows of our lives were heading for a mighty confluence.

That we were "in love" with each other was obvious to us—and to all! But we had no time or opportunity to become absorbed or obsessed with each other. We were too busy. I have noticed all too often that when young people meet the love of their lives, all other interests recede, other activities cease, and other relationships are eclipsed. They are experiencing something strange, exciting, and indefinably wonderful that can sweep them away. As the old song says, they live as if they "only have eyes for you." That's understandable and to a certain extent forgivable, but it can slip-slide into something unforgivable called selfishness—the enemy of servanthood and, not incidentally, the killer of marriage. We grabbed our quiet moments and cherished our romantic interludes, but we continued to live most of our lives as we intended to carry on—serving. As Jill lived in Liverpool and I was based fifty miles to the west in Manchester and rarely at home there because of business travels, we didn't see each other very often. Phone calls were special and letters were frequent, but both of us knew we were settling into a calm, sweet relationship that was based on mutual trust, encouragement, support, and enjoyment all in the context of a deep desire to serve and honour the Lord who had brought us together because he made us for each other. We didn't spend a lot of time discussing, testing, and probing to see if we were "right for each other." In fact, we didn't spend a lot of time at all until we became engaged, and about eighteen months after meeting we were married.

We were embarking on a life of learning how to live in love and to love living with each other. And we had something huge going for us—the models of Bill and Peggy Ryder, Stanley and Mary Briscoe, and assorted other couples like Harry and Dorothy Green. We had seen their marriages at close quarters. They had marriages that worked, and we were determined to build one too.

The wedding day came quite quickly, surprisingly quickly in my mind, given the enormous amount of preparation. Our honeymoon was spent tearing round Europe in a small, grey Austin 35 automobile—a present from Jill's parents. Shortly after our return, we moved into a tiny house in a suburb of Manchester, kindly allotted to us by the bank for the princely sum of twelve shillings and sixpence (approximately one dollar and fifty cents) a week. About what it was worth!

We moved in, and I set about demonstrating my domesticity by wallpapering one of the rooms, and showing my lack thereof by giving up after one frustrating evening in which the paper insisted on peeling off the wall with something like a sigh and enveloping me in its sticky embrace. Meanwhile, Jill decided to keep a record of her weekly expenditures on groceries, which she proudly presented for my inspection on my return from inspecting banks. Instead of "Balance," she had written, "Left to spend," and when I asked where the balance ("Left to spend") was to be found, she happily said, "I spent it!" So we agreed that I would not do wallpapering and she would retire from bookkeeping, and we set out on the long, exciting road of making adjustments, without which no one lives happily ever after.

In those days young couples did not decide "if" or even "when" to start a family—that thought did not occur to us. So we were not at all surprised—or perturbed—to discover that we would spend the first year of life together discovering "How to be married" and doing a second course entitled "How to prepare for parenthood."

In theory, at least, we knew that life is not all shadowless sunshine. We were well aware that hard, unpleasant things happen. We just didn't think they would happen to us—or at least not yet. But happen they did, for early one morning while inspecting a bank—actually the one managed by our friend Harry Green—I got a phone call from my brother saying that my father had passed away in his sleep at the age of fifty-four. Although he had been suffering from what the doctors called "angina pectoris," which told us, in Latin, that he had chest pains and nothing more, no one in the family had even contemplated the possibility that his condition was fatal. We rushed to my mother's side, and her first words to me were, "Stuart, what are we going to do?" with such a note of urgency that I could barely look at her. I had no idea what to do—I had never looked death in the face before. And I certainly was not ready to don the mantle of senior man in the family. But once again life had sent me an unavoidable message, "Here, take this. Grow up. Be a man." Life relentlessly thrusts us into situations for which we are ill prepared because we have had no way of being equipped.

I learned in those sad days that marriage truly proves that "two are better than one," because Jill became a tower of strength to my mother, brother, and me. I had never guessed and could not have known that beneath Jill's gentle demeanour and disposition lay resources of strength and stability that would enrich our lives together for many decades. However, in those days they first put in an appearance, and I liked what I saw. More than that, I realised that we can only discover who we really are and who those near and dear to us truly are as we go through life's vicissitudes together.

The Sunday after my dad's death, we all attended the morning service in the Brethren assembly, and I felt constrained to talk to the people about what had been going on in my heart during the hours since his death. I spoke about the words of Jesus, "I must work the works of him that sent me, while it is day: the night cometh, when no man can work" (John 9:4 KJV). I admit I took them out of context and applied them to myself. But they expressed the feelings that had overwhelmed me—that my father who loved the Lord, his Word, and teaching the Word could no longer do it. But I could—the opportunity was open to me, and I wanted to say publicly that I desired to do just that.

Two weeks later we celebrated Jill's sister's wedding, and a few weeks after that the day dawned when Jill informed me, "The baby's coming." After what seemed to her an interminable and unforgivable delay—caused by me responding to her from the depth of my ignorance of such matters and saying, "The baby can't possibly be coming!" I deposited her at the hospital and went to work—in Manchester while she was in Liverpool. I confess that's how we Brits did it in those days. The delivery room was no place for men, both in the minds of the hospital authorities and in the hearts of the men, and so rather than pace the corridors, real men went to work. But on hearing by telephone the glad tidings, "Mr. Briscoe, you have a son," I returned to Jill's bedside and made my son's acquaintance. David Stanley Campbell Briscoe had made his entrance into cold damp Liverpool two months too late to meet the grandfather whose name he bore—while my father went to glory two months too soon to welcome his first grandchild.

As soon as I saw my wife holding our baby in her arms, I was aware of the naturalness of motherhood. She knew instinctively how to hold him, soothe him, make him feel secure, and of course, feed him. I saw a look in her eyes

I had never seen before. She had a contented glow, a quiet knowing smile on her face. She was a mother who had carried this helpless little boy in her body for nine months and now would devote herself to his care and nurture in ways that I could no more understand than I could fathom the mysteries of conception that she had known, the movement of embryonic life that she had felt, and the anguish of childbirth she had experienced.

Jill was a woman, a mother. And I felt like a spare part—a man on the outside looking in. A father who was even afraid to hold the little boy in case I dropped him. But I soon discovered that the girl I loved was rapidly turning into a woman before my eyes, and she who had begun to show me the meaning of marriage was equal to the task of sharing with me the joys of parenthood, which appeared to be far more natural to her than to me. Much later in life I would realise that the genius of God in ordaining two parents per child ensured two things: first that the mother, to whom nurture would flow naturally from the inner experience of conception, birth, and the intimate times of feeding, would meet the child's need for care; and second, that one day the child would need to head out on his own and the nurturing mother would inevitably struggle with relinquishment. Not so the father who, to a certain extent, had been on the outside looking in all along. He would know how to give the lead to the mother in this. So in years to come, after Jill had ministered to me by drawing me into the inner circle of her relationship with our son, I was able gently, I hope, to help her disengage when the time had come for our boy to be a man.

I learned to thank God continually that Jill and I had met, come together, and been made one—like streams that converge. Deeper, fuller, richer. But I must also admit that there were times when her input was not always as welcome. In addition to my busy life in business, traveling all over England, I was preaching most weekends in churches around the northwest of England and increasingly in youth rallies farther afield. Jill, whose spiritual experience had developed in parachurch organisations such as InterVarsity while in college, and who had little experience of churches, was not as committed to the local church as I was. Accordingly, she was not always impressed by the fact that I would travel considerable distances to speak to a relatively small group of people who, as she explained, probably knew what I was saying as well as I.

This led Jill to ask me an awkward question. Pointing to a coffee bar across the street from our little house in Manchester and stating the obvious fact that there were hundreds of young people standing around there with nothing to do, she asked, "Why don't you go and talk to them?" The answer, which I was reluctant to give, of course, was that I felt perfectly at ease talking to "the choir" but less comfortable going outside the sanctuary of a sanctuary. Masculine pride would not allow an honest answer, so I did a less than honourable thing and challenged my wife, holding our baby in her arms, by saying, "If you are so concerned about them, why don't you do something about them?" I'm ashamed, but I said it. Jill was not offended. Just determined.

Jill accepted the challenge, rounded up a small group of youngsters from the church we attended when possible, showed them how to take a survey we had developed, and sent them across the street to the Cat's Whisker.

By a strange coincidence (or divine appointment?) the coffee bar was closed because of some misbehaviour inside and the patrons were put out on the street. Our young people arrived as these events were unfolding and helpfully said, "The lady who lives over there would love to make you coffee." So over the street and into our little house poured a veritable river of youthful humanity. Jill rose to the task, made them coffee, and started to tell them her story.

When sometime later I arrived home from preaching in a small church somewhere, I was unable to open the door. But a young man sitting immediately behind it opened it a crack and helpfully said, "Sorry, mate, it's full," and closed it in my face. The door was promptly reopened when Jill realised what had happened, and I suddenly found myself in my own home, the guest of perfect strangers, who were not only listening with great interest to Jill's story, but were also, I soon discovered, equally eager to hear mine. Thus began a new chapter of our lives.

A few days later conviction overcame reluctance, and I ventured with great trepidation into the Cat's Whisker. Immediately on entering that dark and noisy place, where dozens of young people were listening to loud music and shouting above its noise to make themselves heard, I tripped over a long-haired young man. He looked at me, clad as I was in my business suit and tie, with surprise and not a little alarm. I apologized, and then, incredibly, I asked him, "Excuse me, are you alive?" Why I asked him such a question I do not know! It just popped out.

He blinked and said, "Of course I'm alive."

"Why are you alive?" I ventured.

"Why does there have to be a why?" he responded.

"Well, everything in this room seems to have a reason for its existence, and I thought you probably had one too," I suggested.

"Just because the things in this room have a reason for being doesn't mean I have to have one," he retorted.

"True," I conceded, "but are you greater or lesser than, for instance, that guitar which we know has a purpose, the window which is equally purposeful, the coffee cup, the light switch?"

"I'm greater, of course," he replied with a touch of dignity.

"Then if things lesser than you have a purpose, is it not reasonable to believe that you, being greater, also have a reason for being?" I enquired.

"Well I suppose you're right," he conceded, "but I don't know what it is."

He paused and then added, "Yes I do! I know why I'm alive. I'm alive because I was born and haven't died yet."

He looked triumphantly around at his friends, who applauded his wise and witty response.

"Did you have anything to do with your birth?" I asked. "And do you plan to have any say in your death?"

"No," he said seriously. "I suppose they'll be accidents as far as I'm concerned." Then he added, "I suppose I'm nothing more than an accident suspended between accidents."

That was my opening, and I proceeded to assure him that he was no accident. That there is a God in heaven from whom we come, through whom we live, and unto whom we are accountable. I went on to explain how we have lost sight of these fundamental truths and have fallen short of living life on these noble principles, yet God in love has taken an initiative to forgive and restore us to full and vibrant living. And so on.

He, and his friends, who by this time had switched off the music, listened intently and respectfully for some time until he suddenly stood up and said, "I've got to go. But before I do, I need to say one thing to you, mister."

"What's that?" I asked, interested in what he was going to say.

"You don't believe a word of all this stuff you've been telling us about God," he almost shouted at me.

I was stunned but managed to stammer, "Why would you say that?"

He replied, "That's easy. Because all that you have told us here tonight is so wonderful that if you and people like you really believed it, you would have been down here long before tonight to tell us kids about it." And with that he gave me a scornful look and disappeared into the dark Manchester night. I left too. Much wiser about the young people of my city and much sadder about my lack of love and concern for them. And thankful for a young wife who had pushed me where I did not want to go—and was making me a better man.

In the days that followed, I could not get out of my mind the young man's words. I was required to ask myself, "So do you really believe what you say you believe? Do you really think the gospel is as wonderful as you say it is? And if so, why are you not telling it to the people who most need to hear it?"

Introspection has never been my forte, but the challenge of this "chance" encounter along with concerns about impending transitions in my banking career and the sudden trauma of my father's death all weighed heavily upon me and led to some serious heart searching.

The shock of an unexpected death is mind numbing. It is a merciful gift in the early days of bereavement that makes coping possible. But as it begins to wear off, the pain of loss and the harshness of reality set in with a vengeance. The sudden realisation that I had a widowed mother to care for who was, for the first time in my life—and hers—leaning on me for guidance and support left me bewildered. Thoughts of my own mortality—I was not yet thirty years of age—rushed into my mind. I even began to experience chest pains! Added to all these emotions and uncertainties, I was aware that if I lived as long as my father, I had already lived half my life. And the words of Scripture I had quoted in the assembly shortly after his death would not leave me alone: "I must work the works of him that sent me, while it is day: the night cometh, when no man can work."

Jill knew I was troubled, and she knew I was also coming to a crossroads in my banking career as my four-year assignment on the inspection staff was coming to an end. The big question in banking terms was, "What kind of opportunity will they offer me?" If all was well, I would be on the fast track to the top.

I felt like a chariot pulled by two horses. Unfortunately, they were pulling in opposite directions. Was God calling us to devote ourselves to "full-time" ministry, or should I accept whatever the bank offered me and serve the Lord in the business world and in the church in my spare time? Either scenario appealed, but I didn't know which way to go.

In those days evangelical Christians talked about being "in the center of God's will"—a concept that I did not find very helpful, as it suggested to me that life was like a huge circle and somewhere in the middle was a dot—"God's will"—that I was expected to find. I felt like a blindfolded child at a party being required to pin a tail on a donkey he could not see.

Jill and I searched the Scriptures in our regular reading and found passages that "spoke to us" about service and sacrifice. We talked to people who knew us and understood our aspirations and uncertainties and recognised our abilities. They gave us generally positive feedback, but one piece of advice proved particularly helpful. Nick Carr, at that time the managing director of a well-known and highly respected British company named "Carrs of Carlisle," told me, "Stuart, push plenty of doors; don't try to kick any down." By that he meant explore all the options; don't force any of them, and the right one will open up to you. He believed this to be true—and I joined him—because we both reasoned that if God has a plan for our lives, he by definition would be more interested in us finding it than we could ever be. Therefore, he would not make it obscure but would participate in making it clear. Hence, doors of opportunity would swing open on careful exploration. I found this satisfying because it put the emphasis on God being active in directing but required me to be involved by using my God-given capacities. So Jill and I together agreed we would pray, tell the Lord we would leave the bank and enter ministry as a career *if* a ministry approached us and asked us to join them. Up till then no ministry had ever done so.

Within two weeks, not one, but two ministries asked me to leave the bank and invited us to go and work with them. Then, to complicate matters, within days I received a message from the general managers of the bank telling me that they wished to interview me, so three doors stood before me. At this point, my business brain kicked into gear, and I made arrangements so that I could interview all three over the space of three days and not let any of the others know I was talking to someone else. This meant traveling overnight to London by train to eat breakfast on Saturday morning with Major Thomas, who was en route to New Zealand from Germany, then returning to Manchester to meet a representative of Pocket Testament League at my home in the evening and the bank's general managers on Monday. I told Jill, excitedly, about the upcoming interview with the general managers: I had worked in the bank for eleven years and had never seen any of them; now I was going to talk to all of them. But she was aghast and said, "But Stuart, you promised the Lord that if a ministry asked us to join them, we would do it. So why are you even talking to the bank?" Good question!

I spluttered, "Well, God needs his men in the business world you know." That was, and is, true, but Jill was right. We had taken a step of faith, made a commitment, and I was in danger of taking a step back.

Fortunately, matters were taken out of my hands, because shortly before I was due to leave work on Friday evening to catch the train to London, I received an urgent message: "The GMs want to see you in half an hour." I only had time to "wash and brush up," breathe a prayer, and look desperately in my pocket New Testament for a word of reassurance. I got it! The verse that leapt off the page was, "Lift up your eyes, and look on the fields; for they are white already to harvest" (John 4:35 KJV).

The opening question in my interview with the three imposing gentlemen, after the customary pleasantries, was, "Mr. Briscoe, please tell us your ambitions." The expected response, I knew, was, "I want to serve the bank in any capacity that I can be most helpful."

Instead, to their astonishment I said, "I want to preach the gospel to as many young people as possible in my generation. In fact," I added, "I want to tender my resignation to you, as I intend to enter the ministry." It was done — I had burned my bridges, and the feelings of joy and relief were inexpressible.

But the GMs were not prepared to leave it there, so for the next half hour, they quizzed me about the gospel, youth, and ministry. Then one of them suggested, "Well, gentlemen, we seem to have covered theology quite thoroughly. Do we need to talk about banking for a little while?" No one had any questions, so I thanked them, bade them good-bye, and left their offices to be met by Mr. Forsyth, the chief inspector, who was waiting for me. At this point, I had been appointed his personal assistant.

"How did it go?" he inquired anxiously.

"I think I gave them a shock," I replied and went on to explain my decision.

He sat down with a thump and said, "Don't give me shocks like that. My heart's not good." He made sure I was serious, asked a number of questions, and then said, "Well, let me tell you this. I don't know your God the way you do, but I believe he'll take good care of you. But if anything does not work out for you, get straight back to me, and I'll have you reinstated." He was a great gentleman, a man I greatly admired in the business community.

Noel Brookes, one of my colleagues, got the job I was interviewed for. He became the bank's representative to the European Common Market. And he died of a heart attack before he was forty. I became an ambassador of the King of Kings, and by his grace I am still going strong.

PART 2

A FLOWING STREAM

I doubt if most people in, or close to, their thirtieth year spend a lot of time in quiet reflection. They are too busy for that sort of thing, and anyway life beckons. They have goals to meet, careers to forge, families to establish—and mortgages to pay. But more than forty years after my thirtieth year, with a little more time for reflection and a more mature appreciation for life's unfolding saga, I have noticed what a pivotal time I was entering as my twenties drew to a close. I knew that Jesus began his public ministry when he was round about thirty years of age, as did the Levites in Old Testament times. Presumably it was—and is—reasonable to assume that having negotiated the teens and twenties, we actually put a few things together and can be entrusted with greater responsibilities and opportunities. This was certainly the case in my experience. The various springs and rivulets and tributaries that at times had trickled and on occasion had poured into my life had served to produce a more recognisable flowing stream with an identity of its own and a unique course to follow. It was time.

CHAPTER 5

A FORK IN THE RIVER

When you come to a fork in the road, take it.

—Yogi Berra

Yogi Berra didn't mention rivers, but coming to a fork in the river requires decision time too. That is precisely where we had arrived. We knew what we were not going to do—banking. But what should we be doing in response to the two invitations we had received?

After an all-night train ride and a hurried breakfast in London during which Major Thomas had invited me to join the Capernwray staff, he jumped in the car bound for Heathrow airport en route to New Zealand and said, "If God wants you at Capernwray, you'll come. If he doesn't, we don't want you anyway!" With a smile and a wave, he was gone. The bluntness might have been off-putting for some, but I knew him and his thinking. God would be a compelling influence in the outworking of the decision, and his will was good enough for us. That certainly resonated with both Jill and me.

The other ministry worked hard at wooing us, telling us of opportunities very persuasively, making all kinds of generous offers. Capernwray by contrast seemed almost casually content to trust God to work out what he wanted. This, I think, was one of the first indicators I was given of the remarkable attitude of almost reckless faith that permeated life and ministry at Capernwray. I had heard of it in their teaching, but now I was seeing it in operation. In fact, I was on the receiving end of it, which was unnerving and exhilarating all at the same time.

After considerable heart searching, we opted for Capernwray and made plans to vacate our little home opposite the Cat's Whisker. We said good-bye to the young believers in Montgomery House and those who had come to faith in the unlikely setting of the coffee bar; and with a promise that we would return regularly to encourage them, we set off north with our belongings and little David securely stowed in our A35.

On a number of occasions, I have met people who, after they have enjoyed a holiday in a certain location, have thought, "Wow, this is beautiful! Wouldn't it be wonderful if we could live here all the time?" The idea has taken root in their hearts, and eventually they have made the move and found that living in a place is very different from vacationing in the same environment. Jill and I knew Capernwray well as a vacation center, but now we were going to live there, and we wondered if we would need to adapt, and if so, how long it would take.

I think I had a sense that leaving the bank to engage in ministry would give me a step up in the ecclesiastical pantheon. This would be "full-time ministry." A young man like myself who was discovering a preaching gift and had been given increasing opportunities to exercise it could perhaps be forgiven for imagining that to take this step was rather like an amateur soccer player turning professional. In the circles in which I moved, there was even a touch of glamour attached to being "in the ministry." So we were heading for Capernwray very excited indeed. Starry eyed.

The thought of working solely with Christians in a Christian environment held great promise too, because while the majority of the people I worked with in the bank were quality people, there were some who made life difficult, and the thought of not having to deal with people like them was most appealing. So Capernwray beckoned with visions of paradise. Perhaps it will suffice to say that we were surprised that life was not quite as we expected it to be.

The people I was to work with were fine young people, most of whom were capable of far more challenging jobs than the ones they fulfilled at Capernwray, and accordingly they were fully able to earn much more than they were earning in the ministry. But they knew that when they volunteered to work there and gladly went about their work sacrificially and joyfully. Nevertheless, they got tired like other people, were sometimes disappointed like ordinary people, and had bad days like everybody else. We had to live and work with them in closer quarters than we had been used to while they coped with life's ups and downs like people on the outside. So we discovered that tensions exist among Christian workers, that tempers get frayed, feelings get hurt, and actions and reactions are often misinterpreted and misunderstood. All grounds for less than perfect living conditions. I'm really not sure what we expected — all I know is that it was totally unrealistic. Actually, the only adjustment we were being required to make was to develop a view of life in ministry circles shorn of utopian visions and "supersaint" expectations. We were being reminded that Christians are very ordinary people who know an extraordinary God — and as they mature in that knowledge, it shows.

We had been assigned, as our living quarters, a quaint little gatekeeper's lodge. Situated by the main wrought iron gates set in an imposing stone entrance, it stood sentinel over one of the driveways to the hall. Quaint it was from the outside; cramped and chilly it was from the inside. But we were well aware of the example of the Thomas family who lived in similarly cramped quarters on a busy corridor in the hall, totally devoid of privacy. At least we had plenty of privacy. Our solitude was so complete that it was only disturbed by trees sighing in the wind, bawling cows, and owls that hooted at the moon. Jill was a city girl—Liverpool, Cambridge, and Manchester were the scenes of her life so far. This was countryside!

The lodge—Middle Lodge it was called to differentiate it from similar structures around the estate—had been used as a dormitory for a number of young boys from the Continent who unfortunately had not vacated the premises to make room for us when we arrived. All but one, Klaus Jenne, were persuaded to pack their bags and head for the hall, but Klaus said that he would like to live with us. Not wanting to have a confrontation upon our arrival, we acquiesced and squeezed him in somewhere.

Small living spaces that have been used as dormitories for young men usually need help recovering from the experience, and such was the case in Middle Lodge. So we set to work "spring cleaning" our new abode. Jill insisted that we should start with the chimney—an ancient structure that looked as if it had never been swept since it was a hole in a thatched roof.

So we called in John Dixon, a plainspoken, hardworking man who had been at Capernwray, as he told us regularly, since he was "knee high to a grasshopper." John knew everything about everything and everybody and was always happy to tell anyone who would listen. He told us he knew the best way to clean a chimney, so we followed his advice. When he said that a holly bush on the end of a rope was far better than the traditional brush, we wondered but bowed to his superior wisdom. So John and I clambered on the roof, discovering in the process that some of the masonry had seen better days. We dropped a rope down the chimney that we then attached to a bush. Our intention was to pull the prickly bush up and down, thus dislodging the soot from the chimney. Unfortunately, the bush stuck, the rope came undone, and the chimney, which had a wicked hidden twist in it, was blocked.

"Not to worry" said John cheerfully, "I'll push the brush up from the bottom and release the bush." The brush failed to release anything except itself, so now we had a brush and a bush resident in the wicked twist. Undaunted, John announced he could free everything by dropping stones down the chimney from the roof, which we proceeded to do with the result that we added stones to our stash of brush and bush halfway down the chimney. Resourceful as ever, John decided we could set the chimney on fire, burn the bush and brush, and the stones would come down on their own. He was right. Clouds of ugly, dirty yellow smoke filled the immediate countryside, bush and brush licked by alarming orange flames disappeared into thin air, and the stones came rattling and crashing down, bringing with them enough soot to cover most of our little house in a black shroud. Jill screamed, the baby howled, I ducked, and John disappeared! Klaus decided to leave too. But the chimney was cleaned. We had arrived.

Major Thomas—he retained his military title, an honour his rank entitled him to—was known to everybody simply as "the major." He was a "take charge" sort of person who without trying would become a focal point of every room he walked into. Even though he was only of average height, his personality was such that he seemed to fill a much bigger space than he physically occupied, and he exuded such an air of authority that he was instinctively treated with great respect. He was not loud, and he did not push himself forward. In fact, I suspect he was rather shy, and except when he was preaching, he was quietly spoken. He had a great sense of humour, a ready laugh, and an endless store of corny jokes he told frequently with great relish.

Not surprisingly for a military man, Major Thomas was disciplined and expected those around him to be disciplined too. Failure in this regard qualified the offending party for a sharp rebuke and the clear expectation that improvements would be forthcoming without fail. Even in his lengthy absences for ministry overseas, he cast a long shadow, and on his return there was always a heightened sense of urgency about life. This was clearly felt by his sons and other young people working on the staff, for on the eve of the major's arrival, they were marched off for military-style haircuts.

Major Thomas was a born leader who generated confidence, exercised control, and created a desire in people to follow his example. His knowledge of the buildings that comprised the hall was encyclopaedic. His interest in the minutest details of showers and toilets, dormitories and drains knew no bounds. He kept financial figures in his head. Above all, his ability to make the Scriptures live in the minds, imaginations, hearts, and wills of young and old was legendary. I still meet people to this day all over the world who can tell you exactly what he preached on fifty years ago and the life-transforming impact his words had on their lives. He had competence, charisma, and character all in abundance. This man was a living, breathing lesson in leadership.

It has been said that the quality of a person's leadership is often seen most clearly during the leader's absence. If that was the case at Capernwray, there was no shortage of opportunities to see how good a leader the major was! Some years he was away far more than he was present, yet a full program of winter and spring Bible schools and summer conferences that followed each other week after week ran efficiently and effectively. Of course, much of the credit for this rested on the shoulders of his wife, Joan Thomas, a totally unflappable, untiring, unassuming woman who served behind the scenes in a thousand capacities, none too mean or too hard.

Working alongside her was a former London real estate agent who rejoiced in the name Leonard Alfred Theophilus Van Dooren, known to intimates as "Van" and to the rest as Mr. Van Dooren. "Van" was the quintessential second fiddle player—and he played it extraordinarily well. He was a single, middle-aged man who devoted himself to his work as principal of the Bible school and spent endless hours teaching and counseling students from around the world. When the Bible school term ended, he traveled to remote parts of Europe, bringing hope and encouragement to small groups of believers.

Major Thomas, his wife, Joan, and Van became our mentors without the word being mentioned, the concept being mooted, or the techniques being practised. They went about their business, we went about ours, and all the time we simply watched, assiduously listened, and endeavoured to emulate.

Shortly after arriving at Capernwray, I was introduced to the sewage system that had a well-earned bad reputation for failing at critical times. Major Thomas, whose military decorations included the Distinguished Service Order and the Territorial Decoration, was entitled to display the letters D.S.O., T.D. after his name. It was whispered that they really stood for "Dirty Shirt On, Tinkering with Drains," because when he was home, he was just as likely to be fixing sewers as preaching sermons. He had been heard to say, "No one is qualified to preach on the Capernwray staff until they've had their arms up to the shoulder down a sewer." I know of no seminaries that require students to take Sewage 101 in their first year. But his approach to leadership, by example, meant he would never ask—or tell—anyone to do what he would not do himself. He was no prima donna, and Capernwray bred none. In fact, I suspect anyone with such proclivities would not have lasted long in that environment. Nor was anything too mundane for this man whose name was revered around the world. A salutary reminder for all of us should our opinions of our own worth become dangerously high. His approach stuck with me for life.

When the major eventually returned from overseas, he gave me a few preaching assignments at a special conference we were hosting for about 250 teenagers. To say I was nervous preaching with him sitting a few feet from me, gazing expressionless with his piercing blue eyes, would be accurate to say the least. When he checked something I said by referring to his well-worn Bible, I was sure I had proclaimed a heresy; and when he closed his Bible before I was through, I took it that he had heard enough. So I stopped rather lamely and waited for a verdict. Perhaps a session of correction, a word of encouragement, some practical suggestions—just something! I knew not what. But he simply closed the meeting and walked hurriedly past me in pursuit of his next task. I thought I heard him say as he sped past, "Good message," but I'm not sure. I was to learn subsequently that such a brief affirmation would have been high praise indeed.

We had also discovered that Jill was expecting another baby (so was I!) while turning Middle Lodge into a home and caring for David, who was having a wonderful time running round the many acres of parkland chasing the sheep and being chased by the picturesque Highland cattle. Then suddenly our ordered lives took a jolt. I developed a throat infection, which I characteristically ignored (macho marine stuff!). Up to the point I eventually was unable to talk, I consulted a doctor who took a very dim view of the situation, ordered me not to speak for a month, and warned me that my preaching days may be over if I was not very careful. This was devastating.

I had left the business world to preach the Word, and at last my opportunities for ministry were beginning to flourish in the Capernwray environment. The thought that I may have abandoned one career needlessly and would be unable to fulfill the other pushed me into a depressed state the like of which I had never known and which I have never experienced since. I continued with my administrative work, of course, but under a constant cloud.

With some activities curtailed of necessity, I had a little more time to think. I'm afraid the more I thought about my situation, the more of a muddle it became. A muddled mind becomes even more muddled when emotions are involved. Mine were running rampant. And my throat was very sore. I was a mess.

More than five years had gone by since I had first felt inner stirrings of the Spirit to leave the banking world and devote my life to ministry. The intervening years had been rich and full and thoroughly enjoyable, but in the back of my mind the thought of full-time ministry had lingered like a haunting refrain. When eventually the way ahead appeared to be clear and the decision was made to make the change, we had moved with assurance and confidence and great excitement. A dream was being fulfilled. But now the nightmare thought insinuated itself into the picture—had we made a huge mistake? Second-guessing your "guidance" is unnerving to say the least. The necessary adjustments to life at Capernwray had been safely negotiated, and vistas of previously unimagined opportunities to preach and teach were beginning to dawn. I would be less than honest if I denied that there was an element of pride in my burgeoning acceptance, and I am sure I was feeding on the affirmation I was receiving. But now what appeared to be on offer was being cruelly snatched away. Disappointment set in, disillusionment hovered nearby, and disgruntlement was not far behind. Life and ministry went on without me; others stepped into the vacant space left by my indisposition. I began to feel like an athlete sitting on the bench because of injury, watching a replacement play so well that his place on the team is jeopardised. Was this going to happen to me? Jill and I talked it over at length without arriving at any conclusions. We prayed without any breakthrough in understanding. So we did what we mortals do. We began to doubt God. Not a malignant doubting or even an accusatory doubting. It was a questioning, a longing for clarity. We wanted God to make sense of a senseless happening. And he did, but not as we expected.

One day as I was trying to pray about the situation, the thought occurred to me that maybe my attitude was all wrong. Was it possible, I wondered, that I was so in love with preaching that talking about Jesus was more important to me than the Jesus about whom I talked? Could it be that what had started out as nothing more than the fulfillment of something that was expected of me ("It's time you were preaching"), but had developed into a genuine attempt to make Christ known, had now degenerated into some kind of ego trip? Had I become so enamoured with the sound of my own voice and so enthused by the burgeoning opportunities to address more and more significant groups that I had been seduced into becoming a performer who thrived on and was nourished by his own performance?

Unaccustomed as I was to regular introspection, this exercise in delving into my innermost thoughts and motives was unnerving and unsettling, and I wasn't sure how to deal with it. But of one thing I was sure. I could ask myself a question and try to answer it as honestly as possible. "Would I still love Jesus, who would never change, even if my life changed so radically that I would never preach again?" The answer to that question, I thought, would go a long way to laying bare the motives of my heart. Surely there were ways of honouring him and serving him other than talking about him. Knowing him in times of adversity, trusting him and obeying him when things were not going according to plan was surely honouring to him. Yes, I could and should apply to myself the question similar to the one Jesus asked Simon Peter, "Lovest thou me more than these?" And in my case, the "these" were study books and pulpits and invitations and itineraries and travel and crowds of people. One fine day I knew the answer, and I knelt down and said, "Lord, I will love you and serve you in any way you wish, and if I never preach again, I will be content."

The experience alerted me to the presence of a deadly virus of which I was unaware — warped motives! Now sadder and wiser, I was able to bring my inspector's training to bear on my own inner life. "Accept nothing, question everything" — that meant I should question why I was doing what I was doing rather than simply continuing to do it. I should be very much aware that *what* you do has a *why* you're doing it behind it. It was unlikely that I, more extrovert than introvert, would become chronically paralysed by introspection, but some inner reflection would surely not go amiss.

Whether the possible prognosis had been greatly exaggerated by the good doctor I do not know, but under God it had worked wonders in my life. At the same time it reminded me of something I had forgotten.

You remember John Ward, the man who pushed me into preaching? This dear man whose contribution to my life was immeasurable had been killed along with his wife in a terrifying accident. But while I was still in the banking business he had told me in the simple, straightforward manner of a typical North countryman, "Stuart, preaching isn't difficult. You study your Bible; then you stand up and tell them what it says. That's it." Then almost as an afterthought, he added, "And if you're any good at it, people will ask you to do it. If they ask you, and you're free, the answer is yes." Those words had not appeared very significant at first, because few people asked me to preach. But as time went on, they did, more and more. Free time was at a premium in the business world, but it existed, and therefore, according to the Ward Doctrine, had to be utilised in preaching the Word. This led, of course, to an increasingly filled schedule. I reasoned that as I couldn't fulfill all the opportunities, I had to be selective. But how to select?

Well, I could select:

the one that offered the biggest crowd
the one to be held in the nicest place
the one that offered a chance to go where I had always wanted to go
the one that might pay the best honourarium
the one that was least demanding
or a thousand other things

Conversely, I could decline:

the one that coincided with a soccer game I wanted to see
the one to be held on a holiday
and make an excuse if it meant a long journey when I was tired
and duck the one that would have (a) old people, (b) few people, (c)
    stuffy people

Some of these reasons may have had an infinitesimal degree of validity, but they all had the potential for selfishness to prevail as well. And selfishness and ego are twins that don't like discipleship and are allergic to service.

I had taken a major, once-in-a-lifetime fork in the river when I joined the ministry at Capernwray, and it seemed as if all was plain sailing. However, the more I looked into what was going on in my own heart — how devious it could be and how powerful were inner motives — the more I became aware that life is made up of forks, obvious and less so, and I began to recognise how easily I could take the wrong one. I was wise enough to see that I needed wisdom beyond my years and insights beyond my knowing.

My voice gradually returned, my heart was renewed, and my ministry resumed—with fresh joy and power. But I had been alerted to the fact that while flowing streams do cut their own channels, they need regular dredging if they become sluggish. After a year or two, I was called upon to do less administrative work and more preaching and teaching. Major Thomas said my desk was more often graced by my absence than my presence—and he encouraged the absence.

Representing the Capernwray ministry in churches and youth clubs around the country became part of my role. One such occasion required me to drive in midwinter across England from west to east over the Pennine Mountain chain. The roads were narrow and the weather was abysmal, and after a long, wearying journey, I arrived at my destination in Beverley, Yorkshire, barely in time to eat a quick meal and make my way to the youth club.

A small group of truculent-looking young people casually looked at me as I walked in, regarded me suspiciously as one might view an undesirable alien, and resumed the game of basketball in which they were involved. A leader of the group, hurried over to me and greeted me, flustered, with the following salutation: "I've been in youth group work for years, and this is the worst group I've ever had to deal with. And he," she said, pointing to a slim, wiry youngster, "he's the worst of the bunch."

I thought back to the day's drive I had made through ice and snow to arrive at this less than promising situation and thought warmly of my little home and family far away—and wondered why I was here.

The kids were eventually pushed, shoved, cajoled, and threatened into some semblance of a circle, their ball having been taken away much to their displeasure, and I was introduced as the guest speaker. They looked totally disinterested, and my interest level was by this time not much higher. I remember nothing about what transpired in the next twenty to thirty minutes, but as soon as I finished speaking, the "worst of the bunch" approached and asked, without preamble, in a broad Yorkshire accent, "Where d'ya live?"

"I live at Capernwray," I replied, assuming he knew what that was from my talk.

"What's that?" he enquired.

"It's a Bible school for young people," I replied.

"I'm comin'," he responded to my amazement.

Assuming he had misunderstood, I added quickly, "No, it's a school. You come there to study the Bible."

"I told you, I'm comin'," he repeated.

I knew he wouldn't. But to my incredulity he did.

Graham Stamford actually enrolled in Capernwray Bible School. But first he became, as far as I know, the only English person required to take the special preliminary English class offered to foreign students. I knew he'd never finish the Bible course—or the English.

But he did!

His desk was always cluttered because he insisted on placing his soccer ball there so that the minute a lecture ceased, he could head for the exit and during the brief interval practice his ball control.

At the end of Bible school, he approached me again and said, "How d'ya get on the staff here?"

"By invitation," I replied.

"Then invite me," he said.

"What can you do?" I asked, assuming his skills, apart from soccer, would be limited.

"Anythin' ya want done," he replied confidently.

So I arranged for him to take the place of a gardener who had recently moved on. He proved to be an excellent worker who learned gardening in a hurry.

One day my phone rang and a very cultured voice asked, "May I please speak to Graham Stamford?" I asked who was calling, and to my surprise it was the vicar of a nearby, not particularly friendly, parish.

I brought Graham to the phone and carried on with my work while he listened for a few minutes to the fruity-voiced vicar and then said in his best Yorkshire, "I told ya not to do that. What were ya thinkin'?"

I looked up from my desk and listened in amazement as Graham went on to tell this experienced minister in unvarnished terms that he didn't know what he was doing and that he (Graham) would come over that evening and sort things out. With that he put down the phone and, turning to me with a shake of the head, said, "He doesn't 'ave a clue."

"How do you know him?" I asked. "And why did you talk to him like that?"

"Oh," he said casually, "I know all of them round 'ere. None of them 'ave a clue."

"You know all of whom?" I asked.

"All the vicars. I've been to all their 'ouses and asked 'em, 'What're you doin' about the kids in the village?' None of 'em are doing anything. So they asked me to help 'em."

And that was what our young gardener, who had only recently come to faith and who had worked his way through Bible school, was busy doing in the evenings. He was setting up youth ministries in various parishes—entirely of his own volition. On his own initiative.

Graham stayed with us for a few years, then one day announced, "I'm goin' home."

I asked if something was wrong, and he said that everything was fine, but his hometown needed him more than Capernwray did. So he got a job working at road repair with a group of tough Irishmen. Each lunch hour while they gambled their wages, he read a book of Moody's sermons. One day the men asked him. "What're ya readin'?"

"Moody's sermons," he replied without explanation.

"Moody?" they asked. "Is that a fella's name or what's up wi' 'im?"

"It's 'is name — 'e were a preacher in America."

"Then you'd better read us a sermon," they said amid raucous laughter. So he did, and the men listened in silence during their lunch break. This became a daily event until one day Graham forgot his book.

"Time for the sermon," the men shouted.

"I forgot t' book," Graham replied.

"Then you'll 'ave to gi' us one of yer own," they replied to more laughter.

"All right," he said and proceeded to preach to the men.

When Graham told me this, I asked him, "What did you tell them?"

"I told them about 'ell," he replied. "They'd never heard about 'ell."

"What did they say?" I hardly dared ask.

"They said they liked my sermons better than Moody's," he replied matter-of-factly.

Graham's life spoke as loudly as Moody's sermons. One of his jobs was to pay for the refreshments the men enjoyed during their breaks. He kept track of the amount owed by each man on a chalkboard until he paid, and then the amount was erased. One man refused to pay, and for six weeks Graham continued to buy his drinks while the other men said he was crazy to do so. On his final day at work, Graham wrote against the man's name, "Paid in full," and the other men, when they saw it, remonstrated and said, "Why would yer do that for the likes of 'im?" Graham answered, "Yer're right he don't deserve to be forgiven, and neither do you or I, but God has done it for us. And this is my final message to youse all."

Now in his sixties, Graham surprised me the last time I saw him by turning up in his soccer uniform. I asked his son, "Does your dad still play?"

"No," he said. "He thinks he does. He just stands in the middle of the park and directs traffic."

Graham Stamford became a remarkable evangelist and leader. He whose English was so bad has spoken in colleges and universities on both sides of the Atlantic and taught Bible in Torchbearer schools around the world. He started a soccer league — a league, not just a team — in which every game is preceded or concluded with devotions. He runs international soccer clinics based on spiritual teaching as well. And he has developed and organised regular public school outreaches where thousands have heard the gospel from his Yorkshire lips. Scores of times he has shown me what a flowing stream looks like.

As a kid, Graham was dubbed "the worst of the bunch," but God knew better. A little care and attention, encouragement and guidance, opportunity and support, instruction and correction, and what God had poured in poured out. Graham blossomed into a man of God. Yet another river given the chance to cut its own channel had done just that—and he's still in full flow.

I have often wondered what the youth leader saw in Graham that earned him the "worst of the bunch" label. Was he unruly and unmanageable? Did he question and challenge? Did the other kids follow his example, and was this disruptive? Did he stand out in the group because he didn't toe the party line? Many a volunteer working with young people has been driven to distraction by such kids, and sadly many such kids have been driven away from the kingdom because of failure to see that their "wildness" is often evidence of latent leadership abilities.

I'm not talking about kids who are destructive, rebellious, vicious, and dangerous (although some of them exhibit positive qualities that have gone wrong through neglect or abuse). I'm referring to the ones who are unruly and restless because they have ideas looking for an outlet, energies that need the stopper pulled out. They question and challenge because they are thinking and evaluating and don't know that's what it's called. Their willingness to stand out by being different, while it is annoying and frustrating, at least shows they have the courage and strength to leave the pack and lead it elsewhere. Leaders need these qualities in abundance. They disrupt orderly proceedings because they only need to lift a little finger and those mysterious charisma factors that other kids recognise but can't identify draw them like a magnet. They are often not the worst of the bunch—they are the pick of the crop. They just need managing. Of course, flowing streams cut their own channels. Occasionally some of them overflow their banks and take shortcuts—and for a while this can be chaotic. A little bank repair, shoring up of weak points, and subtle redirection can take care of that. And the river flows on. The further it flows, the more forks it presents, the more decisions it demands, the more opportunities to get it wrong it introduces—and the greater the chances to do it right it brings our way.

CHAPTER 6

OVER HILLS AND THROUGH VALLEYS

By thirty hills I hurry down,
Or slip between the ridges,
By twenty thorps, a little town,
And half a hundred bridges.

—Alfred Lord Tennyson, "The Brook"

If Tennyson's little "brook" had been able to think or dream when it started out among coots and herons, I doubt if it would have envisaged the hills and ridges, the towns and bridges that lay invitingly in its path. The hills and ridges of course would contribute to its direction, the thorps and towns would depend on it for their existence and development, and the bridges would become necessary because the "brook" came that way.

In my growing years, I, like the brook, was just trickling along. But a friend named David Carling in comparison was already a rushing stream. When he was asked by well-meaning adults, "What do you want to be when you grow up, David?" he would answer in an unbroken soprano, "a missionary doctor." He set his sights, went about his business, and became a missionary doctor. I used to look at him in amazement. He actually knew what he wanted to do with his life. He knew where Lake Chad was, way out in the Sahara Desert; he was aware of the people who lived on its floating islands of tangled vegetation; and he was aware of the needs of these "unreached people." Moreover, he knew he was to go to them.

In marked contrast to David's knowledge of Africa, to me the hills and valleys, the rivers and lakes of Europe were nothing more than lines on a map, but in the economy of God, they were part of my destiny. The boys and girls going to school in Alpine villages, learning English in kindergarten, busily growing up as proud of being German or French, Swedish or Swiss as I was of being British, did not appear on the radar of my imagination. In later years, however, our streams would flow together, and the hills and valleys, the towns and cities of Europe, and the people who lived there became integral to my life. We talk about "cross-cultural" experiences today, but in those days I was not aware of such terminology. Nevertheless, I was keenly aware of the value of looking at life through different eyes and of seeing myself from the perspective of others. I was in no great danger of becoming insular in thinking or myopic in vision—huge blessings indeed.

Many of the original group of young Germans who came to Capernwray in 1948 returned home and shared their new life in Christ. Because they had learned about Jesus' promise about "streams of living water" flowing, it is not surprising that blessing began to flow as young people from around the Continent became ardent followers of Jesus. By the time we joined the staff, hundreds of them had attended the short-term Bible school and spread out literally around the world. And when I had the opportunity to teach in the school and to mingle with the students, friendships were born that to this day rank among my dearest relationships.

Peter and Runhild Wiegand went to Upper Austria to start a Torchbearer ministry among the young people who lived in the idyllic mountains and valleys around the region known as the Salzkammergut. Small groups were gathered and developed, and when a centre of operations was needed, a picturesque sixteenth-century *Schloss* became available—a castle adjacent to the ruins of a *Burg* (fortress) that was certainly in existence in the eleventh. They tackled the Herculean task of changing first the *Schloss* and then later the *Burg* into a youth conference centre and Bible school. Under Peter's direction, driven by his relentless energy, vision, and determination, a small team transformed the ancient buildings into a Torchbearer centre named "*Schloss Klaus*." I led the first of hundreds of schools and conferences conducted there in a ministry that has made an impact all over Austria and Germany, behind the Iron Curtain in the days of the Cold War, into the wastelands of Sudan, the islands of Micronesia, and the refugee camps of Kosovo, Albania, and countless other nations.

Bernhard Rebsch, a tall, blond, good-looking Berliner arrived at Capernwray one day. I met him as he was raking leaves clad in traditional lederhosen. *"Guten morgen,"* I said in my best German. *"Wie heist Du?"* ("Good morning. What's your name?") With an impish grin and in impeccable English, he said, "Who are you, and why do you want to know?" Then he burst out in a great guffaw, and I realised I had met another "cocky" young Berliner. Bernhard came to faith, studied hard, showed a remarkable aptitude for languages, and in short order developed into an excellent translator, evangelist, and youth leader. He took over the leadership of a Torchbearer centre and school in Germany named *Klostermuehle* (the old "mill of the cloister" that was set high on a steep, wooded hill overlooking the tiny village of Obernhof an der Lahn).

One day Bernhard was involved in a tragic motor accident that cost him a leg, and during the weeks he spent in a coma, we all thought it had cost him his life too. His wife, Anne, worked tirelessly with the doctors who declared him "brain dead." She refused to accept their diagnosis, and eventually he emerged from unconsciousness a shadow of the man he was before the accident but with a childlike, almost innocent faith intact — a faith that years later still endears him to young people around the continent of Europe. Streams still flow even in damaged watercourses.

Literally dozens of relationships and ministries such as these developed in those years, and Jill and I began to see from our little lodge in the countryside something of the worldwide reach of the church.

People from all over the world began to find their way to us, often in unusual circumstances. A painfully shy, young Austrian from the Alpine town of Schladming named Walter Thaler, traveling home from Capernwray, stopped overnight at a youth hostel in London. A young Japanese boy named Hideki Tanazawa who was roaming the world searching for something — he knew not what — on an impulse went into the hostel for breakfast. He saw Walter, the only person in the room, reading a book, and sat down next to him. In fractured English he asked about the book, and on being told — in equally fractured English — that it was a Bible, he asked what that was. Walter suggested he visit Capernwray, which he did, arriving on the doorstep one evening. That's how "Tana," as he became known, arrived on the scene.

Having no previous contact with Christians, he knew nothing about Christianity but was welcomed, fed, housed, and put to work on the endless number of jobs that always needed attention. As time went by, Tana's English improved until it was occasionally understandable. He became interested in Christianity, not because he wanted to become a Christian, but to understand what writers like Kierkegaard and Camus were talking about. He began to listen in to preaching, and after a long time, he became a disciple of Jesus. After staying on for Bible school, Tana continued to work on staff, and during his long stay with us, as so often happened with young people who drifted in, he became part of the fabric.

One memorable day he was invited to speak at staff devotions — a big step for him. He surprised everyone by choosing to talk about Solomon, with particular reference to the fact that the ancient king had seven hundred wives and three hundred concubines. What attracted this single young man to this extraordinary marital arrangement he never divulged. We gathered eagerly to hear how Tana would apply the behaviour of the ancient king of Israel to a group of young twentieth-century people. Unfortunately, we never found out, because Tana not only had problems pronouncing the English words with a Japanese tongue, but he confused "concubines" with "cucumbers." He astounded everybody by telling us that Solomon in addition to having seven hundred wives had three hundred cucumbers, and he added to the confusion by warning us of the danger of multiplying cucumbers. Stifled sniggers gradually gave way to uncontrollable giggles, and the devotional came to an inconclusive end.

Tana, however, was nothing if not resilient, and none of us was a stranger to language lapses and the hilarity that always attended them, so he recovered from his less than auspicious debut and some time later returned to his native Japan where he opened and continues to run a Bible school named Yamanakako Cove in the shadow of Mount Fuji.

The spread of Torchbearing around Europe meant an increasingly busy travel schedule for me as I began to lead groups of young Brits to the centres for conferences where they would not only learn about Christ, but would have opportunities to learn about each other, their countries and their languages, and of course their faith life lived out in different cultures. In the case of the Brits, they certainly had a lot to learn. On one long train journey to Germany, a young girl in our party excitedly showed me a fistful of German currency her father had given her to spend on her vacation. Noting that the bills were not deutschmarks but reichmarks—which meant they dated from World War II and were worthless—I asked where she got them, and she proudly told me that her daddy brought them back from the war. Sadly, I had to break the news to her that she was broke not rich.

When we arrived in Obernhof, the locals were rather startled by the invasion. The young people I had taken there, most of whom had never ventured out of England before, were equally surprised by what they found. Communications proved problematic. One young gentleman opined, "These Germans don't know much. I didn't find one of them that spoke English!" We pointed out gently that as his Deutsch vocabulary seemed to be limited to *ja* and *nein*, he perhaps should temper his criticism! And needless to say, we sat them down and taught them some basic principles of cross-cultural communication.

My frequent absences from home provoked numerous comments—and criticisms—over the years. But one friend, noting our growing family, had commented pointedly, "At least you get home occasionally."

In 1961 Jill produced our daughter, Judy—much to her father's amazement and delight! I'm afraid Capernwray in those days was a very masculine place. Led by a military major who had three sons (a fourth arrived later) and who barely noticed the girls who clustered around the boys, we were unconsciously male-oriented in our thinking and ministry. So in that kind of environment, the thought of me becoming father to a daughter did not occur to me until my Judy arrived on the scene. But arrive she did, and her arrival was heralded by the ancient bell in the clock tower being rung furiously by a delighted Joan Thomas. A wise woman whispered in my ear, "She'll wrap herself round her daddy's heartstrings." She did. She does. And she always will.

Two years after Judy's arrival, her little brother, Peter, was born in 1963, and our family was complete. The little lodge was crowded!

During my absences, Jill turned her attention to the immediate neighbourhood. Small villages and isolated cottages with neat colourful gardens dotted the landscape. A few miles away, the railway town of Carnforth provided work for a few thousand people, and further afield the historic city of Lancaster, dating back to Roman times, spread out around its forbidding castle. Jill was to be seen regularly walking the country lanes with David running ahead, Judy puffing behind, and Peter surveying the scenery from his pram. She visited the homes of the older people, drank endless cups of tea, and tried to interest them in coming to our home for some spiritual encouragement. Naturally set in their ways and suspicious of anything that wasn't "Church of England," even though most of them rarely visited the church — or any church for that matter — it was slow work, but as time went by, the local women shyly began to attend little gatherings in our cramped lodge. Eventually their daughters also began to attend, the crowds grew, and the meetings were moved to a chapel on Capernwray's grounds. Later on the teenagers from the vicinity were intrigued enough to inquire about what was going on. So a cow barn was turned into a youth center, and eventually a four-story warehouse was purchased in Carnforth, and the work of reaching the neighbourhood took off apace.

A nursery school, a bookstore, youth groups, a youth center, and soccer teams were all started and flourished, and both young and old came to faith. Jill was reminding us all that while there is a certain glamour attached to overseas travel and a definite excitement in seeing the gospel spread in exotic places, great spiritual needs exist close to home too. Furthermore, it is often the case that the people who know us best, in the place where we live, are the hardest to reach, convince, and lead to faith. Jill was reminding us that, as Tennyson said, there are "brimming rivers," but the brook must "trickle down the valley" too!

Very occasionally Jill was able to join me in taking groups to the Continent, but after a particularly rough crossing from Gothenburg in Sweden to Harwich in England, her ardour for such excitement waned dramatically. Nevertheless, she did agree to share in the leadership of a group conference in The Hague in the Netherlands. The return journey included crossing the English Channel by ferry from Ostend in Belgium to Dover. On arrival at the quay in the middle of the night with forty tired teenagers clinging to us, we found great crowds of people milling around. Total chaos reigned supreme. With half our group on board the ferry, we were informed that the other half, still on the quay, would have to wait for the next boat. Jill, who happened to be on the gangway halfway between the quay and the boat, protested strenuously. She was told by the officer of the watch that there was nothing he could do about it. Since I was on the quay with the other half, she could take half to England, and I would follow on with the remnant of the group. She refused, insisting that we were on a group ticket (she was right about that) and must travel together. The captain, who was anxious to sail, called down from the bridge to see what was causing the delay. The frustrated officer said it was my wife. The captain asked her please to get off the gangway. She refused, and like a suffragette of former days, while stopping short of chaining herself to the rail but in the interests of justice and some other things, made it clear that she was not going anywhere. If they wanted her to leave the gangway, they would have to remove her. My wife has a flair for the dramatic, and occasionally it blossoms in all its splendour. Such was the case on the floodlit gangway in the dead of night before the watching crowds! I, meanwhile, was trying to look as if I had never met the woman, because I couldn't see where the problem lay. But Jill has super-developed mother instincts, and in her mind her little brood of bemused British kids were going to stay together or she would know the reason why! She won the day—or the night as it happened—the captain relented and triumphantly our group boarded together and traveled home safe and sound.

In those days Jill demonstrated time and again the leadership gifts that I had first seen as she worked among her group of kids from Liverpool. And now, all these years later, the way she started the work of spreading the gospel in the neighbourhood of Capernwray and the way she readily took control of situations that required courage and conviction showed clearly that the good hand of the Lord rested upon her. Without doubt the Spirit of God was flowing in and through her just as much as through those of us who were being given more and more public exposure and recognition. We were recognising that we really were partners in ministry, and even though we often served apart, there was never any question that we were in it together. "Together apart" became a kind of watchword for us.

One of the great advantages of living at Capernwray was that we had a constant stream of gifted preachers and teachers participating in the Bible school and summer conferences. Men like Alan Redpath, Stephen Olford, Gerald Griffiths, and others greatly enriched my life by their godly example and their ministry expertise. Whenever possible I took the opportunity to listen to them and learned much from them theologically and devotionally, and I was also able to study the way they, as experienced preachers, went about the task of sermon preparation and presentation. This was something I knew I lacked, and their input was immeasurable.

During this time I was also surprised to be invited to join the team of speakers at the Keswick Convention — I called it the "Wimbledon of Evangelicals." Apart from the war years, Keswick, the beautiful little town in the middle of the Lake District, has hosted the convention for 130 years or more, and each year twelve thousand people from around the globe attend. Specifically designed to promote the development of spiritual life and the furtherance of the church's mission, it historically has been one of the great powerhouses of evangelical witness in the United Kingdom and throughout the world.

I was particularly thrilled to be invited to join the team of speakers, which included the men whose names I mentioned above, not least because I was a local boy born not far from the site of the convention. Moreover, I had reluctantly attended the convention as a boy with my parents and perhaps felt that I should in some way make amends for my less than commendable behaviour there. Despite myself, I had derived great blessing from the convention. On one occasion when I was attending against my will, like all teenagers in such circumstances, I knew the only thing I could do was to make people around me as miserable as I felt by my attitude, and this I proceeded to do without paying any attention to what was going on.

Suddenly a loud voice proclaimed, "The way to up is down!" There was a rustle of reaction from the crowd, startled by such an abrupt, enigmatic statement in surroundings where the tone was usually solemn and serene. I too looked up to see a large man with grey hair standing at the podium surveying the audience and presumably weighing the impact of his opening statement. Then he, apparently satisfied, added with equal forcefulness, "And the way to down is up!"

I was hooked. He had grabbed my reluctant attention and proceeded to explain Peter's teaching from 1 Peter 5:5–6 about people who exalt themselves being brought down and those who humble themselves being raised up. I had heard that a dozen times before, but Donald Grey Barnhouse, the great Philadelphia preacher, for he it was who had disturbed my truculent reveries, put familiar truth in unfamiliar language, presented it in an unfamiliar manner, and taught me more about preaching in a few seconds than others had conveyed in lengthy perorations. His method was compelling, his message was equally powerful, and I went away pondering.

It was to this great convention that I was invited to speak — and I did so with not a little fear and trembling!

My streams were flowing serenely through pleasant pastures. But streams sometimes take surprising twists and turns, and when Major Thomas bustled into my small office one day on his return from the United States, my life was going to be twisted and turned!

"What are your plans for the first three months of next year?" he asked.

"I have just a few engagements lined up," I said.

"Good," he replied. "I've just completed three months' ministry in the United States, and in each place they invited me to return, but I was already booked. I suggested that you would be a suitable replacement for me, and they all agreed. Here is your itinerary for the first three months of next year."

I don't recollect him asking me if I wanted to go or if I would go. He apparently assumed I was ready, willing, eager, and halfway packed to go.

He continued with great enthusiasm. "You'll be there for thirteen weeks starting January 1," he said. "The first week you'll be in Chattanooga, Tennessee, with Dr. Paul Rees."

My heart stopped! Paul Rees was my all-time favorite preacher, a master of exegesis, cultured, polished, easy to listen to, humourous, serious, compelling, and pastoral. In my book he had it all. I had listened to him whenever he came from his church in Minneapolis to England. On occasions I had even traveled specially to hear him preach. The thought of being in a strange land far from home and preaching in the company of this spiritual giant was totally too much. The major went on.

"The second week you'll be with Alan Redpath in Dallas."

Now Dr. Redpath was probably England's best-known preacher at the time. A former rugby player and businessman, he had pastored one of England's renowned churches in Richmond, Surrey, before heading to America to become the senior pastor of the great Moody Memorial Church in Chicago. He was as powerful in his presentation as Dr. Rees was polished, and he could overwhelm people by the sheer force of his personality and the respect he commanded. But it got worse.

"Then you'll be in New York with Stephen Olford," he said.

Another great British preacher known for his fiery eloquence and burning intensity. I had listened to Stephen preaching to the biggest crowds of anyone in Britain with the exception of Billy Graham. I had heard enough.

"I can't do this!" I blurted.

Major Thomas, who appeared to have difficulty understanding the word *can't*, looked surprised and replied without hesitation, "Jesus Christ in you is adequate. You'll have to get on with it." And with that he left.

My immediate emotional response to the challenges presented to me I have already outlined, but on the other hand, the thought of traveling to America was vastly appealing. Yet when I went home to the Middle Lodge and told Jill about my assignment and saw the look in her eye and heard her say quietly, "But, Stu, when we came here, I thought we were going to have a chance to be a family," I was torn. Feeling the warmth and excitement of my three small children as they greeted "Daddy" home in the evening and knowing they and I would miss it every day for three long months was far from appealing. I discovered later that Jill had rightly suspected that if I started traveling to America, I would be away from home for extended periods of time as Major Thomas was. Thus she was concerned.

Underlying this turmoil of mixed desires and tangled aspirations were two incontrovertible truths that we had embraced, we thought, wholeheartedly. Discipleship involves carrying a cross, and crosses are not ornaments for decoration but instruments of submission. Second, "Jesus Christ in us is adequate." But—and it was a big *but*—did the fact that Jill and I might be willing to die to some aspects of marriage and family life give us the right to deprive our children of the presence of a father for extended periods in their formative years? And what exactly did it mean that Jesus was adequate—there were obviously limits to the adequacy he provides. I knew for a fact that he would not make me adequate to teach nuclear physics in a university! Would he be adequate to equip for separation and periods of single-parent parenting?

I cannot say that either Jill or I came to thoughtfully worked-out positions on either of these questions. But from a practical point of view, we decided that as the children, ages six, four, and two, were naturally more in touch with their mother than their father (at least that was the way British people thought in the 1960s), they would not suffer any lasting harm from my absence. We were also children of World War II; we knew men who had gone off to war for years and their children had survived—and anyway we were in a warfare against evil, and that meant that sacrifice was normative.

As for the response that I had been given to my feelings of inadequacy, I knew Paul's teaching from 2 Corinthians 2 and 3. I had preached on it! Paul had outlined a wonderful picture of ministry based on a picture of the triumphal return of a conquering hero to his home city and the thunderous welcome of the hometown crowds. He had described being part of Christ's triumphant procession—either as an exhibit of his victory or as a participant therein. He had graphically explained how the proclamation of Christ through his lips was like a breath of fresh air or the fragrance of incense to those responding, and a deadly odor spelling out doom to the rebellious. He went on to say that in the same way the priests welcoming home the conqueror did so with sacrifices, the odor of which permeated the city, so the life of God's servant is to the Father a sweet reminder of Christ and the efficacy of his work of salvation. In Paul's mind ministry was to be a triumphant procession through life demonstrating the power of Christ's victory, bringing delight to the watching Father, conviction of spirit to the reluctant, and unspeakable blessing to the responsive. It is no wonder that he, grasping the enormity of it all, stopped and asked the great question, "Who is sufficient for these things?" (2:16 KJV). When we get past an approach to ministry that can easily become manageable and doable, routine and even mundane, and remind ourselves of the immensity of what we are called to be and to do—as Paul did in this passage—these questions must never be far from our minds.

The question of sufficiency was certainly dominating my thinking. Like a good preacher, Paul answered his own question. "I'm not sufficient. I'm not adequate," he said. That was where I was and where I wanted to stay—and stay home. Staying home feeling totally inadequate was fine by me! But Paul—and the major—would not let me. They both insisted that "our competence comes from God." God calls us and makes us sufficient, adequate.

The question for me was, sufficient for what? I knew the answer: sufficient for all that God calls us to. So the question became, "Is this what God is calling me to?" Because if it is, I cannot claim insufficiency—or inadequacy—and leave it there. I cannot say, "I can't." That response is ruled out by the simple but powerful principle, "God never calls without equipping." From early days I had been nurtured with that concept in a technical sense and later introduced to it in practical ways in my Torchbearer experience. If "I can't" is ruled out, I can only say, "I will" or "I won't." That was clear.

Then another old principle came roaring back into my consciousness—"If they ask you and you're free, the answer is yes." That, along with responsible affirmations of effectiveness from knowledgeable, godly people had become our understanding of "calling." We were being asked; we were being affirmed; there were evidences of blessing following the ministry—if this was not a calling, what was it? Jill and I worked through all this—inadequately, I have no doubt—but we answered yes to what we assumed was a call. I would go—and yet another bend in the river loomed ahead.

Somewhere round the bend I had visions of an America practically everybody in those days viewed as the land of opportunity—and many still do despite the plethora of criticisms, deserved and undeserved, so often leveled at the world's remaining superpower. Gradually feelings of inadequacy and uncertainty and worries about family were superseded by positive thoughts fueled by excited studies in atlases to find out where exactly Tennessee, Alabama, Mississippi, and Arizona were—and how these strange place names were spelled. But Jill was contemplating long, lonely winter nights in a small cottage in the countryside, with small children asleep in bed and a husband far from home. She said little, but I knew she was struggling. I was concerned about her but didn't know what to do except to "trust the

Lord." This was a perfectly legitimate and appropriate approach but, sadly, not without a hint of irresponsibility in the way I went about it. Yet the trustworthy Lord who "works in wondrous ways his wonders to perform" already had something in the works of which we were totally unaware.

My secretary, a bright, perky, petite woman named Catherine O'Connor, who spoke fluent French and had a strong attraction to French people, had been wrestling for some time with a decision regarding her future. She loved being at Capernwray and was highly efficient and a constant spark of good humour and wit—a delight to have around the place. But France constantly beckoned her, and she was becoming more and more traumatized by indecision. One day, seeing her looking with a faraway gaze out of the window and knowing that while her eyes registered the English countryside, her mind saw the Eiffel Tower, I said to her, "Catherine, you need to make a decision. You can't go on like this. So put on your coat and go for a long walk and don't come back until you've decided whether you're going to France or staying here." I don't usually place things so directly before people, but I knew this sweet girl very well and was convinced in my mind where she really belonged, although I was reluctant to tell her—or to lose her.

So off she went, bundled up against the chill winds. A couple of hours later she returned with a smile and her old buoyancy and announced that she was going to France to serve the Lord. That evening a missionary from France arrived unexpectedly at Capernwray and stayed overnight. During dinner he said to me, "I felt a strange compulsion to come here tonight. I'm looking for a spiritually mature assistant with good secretarial skills, fluency in French, and a heart for the French people."

"Let me introduce you," I replied, and to his and Catherine's surprise, I brought her into the room and they made arrangements for her to join him in his work in France. Fifty years later she is still there—the same Catherine so immersed in French culture and committed to serving the French people that now she has to try hard to remember English, and when she does remember it, she pronounces her native language like a lady from Paris.

Catherine's leaving left me secretary-less at a critical time. But my sister-in-law, Helen, had called and said, "A school friend of mine named Angela Mills has recently been converted. Could she come and spend a weekend with you both as she needs some advice and encouragement?"

So Angela arrived. She was employed by British European Airways as a stewardess and had, as she explained graphically, "got tired of emptying sick bags." She was looking for a change. She was a fresh, new believer who had an endless enthusiasm for anything and everything she touched. She was boundlessly energetic in her pursuit of anything that took her fancy and was lively and funny. Furthermore, she was fluent in French. So I offered her a job. She immediately accepted, and Catherine moved on and Angie moved in. She stayed for more than forty years!

But Angie did much more than take over as my secretary, for she and Jill became close friends and partners in the burgeoning ministry to the neighbourhood. In his grace and kindness, God had brought someone to help fill the loneliness for Jill and to share the burden of the ministry to the locality—and an "auntie" who won her way into the hearts of our three children like none other.

Angie became the implementer of Jill's wildest ideas, the pricker of Jill's most impossible balloons, and a cheerleader extraordinaire. Years later when we as a family emigrated to America, Angie took over the leadership of the neighbourhood ministry, which had grown beyond our imagining, and led it to new heights. God is good—and he is adequate.

In my imagination I'm standing on one of the half hundred bridges looking back across the years through the hills and ridges, the towns and thorps, tracing the course of the river that is my life. And I see people on the banks. They are the people who in a thousand ways made me who I am, and some of them are who they are because we met in some backwater or on some promontory overlooking the Rhine or the Rhone or the Danube. I see again Peter Wiegand and the unquenchable energy and determination that turned the ruins of a fortress into a powerhouse for God, and I feel the challenge of his example all over again. And there is Anne Rebsch, tiny and afraid but unflinchingly taking on the doctors and fighting for the life of her husband, a life they have already abandoned. Her courage warms my heart all over again. I laugh as I think of Tana and his cucumbers, but my laughter dies as I remember that this young man read Kierkegaard and Camus and was willing to study Christianity in a foreign language because he had an insatiable appetite for truth. I feel ashamed of my shallowness.

And there is Jill with our three small children, a city girl content to live in the country among the cows she fears and the mice she fears more. She's adjusting to the unfamiliar because it's the right thing to do. It's her calling, and she'll do whatever it takes. If necessary, she'll stand on the gangplank of a channel steamer in the dead of night in a foreign land and do the right thing by the kids she loves and serves. And I love her all over again, and I thank God for the places my river has flowed, the things I've seen, the people I've met, and the things I've learned. Above all and through it all, the abiding lesson I have learned is that he who lives by his Spirit within is adequate.

CHAPTER 7

STREAMS OF ABUNDANCE

Blessed be Your name
In the land that is plentiful
Where the streams of abundance flow
Blessed be Your name.

— Beth Redman and Matt Redman,
"Blessed Be Your Name"

It was New Year's Eve 1964 when I boarded a plane for my first transatlantic flight. Jill was supportive of this new development in our lives. She promised to try to be Mummy and Daddy in my absence and asked only that I would write often. As we couldn't afford regular international phone calls (and Jill found that the sound of my voice exacerbated, for her, the feelings of distance) and the Internet was not yet invented, old-fashioned airmail letters had to suffice.

Safely navigating the international airport in New York, recently renamed for the slain U.S. president John F. Kennedy, was a challenge even though I could read the signage and understand some of the announcements. But the noise and the bustle of the crowds in what according to my biological clock was the middle of the night was not the most pleasant experience. I made a mental note to avoid JFK whenever possible — a commitment I religiously keep to this day. And I spared a thought for the befuddled individuals who, without the language, the currency, or people to help them arrived in huge numbers in such a whirlpool of confusion.

On arrival in Chattanooga, I was met by the local pastor and taken immediately to the Read House Hotel in the centre of town. This was new — I had rarely been accommodated in a hotel before! The room seemed unbearably hot — it was seventy degrees — a temperature that makes railroad tracks warp and blacktop melt in England! But all my efforts to open the window failed, so I literally had to sweat it out. Waking up disoriented early the next morning with an unaccustomed low-grade headache, aching muscles, and unusual lethargy (I discovered later it is called "jetlag" and have since learned to live in it as a continual state), I waited for the dining room to open and went in for breakfast.

Oak paneled with great chandeliers and tables covered with perfectly laundered linen, the ornate dining room was a masterpiece of classic Southern gentility. I was greeted by three or four smiling black waitresses dressed in the kind of black dresses and white aprons I had seen in the movies. One of them said something that sounded like "Yallhagrits?" Assuming this was a greeting, I politely said, "Good morning," to which she repeated, "Yallhagrits?" Gathering that greetings were repeated in America, I repeated mine, but to my surprise the young woman, backed like a singing group by her companions, in forceful unison asked, "Ah say-ed, 'Yallhagrits?'"

I assured them as best I could that I could hear them perfectly but was having difficulty understanding, and I asked if any of them perhaps spoke German. They didn't unfortunately! But they took pity on me and served me a kind of hot cereal that I discovered tasted only of what you put on it. It was some time later, after careful inquiry, that I discovered the cereal was called "grits," which allowed me to parse their initial enquiry into "*Y'all* [an abbreviation of 'you all' that was addressed to me even though I had always assumed I was singular, not plural] *ha* ['have'] *grits* [tasteless cereal beloved of people living in the South]?" When translated, "You all have grits?" meant that they were asking me if I wanted some cereal. But it got worse.

The next day as I was being transported to a speaking engagement, the driver leaned toward me and asked, "Would you like a chocolate kiss?" This was quite startling until I saw the candy (sweet) being offered.

I wondered how on earth I was going to communicate to those who spoke such a strange tongue, but I found the people incredibly warm — I had never been hugged by large men after sermons before — and my program was so full (I preached seven times each day the first week) that I had little time to do anything but catch my breath!

My fears of working with my hero Dr. Paul Rees were totally unfounded. I reveled in the opportunities to listen to him and grabbed every chance to ask him questions about ministry. Particularly preaching. In one of his talks, he quoted from Hamlet's soliloquy — "To be or not to be — that is the question." (That to me was startling, because in my upbringing my interest in classical literature had been treated with a little concern — worldliness always loomed and had to be guarded against — and the thought of using it in a sermon was frankly unthinkable.) He used the quote to illustrate Paul's statement, "For to me, to live is Christ and to die is gain.... Yet what I shall choose I wot not. For I am in a strait betwixt two, having a desire to depart, and to be with Christ; which is far better: nevertheless to abide in the flesh is more needful for you" (Philippians 1:21 – 24 KJV).

Hamlet, he said, was torn because, as he looked at what life had to offer, he was appalled, and suicide seemed the only option. But on contemplating suicide, he was terrified. So to be or not to be—neither held any attraction for him. He was overcome. Paul on the other hand was confronting two possibilities—either he would live or he would die. Should he live, Christ would continue to be the essence, the power, the reason, and the goal of his life. Serving him was joy. On the other hand, should he die, he would be released from many unpleasant situations and find himself "forever with the Lord." To be or not to be—both options filled him with delight! The illustration was vivid, the point inescapable. The contrast between the hopelessness of despair on the one hand and the hopefulness of faith on the other presented modern men and women a clear-cut option. And it gave me the encouragement I needed to pursue my interests and aptitudes in the service of the Lord who was, after all, the Lord of all things. This was liberating—and Paul Rees did it for me!

One of the planned events was a gathering of pastors, and for some reason, I, who had never been a pastor, was asked to speak, while Dr. Rees, who was a consummate pastor, was required to listen. Unsuccessfully I tried to change the program, and when I asked Paul if he would please take my place as I didn't know what to say to the pastors, he replied, "Stuart, you know what to say. Whenever you talk to men and women in ministry, talk to their hearts. They are the hungriest people in the world." I follow that advice to this day.

Despite the fact that I had prayed fervently that Paul would not come to my sessions (I wisely made no suggestions on how God should stop him), he came, sat on the front row—and took notes. He was the essence of courtesy. He and his wife adopted me, showed me the ropes, steered me through menus, and translated waitresses for me. Incredibly, they thanked me profusely for my ministry, which they said had been an encouragement to them. Paul Rees was Barnabas—son of encouragement—to me. And how I needed him that first confusing, unnerving week in the good ol' U.S. of A.!

I was invited to speak on radio programs on which people called in to ask me questions in accents I could barely understand. As I was about to make my debut on a noontime television show, the host announced that Winston Churchill had just died. Then, without missing a beat and sounding as if it had been presciently arranged, he said that they had an Englishman in the studio. I was quickly bundled onto the set. Blinking in the lights, I found myself being interviewed on the great man's impact on my life! I was being introduced to "thinking on my feet" sitting on a set.

Another time, at a dinner party in a fashionable home, I was suddenly asked by the hostess, a most gracious woman, impeccably dressed and coiffed, "Mr. Briscoe, we thought we could see the hand of God in the assassination of Kennedy. What do you think?" Stunned, I stuttered something to the effect that I didn't know about the hand of God, as I thought the

Bible taught that it was the devil who was a murderer from the beginning. That was not the most diplomatic of answers, I'm sure, and it did have a chilling effect on the rest of the evening. I was in a room full of members of the John Birch Society, a political group of whom I had never heard and whose politics I had never imagined. This was what the Americans called "being in way over my head"—the English equivalent of "being out of my depth." In either language it meant I spent a lot of time floundering, splashing, and spluttering!

Free time was so rare in the three months I traveled the States that I was delighted when I was invited to attend an American football game between Baylor University and Texas Christian University. In England in those days most people stood during an entire soccer game. They were crammed in like sardines in a can, and understandably women rarely ventured into such a rough and ready male preserve. Old clothes were worn because the possibility of being soaked in a downpour was very real. So I arrived dressed as if for an English soccer match. What I didn't know was that I was invited first to a brunch beautifully served by uniformed attendants in a magnificent home. Large numbers of women clad in expensive clothes in the colours of their team were there with their husbands, all of whom seemed to be attorneys or stockbrokers—obviously very successful. Wanting only to hide, I was seated in a place of honour and peppered with interested, intelligent questions about the talks I had given during the week. After a sumptuous meal and a challenging discussion, we drove to the stadium in fine automobiles and took our places on the fifty-yard line.

The idea of a Christian university was new, so I asked about Texas Christian University and found that nobody wanted to talk about it, as they were all Baylor people—and Baylor was a Southern Baptist university. Sitting there among these charming, generous people so deeply committed to the Lord and obviously committed to their university, which was in some way linked to their denomination, and seeing the partisan support of both men and women for their football team, I thought, "I wish my old dad could see me now. He who thought football was the essence of worldliness!" But I assumed he was too busy in glory to be watching, so I went ahead and enjoyed myself!

Just before the game started, we were all asked to stand for the national anthem, and then I was flabbergasted when an "invocation" was announced in which a clergyman invited the Lord to join us, asked that no one would get injured, and implored the Deity to "deliver us from idle pursuits." As we had just been watching a spectacle in which scantily clad young women twirled blazing batons and dangerous-looking swords around their necks and grown men played with a couple of bears, I wondered what would count as idle pursuits if they didn't. I was on a learning curve so steep I was in danger of slipping off.

On the way home, I was also introduced to "fast food" in the form of "Arby's," which I learned stood for "R.B.'s," which in turn stood for "roast beef." I thought that was a perfect example of the American genius for streamlining everything. I also was struck by the way in which these people who lived easily in luxury quite casually stopped to eat in something that looked like a roadside shack. Americans, unlike Brits, seemed to be without any "class" consciousness and seemed equally at ease being formal or informal, casual or correct. I liked it, but I was continually surprised that I was having more difficulty adjusting to life in the United States than I ever had when traveling in European countries where I could not even speak the language. I think I was put off my stride by the increased pace of life, the abundance of resources, and the grand lifestyle of so many of the people I was meeting that was far above anything that I had known.

People's extravagant appreciation of my preaching was at first embarrassing to my British ears. "Oh, God blessed ma soul today! Ah've never heard anything like that my whole life long." It could not possibly be sincere, for I knew that the same message in England had elicited nothing more than a shy "Good night." But as time went on, I concluded that I was dealing with people who really were open to and ready for and anxious to respond to God's Word. After a talk in which I had mentioned giving for cross-cultural missions, one woman informed me, "Ah was so blessed, Ah upped ma pledge." I had not previously encountered the verb "to up." Neither had I known, until I was informed, that "you can verb any noun"—a common practice, I discovered, as we "fellowshipped" with each other and "accessed" various things.

Jill's letters were full of news about the children and tales of the ministry among the local people. Everything she was experiencing was smaller and simpler but no less real, and the interplay of our news to each other served to remind us that as rivers flowing in different geological strata take different courses, so our lives and ministries at that point were being lived out in different spiritual environments, but both rivers were flowing nevertheless—and we rejoiced in each other's joy.

I had little time to be lonely, and only when I was passing through an airport and saw a British Airways jet bound for London did I have a heart pang. The thought, *If I jump on that, I can be home for breakfast in the morning!* had to be quickly corralled and the next assignment embraced. Eventually the thirteen weeks were concluded, and I flew home on the first plane, tanned and tired and much better equipped to understand people and ministry, particularly Americans—and myself!

Jill and the children were waiting for me at the Manchester airport, and I remember savouring the sight of them standing together in the crowded concourse before they saw me. When one of the children saw me, he shouted, and all three ran toward me. As they came through the crowd, as if in slow motion, I wondered, *What will they say? "Daddy, how are you? Daddy, we love you! Daddy, we missed you"?* None of these words of endearment fell from their lips. "Daddy, what did you bring us?" was uppermost in their minds. Smiling just a little ruefully, I realized they were just normal kids and apparently had experienced little or no harm during my absence, under their mother's care. And I was glad.

When we were safely home, Jill wanted to know all about my trip. Starting with the time spent in Chattanooga, I told her how toward the end of the week the pastor told me that a woman from the church where he ministered had asked that I have dinner with a group of teenagers before the evening service. As I had been going nonstop since arriving in America and had already spoken six times that day, I said I was really hoping for a few minutes' break. But he said that the woman in question was quite persistent, and he was sure I would enjoy being with the young people. So I agreed to go—reluctantly, I admit—and young Drew Trotter, a freshman at the University of Virginia, arrived in a sports car fit for the Le Mans twenty-four-hour race and drove me expertly up the hairpin bends of Lookout Mountain.

Arriving at his beautiful family home, I was introduced to his mother, Hazel, who I discovered quickly had a wry sense of humour and an easy rapport with the large group of immaculately mannered, preppy young people who surrounded me. All were neatly groomed, the boys with short hair; and the girls all seemed to have perfect even teeth. They addressed adults as "sir" or "ma'am" and seemed poised and totally at home in the company of adults. Andy, the man of the house, dressed in a polo shirt and Bermuda shorts, was physically small but a man of great presence and integrity and considerable business acumen. A devout Presbyterian elder and supporter of and adviser to ministries, he became a firm and fast friend for many years.

For an hour the young people peppered me with intelligent, informed spiritual questions of deep significance as we ate something called "sloppy joes." My tired mind was not too tired to realise I had met an unusual family with access to a remarkable group of young people. Their home and family became my home and family far from home and family. I told Jill that I was so impressed with Drew and his younger sister, Polly, that I had invited them to visit us, and they were coming.

Drew was studying literature and loved to engage me in discussions about the English poets—he knew more about them than I knew. He moved easily from literature to movies and showed a remarkable ability to grasp and evaluate the philosophies and presuppositions behind the narratives of the movies and contemporary popular songs. I had spent years working with young British kids who watched the movies as if they were chewing gum for the eyes, but often didn't know what they were being shown. They endlessly played the Beatles, the Pretty Things, Herman's Hermits, and the Rolling Stones but had little idea of what they were humming. Thus it was stimulating for me to befriend and engage a bright young student like Drew. He was about fifteen years my junior, and he taught me a lot—and would continue to do so for many long years. He is still on top of who is writing what and why. He knows all about what is being filmed and what the images are really saying. He knows what is being sung and what exactly the rhythms and lyrics are conveying. And he is still trying to get Christians and pre-Christians to be dissatisfied with simply being entertained mindlessly and encouraging them to bring discretion to bear as their lives are moulded by video and audio technology.

Not surprisingly, Drew went on to complete his PhD in New Testament at Cambridge and then joined me on the staff of the church I was called to pastor. Drew's sister, Polly, and her husband, Phil, who also completed a Cambridge PhD, went on to teach at Regent College in Vancouver. And I nearly missed meeting them all because I felt tired! As I had learned in the marines, being pushed further when you're tired presents you with opportunities to discover resources and reserves that otherwise lay untapped and underutilised! Life has consistently given me endless opportunities to press on while tired and discover what I might be missing by collapsing too soon.

Jill had been introduced to the ministry of the Billy Graham team in London shortly after she was converted. So she was well familiar not only with the powerful preaching of Billy Graham but also the warm charisma of Cliff Barrows, the team's song leader and choir director. Although she had only seen him from a distance in the huge Harringay arena as he compered the vast gatherings, she knew he had the remarkable ability to project effortlessly a genuine friendliness and transparent believability that quickly endeared him to the British crowd—the people who were initially skeptical of American showmanship and the hard sell they associated with American methods of selling everything, including the gospel. Cliff did more to win people over to a fair hearing of what Billy Graham was saying than anyone, and his contributions were immeasurable. Imagine therefore her excitement when she had heard that the Barrows family had invited me to spend time on my rare free days in their large home in the hills of South Carolina.

She wanted to know "What was it like?" I told her the first thing that impressed me about staying in their home was how utterly unpretentious the whole family were, how natural and welcoming and what down-to-earth, friendly people they were. Cliff, who on the stage or on television was always immaculately dressed, clearly favoured blue jeans, cowboy boots, and wide-brimmed hats as daily wear. In between meeting with all kinds of dignitaries and making arrangements for large evangelistic enterprises and projects, he seemed to be most at home hewing wood, chopping down brush, and working hard on the land. Music, not surprisingly, played a significant role in their family life, and in the evenings it seemed perfectly natural for Cliff and Billie, his wife, to gather the five children and assorted guests such as myself around the piano for a lively and harmonious sing-along. Over the sink in the kitchen, Billie had hung a sign saying, "Divine service conducted here three times daily," and that encapsulated the way the family was being brought up to see life as a worship experience however mundane or ordinary.

The lifestyle of those who lived at Capernwray, while to my knowledge it was never articulated, was clearly modeled by the senior leadership and could best be described as "simple and modest." We gladly embraced it and lived well in it. But travel in America, I quickly discovered, involved living and moving among people and ministries that by comparison were much more upscale and resource rich. This required an adjustment on my part, which of course came very easily; although I must admit there were times when I was embarrassed by abundance.

One woman decided I needed a car so I could travel from my hotel to the church approximately a mile away. Try as I might to persuade her that I really didn't need a car, that I was very grateful for her generosity but needed some exercise and fresh air, she nevertheless ignored me and delivered her car for my use. A huge, brand-new Cadillac! It resembled an aircraft carrier with tail fins, and accustomed as I was to a small British car ideally suited to the narrow winding roads of the countryside back home, I could not imagine driving such a magnificent behemoth. So, unwisely, I told the woman I would really prefer not to drive such a beautiful car and I honestly did not need it. She, assuming I was uneasy driving a car that looked a little too feminine, said, "Oh please don't worry; I'll bring you my husband's car tomorrow. He'll be so glad for you to use it." As good as her word, she arrived with her husband's car the next day — a Rolls-Royce Silver Cloud! And she, with a rather worried expression, inquired if it would be all right for me. All right? I was terrified I was going to wreck it, yet I worried that if I demurred she might offer me her son's car, and it would probably be a Maserati. I accepted the Rolls, but I drove it back and forth the mile to and from the church at no more than thirty miles per hour.

Adjusting from what I was used to, to the lifestyle on the other side of the Atlantic was therefore not difficult at all, but on returning home I realised the adjustments that Jill had gladly accepted when we left the business world and entered the ministry. Her father had recently bought a retirement home — an old manor house with its own stretch of salmon river in a beautiful Yorkshire dale. Her mother had scoured the countryside for antiques, and between them they had created a country home of elegance and comfort. Without a complaint Jill had made the move downscale—but I was moving in the opposite direction. As I described the lifestyle I was enjoying, I became more aware of the adjustments Jill had made and was making. And I was more appreciative of my wife than I had been for quite awhile.

We talked about this and together studied what Paul said in his letter to the Philippians about being content wherever he found himself. He specifically talked about having an abundance and having to do without and being content in either or both. Jill was being given the chance to move from relative abundance to something simpler and more modest. On the other hand, a move in the opposite direction was on the cards for me! Both were riddled with danger—the one of disgruntlement, the other of selfish indulgence. We had to help each other, like Paul, to *learn* how to be content either way.

Jill's eyes glistened with excitement when I spoke of Christian universities where I had been invited to speak to literally thousands of sharp young people. She found it hard to believe that sizable groups of men would rise at unearthly hours of the morning for Bible study in a restaurant. And she laughed uncontrollably at the thought of me attending lavish luncheons and watching glamorous women give exhibitions on makeup and something called "Colour Me Beautiful" before preaching to them. I described speaking to prisoners on death row, seminary lectures, radio, and television. She was thrilled—she shared my joy.

However, when I told her another three months' invitations were already in hand, her joy was tempered. She had suspected that once I went to America, I would be asked to return, and her suspicions were proving accurate.

One of the unexpected results of ministry in America came from the missions conferences I was invited to address in a number of churches. These events, quite unlike anything I had experienced in the United Kingdom, were attended by cross-cultural missionaries (those who had left their homeland to work overseas) supported by the American churches and church leaders from the indigenous churches (overseas church leaders) who were brought over for the event to inform the congregation on the work of the church overseas. They were festive but challenging events that included colourful national flags and costumes, meals where "national food" was consumed, expertly produced video presentations, and stirring testimonies. I found the missionaries and church leaders particularly responsive to my preaching, and as a result I began to receive invitations to visit them in their places of ministry to encourage and help the local believers around the world. The brimming river was beckoning me.

CHAPTER 8

STREAMS ON DRY GROUND

I will pour water on the thirsty land,
and streams on the dry ground.

—Isaiah 44:3

My first invitation to travel further overseas to meet with missionaries and indigenous church leaders took me to South America. Flying out of Lima, Peru, through cloud-shrouded Andean passes in an old unpressurized DC3, two options were available. Stop breathing or suck a strange looking tube found dangling under the seat. I sucked, and life-sustaining oxygen flowed! Arriving in Pucallpa—now a modern city but then a frontier town on the banks of the Ucayali River, one of the vast Amazon headwaters—I saw many small stocky Indians clad in hats, jackets, and loincloths. Apparently the townspeople insisted that they dress properly in town. Their attempt to comply resulted in them looking like townspeople from the waist up and denizens of the forest from the waist down. To my mind, this was a parable of the challenge facing the missionaries. They have no desire to produce cultural and spiritual schizophrenics—metaphorically clad in Christian hat and jacket while still girded with pagan animistic loincloths. They want to nurture committed disciples of Jesus who can transform hearts, restore lives, and revolutionise cultures.

We flew on from Pucallpa in a World War II Catalina flying boat that roared across the waters of the lagoon, coming perilously close to swamping canoes laden with corn and bananas, before lumbering into the air spraying water in every direction. I was given a special seat in a former "blister" machine gun turret on the side of the aircraft, which afforded a magnificent view of the endless forest intersected with winding muddy rivers and occasional spirals of smoke that indicated a village hidden under the splendid canopy of majestic trees.

Sitting around campfires with the sounds of the jungle filling the sultry night air, I listened eagerly to men who had actually followed the tracks of Indians who had never seen white people and had camped out in the forests and lived like Indians while seeking to make contact with them. These unassuming men opened my eyes to new vistas of discipleship and service. I heard tales of first contacts that ended in a hail of poisoned arrows and hasty retreats through dense jungle. They told me about the painstaking work, once contact had been made, of being accepted in the tribe and of building primitive shelters for their families in the midst of the rotting vegetation and filth of the Indian villages. They told of the endless hours spent learning the language, translating the Scriptures, and then teaching illiterate disease-ridden people about the gospel of grace. Their stories were eye-popping and heartwarming. These missionaries were the salt of the earth, unsung heroes.

I met Indian elders who welcomed me with wide grins that displayed toothless mouths and handshakes that threatened to crush my lily white digits. One carried a long bow—as long as me and much longer than him—and a quiver full of arrows. I borrowed his bow, but when I tried to stretch it, he almost fell over laughing at my weak efforts. He took it back from me, effortlessly stretched the bow to its limit, and indicated that an arrow should be fired straight up in the air. He understood, "What goes up must come down." I would have fired it into the jungle, and it never would have been seen again. There's education and there's intelligence. I had some of the former; he was full of the latter. This was also evident as we taught basic biblical truth. The Indians, I realized, had insights into spiritual dynamics of which I was ignorant. They often had an instinctive grasp of spiritual truths, which once explained to them and illustrated—not by talking about television, newspapers, politics, or sports, I might add—they quickly embraced and started to apply to their culture.

In my ignorance—and arrogance—I had not even considered that they, being in my mind primitive people, would know anything about "civilisation." Imagine my surprise when I was told about what happened in one tribe when a young girl arrives at puberty. She climbs a tree and sings a song that is recognized by the men and boys of the village as an announcement that she is ready for sexual activity. A mad dash for the tree ensues, and the first male to reach her takes her. In time she becomes pregnant, but as the couple does not wish to settle down and start a family, they bury the child alive. This may be repeated a number of times until the couple signal they are ready for marriage by keeping a child born to them. Once they are recognized publicly as a married couple, rules of adultery apply and are strictly enforced. A village elder showed me a sharp knife that was described as "the adulterer's knife." Should a married man in the village be suspected of committing adultery, he was apprehended and tried. If found guilty, the back of his neck was slashed open and his blood was shed to punish him. Perhaps in some way that death was also thought to atone for his sin.

"That's primitive," I said to my missionary friend.

"Not so," he explained. "They have a very clearly defined culture that bears some embarrassing similarities to our own and sometimes shows ours in a poor light."

That I could not see, but he went on, "When I return home to the United States after four years in the jungle, I'm amazed at the way young women dress—or don't dress—in public. They don't sit up in trees announcing they are available, but their signals look very obvious to me. I see the promiscuous behaviour of men when I'm back home, and it doesn't seem very different from the men down here. In the jungle when they have an "unwanted pregnancy," they bury the child alive, while at home hundreds of thousands are aborted. But remember that the Indians bury the child alive because they believe if they kill the infant the spirit will live on—and haunt them. So they bury body and spirit intact so they'll die together. Primitive? Yes, but at least they believe the child, or the 'unwanted pregnancy,' is spirit and body, which as far as I can see, is way ahead of the attitude back home where what is aborted is regarded as little more than a piece of protoplasm. And then there's the adultery rule. Adultery certainly is common here and is common back home too. Here there is at least some disgrace attached to the behaviour, but I suspect that back home it is being accepted more and more as something 'everybody does.'"

There was time for reflection on the local cultures and the unique difficulties facing the missionaries in the villages and camps of South America. There was also much food for thought on the cultural environment in which I live. I saw afresh that both cultures have deep problems and are riddled with flaws. But the more I explored how the other half of the world lives, the more I was driven to look critically, from a new perspective, at the way we conduct ourselves in the "civilized" West.

I saw poverty firsthand that I had never dreamed existed. I witnessed living conditions so unhygienic that it was a wonder anyone survived. I heard of encounters with evil spirits and learned how what anthropologists regard as fascinating photogenic and telegenic cultural events are actually frenzied drunken dances designed to thwart the spirits seeking to destroy the jungle dwellers. But as I watched bright young Christian women trained in squeaky clean hospitals in the West prayerfully using pitifully inadequate resources to care for people with diseases they had never read about in nursing school, I saw prayer work—or rather, God intervene in answer to prayer.

I saw elementary hygiene classes being taught, open sewers being redirected, water being boiled, and babies being cleansed. I listened as the stories of creation and fall, of Abraham's call and God's covenant, of Israel's declension and the prophets' promises of Messiah, of Jesus' birth and his loving, powerful life, of his betrayal and crucifixion and glorious resurrection, of his ascension to the Father and promise of his return were told to rapt groups of ill-clad, poverty-stricken people in "churches" without walls or floors or seats, where babies crawled in the mud and chickens pecked among the rows as mosquitoes feasted on our fresh Western blood. Morning and evening I opened the Word of God to both spiritually hungry missionaries and simple new believers from the tribes, remembering what Paul Rees had told me: "Speak to their hearts."

Although I was now traveling further afield, Europe had not escaped my attention. I was in Germany in August 1961 when construction of the Berlin Wall was begun and the world saw Communism shooting itself in the foot with one of the biggest publicity disasters of all time. No one believed the wall was built to keep westerners from flooding into the Soviet bloc to enjoy the Soviet lifestyle. Everyone knew it was a tacit admission of the bankruptcy of the system that held millions under its control. But many years passed until, on my birthday in 1989, the wall finally started to come down. In the interim I visited Berlin and saw for myself the ugly barrier that divided a great city and decimated families. I saw the death strip that had been cleared on the eastern side so that guards could get a clear shot at desperate people trying to escape. A Lutheran pastor named Klaus Eichoff invited me to preach in the church he pastored close by the wall. After the service, during lunch with Klaus and his wife, Renate, they served a long glass of dark liquid. Klaus, seeing me look suspiciously at the proffered drink, inquired in his broken English, "You trink beer?" I, in equally tortured German, replied hurriedly, *"Nein danke."*

"Why you not trink beer?" he asked, surprised.

I had to think quickly and said, "Because English Christians don't drink beer, and I don't like it."

I thought he would say, "Ah, you English Christian not trink it; how you know you not like it?" Fortunately, he didn't.

He said, *"Ich bin erstaunt!"* ("I am astounded!") Then turning to his wife, he said, *"Renate, wir wollen beten."* ("Renate, we will pray.") She replaced her glass and folded her hands demurely, and he prayed, "I sank you, Gott, I am Cherman Christian!" We laughed and discussed as best we could what I call "cultural worldliness," because my travels have unearthed some strange anomalies on the subject.

Shortly after leaving my friends Klaus and Renate in Berlin, I arrived in Sweden where I stayed in the home of the delightful Johannsen family. Their two teenagers had come to faith in England and, on returning home, had influenced their mother for Christ and invited me to spend time with them to meet their friends and preach in their church. Greeted at the door by the father of the family, I was surprised when he immediately said, "Welcome, dear Stuart. Thank you for blessing my family. But I am not a Christian myself."

We immediately embarked on a discussion of the gospel, in which he explained, "I cannot become a Christian because I smoke, and in Sweden it is not possible to smoke and be a Christian, and I cannot break the habit." I stayed for a few days, explaining to him that it is God who transforms and releases by grace through faith, not man who changes to be accepted on merit and effort. But he was adamant, and I left feeling that he was very close to the kingdom yet thwarted by a tradition that was a human construction, not a tenet of Scripture. (I might add that I have never smoked. I encourage people not to start and those who have to quit—but not in order that they might merit or earn salvation.)

Ironically, I drove straight from Sweden to Copenhagen, Denmark, spoke in a church on my arrival, and after the service was amazed to see the most sumptuous meal prepared for us all during which cigars were produced and enjoyed by most of the congregation as we sat in an increasingly dense haze of blue smoke. I thought about calling my Swedish friend and advising him to emigrate to Denmark. Still, it raised for me yet more questions about communicating the gospel in one culture as opposed to another. What are the essentials that we must teach without confusion; where do the nonnegotiables lie? What are the hindrances to belief that we sometimes unwittingly place in the way of honest, earnest people? What part does tradition play in the life of the church? And how do we react to those whose traditions appear to take the place of doctrine?

In the midst of all the hard work of travel and ministry at home and overseas, there was always time for lots of fun. So one day when I received a postcard purporting to come from Poland inviting me to the Polish Millennium, I assumed that some of my fun-loving colleagues had gone out of their way to play a practical joke on me. In those days before political correctness reigned supreme, it was normative to enjoy ethnic jokes mostly at the expense of the long-suffering Poles. I was surprised that my friends had gone to so much trouble as to get a Polish postcard and Polish stamp and give the card the appearance of having suffered at the hands of Soviet bureaucracy, but I knew it was a joke and made a note to say nothing and quietly find out who had sent it. A couple of weeks later, I received a phone call from overseas. A voice with a heavy accent explained. "My name is Kapitaniuk. I come from the Ukraine. I sent you a postcard, but you have not answered it." Oops!

I hurried to apologize for not answering and said, "Oh, thank you, Mr. Kapitaniuk. What exactly is the Polish Millennium?"

"We are celebrating the thousand-year anniversary of the arrival of Christianity in Poland," he explained. My face was red! I was glad I was on telephone and not television.

"Oh, I see," I replied. "And what exactly did you have in mind?"

"Well, to be perfectly honest," he said, "the Catholics wanted to invite the pope, but the Communists said no. And the Protestants wanted Billy Graham, but the Catholics were able to stop that. But we thought that as nobody has ever heard of you, we could perhaps sneak you in and nobody would know."

That was good enough for me, and a quick look at my calendar showed I was free, so I said, "I'll be glad to come!" The year was 1967, the depth of the Cold War when the U.S.S.R. and the United States were spending billions arming themselves to the teeth and reminding the world daily of the possibility of mutual destruction in a nuclear holocaust. It was also the fiftieth anniversary of the Communist revolution.

It was surprising how many people were nervous about anything to do with the "Iron Curtain," a term popularized by Winston Churchill in 1946. A number of people questioned me on whether I had the right to go with three small children at home. The old adage "If they ask you and you're free, the answer is yes" had not, as far as I knew, been rescinded, so off I went.

Landing in Warsaw in the middle of a November night, in the middle of winter, in the middle of the Cold War, was neither glamorous nor fun. Not being met as promised proved even less amusing, and when the airport began to close and truculent workers began literally and metaphorically to show me the door, I wondered what to do and where to go. I had been advised not to bring addresses, names, or phone numbers, so I was stuck. I knew no Polish, and no one I came across knew any English. I stood outside the closing airport and noted the difference between "alone" and "lonely." I like the former; the latter can be troublesome.

Fortunately, as the snow was beginning to fall and the night was getting decidedly frigid, I was not kept waiting too long. Suddenly a voice behind me said, in what appeared to me to be a conspiratorial tone, "Briscoe?" I turned. A man stood there in a long leather coat with the collar turned up and in a wide-brimmed hat with the brim turned down. His face was hidden, his hands were deep in his pockets. He looked like Orson Welles in *The Third Man*. In that moment I knew I should not have ventured behind the Iron Curtain.

"Yes," I squeaked, trying to display a confidence I did not feel.

His reaction bowled me over. Instead of arresting me, which I was sure was his purpose, he grabbed me, kissed me fervently on both cheeks, and said, "Welcome, my brother, I'm sorry I'm late. We are so glad you came! Come, we must catch a trolley bus." Relief washed over me like a tide, and I hurried after him.

As the trolley bus clanked along the cobbled streets, my new friend and I hung on to seriously worn straps and swayed and lurched with the terrain.

He spoke openly and in quite a loud voice about spiritual issues, and I, with the *Third Man* image still firmly implanted, fully expected him to be arrested at any moment. But when he urged me to "speak loudly of Jesus," I protested that I knew no Polish. He replied, "Then speak in English and German. They will listen." And they did. People moved in their seats to catch our conversation, and slowly but surely I began to feel thoroughly at home in the middle of Warsaw in the middle of the night in the middle of winter in the middle of the Cold War. My conscience also required me to ask why I had forgotten that Jesus had promised to be with us always and that had not been enough for me until my friend came along.

I was taken to a clean and frugal hotel where the menu was fresh bread, lean ham, and scalding hot tea presented in glasses too hot to pick up. Sometimes the menu changed to fatty ham and stale bread, but always there was scalding hot tea. I noted that everyone but me seemed to have hands of asbestos and throats of steel.

The conference I had been asked to attend was a united gathering of Baptists, Brethren, and Pentecostals. These groups, in my experience, did not always coexist with any discernible degree of harmony, and I mentioned how good it was to see the obvious love they had for one another.

"It was not always like this," I was told. "But one day Stalin ordered all evangelical pastors arrested. Finding themselves in the same cells for the same offence — loving and preaching Jesus — they decided wisely that as they were all suffering for him, they should work together for him too. So the Evangelical Alliance was born in prison."

In the Polish church in those days, when the saints gathered, they didn't easily part, so services went on — and on — and on. I preached on Sunday morning, and after my message we had Communion. Then the pastor leaned over to me and said, "Now you preach."

"Again?" I inquired, bewildered.

"Again," he said with a smile.

So I did. And after that we had an ordination service for new deacons and elders. Then the pastor inclined in my direction again and said, "Now you preach again." This was turning into preacher paradise. I could not believe my ears or my luck! Well, maybe not luck — opportunity! Three times that morning I opened the Scriptures to these wonderful people who listened with intensity and obvious hunger.

When the service finally ended, we had lunch together — bread, ham, and you guessed it, scalding hot tea! Then it was time for the afternoon service.

Each day I walked to and from my hotel in the frigid temperatures along grimy snow- and ice-covered streets past the massive, monolithic Soviet-style architectural monstrosity named by the authorities the Centre for Culture and by the locals who had no love for Joe Stalin, "St. Josef's Cathedral." It dominated the skyline, and years later in Moscow I saw at least four identical monolithic monstrosities. As far as I could tell, there was only one coloured neon sign in the city. It was a green and yellow image of a sower sowing seed as he walked, and I recognized it at once as identifying the headquarters of the Bible Society, which continued to function even in the Soviet era. Because the authorities, not the Poles, were celebrating the fiftieth anniversary of the Revolution, huge red banners with Marx and Lenin prominently portrayed on them hung from the top stories of the highest buildings to street level. Underneath them the sidewalks were regularly crowded with people wrapped up warmly, standing in line to enter the churches in time for Mass. Stalin, Marx, Lenin, and the other powerful men of the Communist regime with all their ideologies, strategies, and cruelties had not been able to destroy the deeply embedded Catholic faith of the Polish people.

One evening I was put in a rickety car and driven along poorly lit streets until they weren't lit at all, and then they ceased to be streets, and we bumped and swerved along dark trails through dense pine forests. As I did not know the people who had picked me up, this was interesting to say the least. About an hour later, we arrived at a large isolated building shrouded in darkness. We struggled through deep snow to a door that was opened in response to our knocking, and we were ushered into a large, sparsely furnished room packed—and I mean packed—with young people. I was told I was in a Bible school and the young people wanted me to speak to them. Duly bidden, I wasted no time talking to them through an interpreter about "the Vine and the branches."

Partway into the talk, to which they were listening avidly and taking notes busily, the light suddenly went out. Being in the middle of the forest, we were plunged in the darkest of darkness. A loud, deep voice through the gloom said, "Keep speaking!" So I did. Just as I finished, the lights came on again. Everybody in the room was kneeling. During the talk they had spontaneously started to pray about what I was teaching. I was told later by one of their teachers, "They told me they had never heard about abiding in Christ, and they wanted to make sure before the Lord that they understood what Jesus meant when he told his disciples to "abide in me.""

People like that make me feel small. I feel that they should be teaching me, which of course they did—and they do!

From Warsaw I traveled to Prague in Czechoslovakia. Years earlier a young man named Peter who had lost a leg because of cancer had arrived at Capernwray. On returning home he had said, "If ever you come to Eastern Europe, please come to visit." I was met at the airport by Peter and his father, both of whom spoke English well. They told me immediately that I was most welcome, thanked me for coming, and said mysteriously, "You will not be allowed to preach of course, but you can bring greetings." Further explanation followed, and I learned that Soviet rules did not allow me, traveling as I was on a tourist visa, to play any part in their restricted church life. They explained with a twinkle, however, that my greetings should last about fifty minutes, after which the pastor would preach for about five. *Wink, wink.*

Church life behind the Iron Curtain was slowly coming into focus for me. These stalwart believers were experts at bending the rules without breaking them. Apparently visitors could bring greetings, but the pastor must preach — and only the pastor. So redefinitions became the order of the day, and the churches went about their business under the watchful eye of the authorities. I was advised not to say anything political when I brought greetings, and I assured them that I had no interest in delving into Communist politics, but asked, "What would happen if I did?" They replied, "They would send you out of the country and not allow you back in. And we want you to come back."

"But how would they know?" I asked.

"The informer will tell them," they explained.

"You have an informer in your midst?" I asked aghast.

"Yes," they replied, laughing at my surprise.

"Would you tell me who it is?" I queried.

"There's no need," they said. "There's only one person taking notes."

So the next time I brought greetings (based on Romans) I saw the only note taker. A little grey-haired old lady.

Life for those godly people was not easy during the long, hard years of Soviet occupation. Some of them suffered terribly, and others lived with continual frustration and restrictions, but they learned how to live well under them. Young Christians were indoctrinated with Marxist philosophy, and they were grossly discriminated against, yet I met many who were stalwart in their faith. As I grew to know the believers who had suffered for their faith and had stood firm in hardship and distress or had grown up in primitive and deprived areas, I could not avoid seeing certain qualities that suffering and deprivation had produced in them. Their faces were often lined deeply beyond their years, but their eyes shone. They were frequently close to tears, but smiles and laughter quickly lit up their faces. They conversed readily on serious topics but loved a joke. They spoke little about their hardships and always with a shrug of the shoulder. And they were hungry for God, they loved the teaching of his Word, their praise was infectious, and their prayers shook the rafters. Often at the end of the day, as I returned to hammock or lumpy bed, I would shake my head in amazement. God in his grace had allowed me to go to many a "thirsty land" with the water of the Word in hand, and there I had met thirsty people. He had called me to travel to the driest of "dry ground" and in his mercy become a conduit of "streams of living water." I reminded myself afresh that my job was to stay in tune with the Spirit and to teach the Word I had been taught. Then—and only then—would there be streams on dry ground.

CHAPTER 9

RIVER BENDS

With many a curve my banks I fret
By many a field and fallow.

—Alfred Lord Tennyson, "The Brook"

Dr. Berry, the local physician, was a practitioner of the old school, and all at Capernwray were greatly blessed by his expert care. He regularly visited patients in their homes, and quite frequently he would "drop in" to the lodge and say, "I was just passing the door and felt like a cup of tea, so put the kettle on, Jill, and let me take a look at David's tonsils while I'm here." This kind man never missed a chance to tease us about our Christianity, and we would talk to him about his agnosticism and remind him that if we were wrong, we had lost nothing, but if he was wrong, he had lost everything. In any case, we could not have wished for a better family doctor.

So an international phone call from Dr. Berry as I was on my way to Berlin demanded and received my immediate full attention. He got straight to the point. "Stuart, you've no business driving to Berlin. Get yourself home at once. Jill is sick, and she needs you more than those Germans need you." Like many Brits of his generation, he had vivid memories of World War II and was no fan of the Germans, although he often cared for them when they needed his medical skills. He did not go into details, and when I asked him what was wrong, he simply repeated, "Get yourself home. She needs you, and she's more important than anything you were planning to do over there."

Jill, unknown to me, had been struggling for some time. She had not been feeling well, and she was worried about the children, who were showing signs of being disturbed by my frequent absences for many months in the year, but she did not want to tell me as, to use her words, she "didn't want to disappoint me and let the side down" (an English expression describing what happens when a team member makes a mistake leading to the team's defeat).

It is quite possible that Jill had not found it hard to hide from me what she was going through, because I had become so engrossed in and occupied with my burgeoning ministry that I was in danger of neglecting her and the children in the name of ministry. Occasionally I heard complaints from her about my workaholism—although I think the term should be strictly reserved for men and women who forget to live and learn and love and know only how to work. I don't think I was ever in danger of lapsing into that sorry state. But ministers of the gospel are susceptible to imbalance in this area because we see ourselves as "called" and our work as "ministry." This, in our minds, can place our daily activities at a level slightly higher than the norm and therefore demand more than normal time and energy expenditure. I will not dispute that we are called to ministry and this is a high privilege with correspondingly high responsibilities. Danger arises, however, when we begin to lose track of other responsibilities and explain that our call to ministry necessitates this aberration. That was where I was in danger of heading. It was easy for me to take comfort in the fact that my wife was a great mother and was more than capable of caring for the children and thus leave the task to her.

Not that I hadn't given thought to my responsibilities. In fact, I had been forcibly reminded of them by a dear friend. Dr. Robert Wise was a prominent surgeon and highly regarded Christian leader from Manchester. During the war he had crawled under the precariously balanced wreckage of his own hospital to amputate the leg of one of his nurses who was trapped and dragged her to safety. For this he was awarded the George Medal, the highest civilian award for bravery. He it was who drove up specially to talk to Jill during one of my absences.

"Jill," he asked her pointedly, "how can Stuart be a father to his children and be away so much?" It so happened that we had a missionary living with us at the time who, on overhearing this question, said, "Dr. Wise, that's only half the question. The other half is, how can Stuart be the international evangelist God has called him to be and stay at home?" That was the essence of my dilemma.

On arriving home from Germany as instructed by our family doctor, I discovered that Jill was struggling with an ulcer. But perhaps more than that, she had concluded that she had gone as far as she could caring for the children on her own. She told me, in tears, that she felt like such a failure. I, however, felt that I had failed her in not reading the signs of the stress she was under. But what to do about it was another matter.

When I started traveling, Jill and I had agreed that we believed God was calling us to this unusual lifestyle, and that if that was true, he would equip us to do what was necessary. We assumed this would apply to the children as well. If God was calling the father of the children to be away from home for extended periods, then presumably he would enable the children to cope and ensure they were well cared for. But we had also agreed that if we ever sensed they were being put under undue pressure, we would make the necessary changes. It looked as if the conditions were ripe for a change, and I was ready to do whatever was necessary if only I could find out what that was!

One or two other things had developed that were affecting my thinking as well. At Capernwray we held a winter Bible school and summer conferences, but there was a period of about six weeks in late spring and early summer when the school had concluded but the weather in England was such that no one would think of taking a summer holiday in it! The result was that Capernwray was not fully utilized during that period. So we decided that we would try a six-week Bible school, and I was invited to lead it.

I jumped at the opportunity for two reasons. The first one, of course, was that it meant I could plan on having six weeks at home, and the other was that it gave me an occasion to do what I was secretly longing to do — remain in a place long enough to do some consecutive teaching. Usually my itinerant ministry required me to visit a church or a similar environment for no longer than a week and then move on to the next place. But I often wondered, *What happens after I've gone? Does anything take root from what I've been talking about? And what about the practical questions that will surely arise as the people put into practice what I was trying to teach?* So spring school offered me the chance to teach systematically and be around to help in the practical application of the teaching.

I appropriated for myself the first hour each morning and began to work through Paul's letter to the Romans. This meant that I had to teach parts of Scripture and deal with aspects of biblical truth that I had never before encountered. The challenge was invigorating, the opportunity to sit down with students and talk through what the Bible was saying was exhilarating, and the longer I taught spring school, the more it began to dawn on me that maybe I really wanted to be a pastor!

Added to this, I had been preaching in Calvary Baptist Church in New York City, where Stephen Olford was the pastor. Stephen was an extraordinarily gifted preacher who had encouraged me in many ways — not least in the fact that he invited me to speak on a number of occasions at New York City's annual Christian Life conventions. One year I was asked to share the ministry with Festo Kivengere and Vance Havner. It is hard to imagine a more diverse pair of preachers than Festo and Vance. Festo, from Uganda, was a typical East African Anglican bishop. He spoke much about transparency and honesty, confession of sin, and heart revival. People listened when he spoke, because they knew that he had courageously confronted Idi Amin, the tyrannical, murderous ruler of his native land. He escaped with his life but had to flee his country. He had actually written a book entitled *I Love Idi Amin*, and such was his integrity that he left you with no alternative, amazing as it was, but to believe he meant it! Quietly spoken and gentle in demeanor, he was a powerful presenter of the truth of Scripture both in word and life.

Vance Havner, on the other hand, loved to tell us that he came from Hickory, North Carolina, and he did so in an accent that could not have come from anywhere else. He had a droll sense of humour and was well known for such epigrams as "We sing 'standing on the promises' then spend all our time sitting on the premises." Or "We sing 'not a mite would I withhold' and then hold on with all our might." Or "Take my life and let it be!" While he spoke with a sprightly light touch, he never failed to speak with power and grace. Then if you added to the mix the fiery impassioned preaching of Stephen Olford and threw me in there somewhere as well, perhaps you can imagine what a rich blessing it was for me to be part of this strategic convention.

Stephen was never reluctant to tell me exactly what he thought about my ministry, and I greatly benefited from the input of such a seasoned pastor. One day during the convention, he startled me by saying, "Stuart, my boy, your theology includes no ecclesiology, and that means it is a truncated theology."

I think he had heard me say something positive about the Lord Jesus and critical of the church in the same sentence. I protested warmly that I thought my ecclesiology — the branch of Christian theology devoted to the biblical teaching on the church — was in good shape as I believed wholeheartedly in the church and was more than ready to say so if people asked me.

He replied, "Tell me about this church you believe in."

"I believe" I replied, "in the universal, invisible, mystical body of Christ."

"Good," he responded. "And what about the local, geographical, visible, tangible expression of the universal, invisible, mystical body of Christ?"

I spluttered something, and he went on. "You're right — the Scriptures do talk about a universal church, but they also refer pointedly to the church in such places as Antioch, Jerusalem, Ephesus, and so on. They were not invisible. They were highly visible and tangible, and in addition to teaching about the universal church, we need to be teaching the role of the church in a local area in corporate worship, discipling, evangelism, and ministry to the community."

The more he went on, the more uncomfortable I became. I'm afraid that since my early experiences of the church had not been so exciting, and because we had gotten very little help but considerable criticism from a number of churches during our coffee bar outreach days, my attitude toward the local church was in dire need of a major overhaul. And Stephen was setting about administering it!

He pressed on. "Stuart, you must realize that your ministry is focused entirely on the individual. You speak frequently about a personal relationship with the Lord, which is part of the story, but the corporate dimension of spiritual life must not be overlooked or ignored. What are you doing to incorporate people into the local church?" I mumbled something like "the Great Commission is all about making disciples not building churches," only to be reminded that the place disciples are made is in the community of believers. And so on. I put up a vigorous defense of my indefensible position, all the time knowing I was wrong, and when the conference in New York ended and I moved on to my next preaching appointment—in another church!—I made a quiet commitment that I would spend time studying the subject of the church.

Shortly after this, I stumbled across something that challenged my thinking even more. For some reason, which I have long forgotten, I decided one day to look up the etymology of the word *church*. My dictionary explained that the modern word *church* was derived from the Middle English word *chirche*, which in turn readily betrayed its connections to the German word *kirche*. The dictionary then made a brief excursion into the obviously related Scottish *kirk* before informing that all these words were offspring of the Greek word *kyriake*, which in turn meant "belonging to the *kurios*." But as *kurios* means "Lord," the etymological root meaning of *church* is "belonging to the Lord."

Immediately a verse that I had known, certainly from my first sermon, and possibly from childhood, came to mind. "Be shepherds of the church of God, which he bought with his own blood" (Acts 20:28). I knew this was an instruction to some real live elders who were to look after and care for the church at Ephesus, not some "invisible, mystical, universal body." The church at Ephesus belonged to the Lord because he had bought it with his own blood.

Dredging up my studies from my preaching debut at seventeen, I also remembered that some time after Paul said these powerful words to the Ephesian elders on his farewell visit, John the apostle wrote the chilling words of Jesus to the same church: "I hold this against you: You have forsaken your first love" (Revelation 2:4). So the church that "belonged to the Lord," which he had bought for himself, was not a perfect assembly made up of unbelievably mature saints. It was a far from perfect community of apparently deeply flawed but redeemed sinners who were uniquely the possession of the risen Lord.

I recognized at once that while I had been quite comfortable in my skepticism of the "meetings" in the Tin Chapel and felt perfectly justified in my critical spirit toward the churches that would not aid us trying to reach the kids on the streets, the attitude of Jesus was "This is my church—it belongs to me, the Lord!" I vowed there and then that in future when I thought and talked of the church I would—albeit clumsily and ponderously—think and talk about "that which belongs to the Lord." What an attitudinal change that decision developed in my life—in a hurry!

The more I thought about the local church, the more I began to see that what had been peripheral at best and irrelevant at worst in my mind was central and crucial in the mind of the Lord. And I found myself thinking, "I wouldn't mind being a pastor if I could ever find a church that would give me a chance." But because I had no credentials, no training, and no experience, I wondered who would be interested in me—and I had to admit that if I were looking for a pastor, I wouldn't look at me. So for a brief moment, Jill and I had entertained a flash of light, but it died as quickly as it came, and the old uncertainties returned—and I left on yet another overseas trip.

My itinerary included a visit to a church called Elmbrook in Milwaukee, Wisconsin, pastored by my friend, Bob Hobson, a long, lanky Texan as casual and relaxed as his blue jeans and cowboy boots. On arrival at the airport, I saw Bob standing at the top of the escalator as I ascended, and he shouted down to me, "I'm resigning in the morning! I'm joining Torchbearers!" Knowing full well that a week's meetings would be lost in congregational consternation if Bob announced his resignation at the start of the week, I shouted back, "Don't do that. Tell them next weekend." We agreed on that arrangement on one condition—that I would try to help the church find a pastoral replacement for Bob.

The church had been founded with thirteen members about fourteen years earlier, and Bob's ministry there had been most effective. Something of his joyous, relaxed spirit was to be seen in the attitudes of the people and the tone of the fellowship that had grown to more than four hundred people. There was a relatively small group of mature believers, and the rest were new believers or those who hadn't got that far.

Two men who were close friends, Willi Treu and Burton Keddie, stood out in the crowd. Willi had arrived in America as a young man from his native Germany after escaping from the Communist regime. He had landed in Texas, where he made a living picking watermelons before moving to Wisconsin. Then, with the help of relatives, he started a business and became very successful. He flew his own plane, loved to sing in a male quartet, and went out of his way to make me feel at home. "Burt" Keddie was an extremely gifted entrepreneurial businessman. In his younger days, he had been an outstanding athlete, playing for his university in the Rose Bowl. In middle age he was still capable of beating men much younger at a variety of sports. He too showed me extraordinary kindness during the few days I visited the church. Both men were deeply committed Christians who were well known in the business community and social circles for their clear-cut faith and solid integrity.

During lunch with Bob, Willi, and Burt one day, someone raised the question of a pastoral replacement once again. It had become a regular topic of conversation. On an impulse, I said, "What about me? Would I do?"

Willi immediately responded, "As soon as I met you, I knew you'd be our next pastor!"

"Really!" I exclaimed. "What else do you know about me?"

Burt and Bob were ready to explore the possibility, and so we began talking seriously about the unthinkable—that a church might be interested in me being their pastor.

As I had no experience discussing a possible call to a pastorate, I had no idea what to ask or what to say. So I made a hurried call to Stephen Olford in New York, who encouraged me to explore the possibility and told me to make sure I would be in charge of the pulpit and to get a copy of the church's constitution. (I didn't see the significance of the former and didn't know what to do when I got the latter!) I insistently reminded them of my lack of formal training, but they simply said, "We've heard you preach, and you come from Capernwray," and that seemed to satisfy them.

I phoned Jill. She was surprised to receive my call and was even more surprised when I asked her, "How would you like to live in America?"

"What would we do?" she asked.

"A church has asked me to consider being their pastor," I replied.

"Really?" she responded. "That means we could be a family!" And it didn't take long before she added, "Let's do it!"

During a previous trip to America, Jill had joined me for a few weeks, and after getting over stress-related migraines and chronic shyness, she settled into American life surprisingly easily. At the end of the trip, as she was boarding the return flight to England, she turned to me and said, "I don't know what this means, but I feel we're being called to North America."

Jill quite frequently demonstrates that she possesses a spiritual antenna that makes her much sharper than I at detecting what could be promptings of the Spirit, and she is also much readier to grasp an opportunity than I. In fact, over the years I had learned to appreciate the value of a wife who is actively involved in the major decisions of life, family, and ministry, and I fear for the couples who seem to operate on the principle, "Father leads, and Mother goes along." Jill has often said, "I have no problem accepting that Stuart is my head, but that doesn't mean he's my brain." In other words, she does not believe that because she is a woman, God gave her spiritual capabilities and insights in order that they might be disregarded or discounted in marital decision making. Accordingly, we have benefited enormously from the indefinable insights and intuitions of my wife that frequently have raced ahead of my carefully logical, calculated decision-making processes. In fact,

I have often said that when it's decision time in the Briscoe household, it's a matter of Jill saying, "You pray while I pack!"

The dramatic differences in our temperamental, psychological, and spiritual makeup have become a rich resource for us. They complement our eager attempts to discover the right thing to do. And they serve to correct imbalance and guard against (Jill) rushing ahead or (yours truly) lagging behind. We believe that spirituality is lived out in the context of personality. There is nowhere else for it to function. It thus follows that God intends for us a spiritual experience that is enriched by insights and contributions of both partners, which are as diverse as the personalities through which they come into being. So I took Jill's positive response as yet another pointer in the direction we should go.

During the rest of the week in Milwaukee, the church leaders and I discussed further aspects of the ministry although in surprisingly little detail. The church asked us to come with two suitcases each, and they promised to equip a house for us that would become our new home. Remuneration was not discussed at any great length because I had no idea what the needs of a family living in suburban Milwaukee in 1970 might be. I told the deacons, "I will come to minister to you, and in return I am sure you will minister to my family and me. You know what it takes to live in Brookfield, Wisconsin, so that we can minister there, so please make it possible and we don't need to say anymore." They agreed, and they did as they promised.

Still, there was a major issue that needed to be carefully addressed—my existing itinerary. In those days I was regularly booked as much as five years ahead, and that was certainly the case as I planned to move from itinerant ministry to the pastorate. I did not believe I should cancel commitments that I had made in good faith. Let your "yea be yea and your nay be nay!" I asked the leaders if they would be willing to release me for overseas ministry on occasions so that I could fulfill commitments already made and stay in touch with people to whom I had already ministered over the years. Understandably, their first question was, "But what about pastoring the church?"

My reply was, at first, confusing to some of them, for I said, "I will accept it as my responsibility to see that the church is pastored."

They thought it over and replied, "And what exactly does that mean?"

"Let's look at Ephesians chapter 4," I said.

So we turned there in our Bibles, and I read to them verses 11 and 12: "It was he who gave some to be apostles, some to be prophets, some to be evangelists, and some to be pastors and teachers, to prepare God's people for works of service, so that the body of Christ might be built up."

"What is the role of the pastor-teacher according to Paul?" I asked them.

"To prepare God's people for works of service, so that the body of Christ might be built up," they replied. Some were looking very doubtful as they sensed where this might be going; others quickly caught a glimpse of what I hoped would become a fundamental principle of the church's life.

"And look what else Paul said," I continued. " 'From him [Christ] the whole body, joined and held together by every supporting ligament, grows and builds itself up in love, as each part does its work [v. 16].' "

"Do you think each part of the church here is 'doing its work'?" I asked.

" 'Fraid not," someone replied.

"Are there things that could and should be done that are not being done in the church?" I went on.

"Oh yes," they replied, "of course there are. But isn't that true of every church?"

I admitted it probably was, but it need not be if pastor-teachers encouraged people by equipping them, getting out of their way, and freeing them up to engage in ministry that would extend and enrich the body of Christ. To illustrate the point, I showed them a Coke bottle with a narrow neck and reminded them that all the liquid contained in the bottle had to pass through the neck—a neck much narrower and constricting than the body of the bottle.

In many churches, particularly traditional churches where the ordained minister is the only person allowed to fulfill numerous functions in the church, that minister can unwittingly become the bottleneck. But if others are trained and equipped to function in those areas and the minister encourages them to do so, far more people are mobilized, more ministry is embarked upon, and, as Paul said, the body is built up.

"Now, if I'm here all the time, I know lots of people will leave it all to me," I said. "But if I'm gone at times, they will have a chance to shine, to grow, and to develop, and the church will be the richer for it. My pastoral role as I understand it is to make sure this happens, and God enabling me, I will." They understood what I meant when I said that I did not intend to be Reverend Narrowneck.

God bless those dear men—they agreed.

My upbringing in the Brethren Assemblies where there were no ordained ministers but all the men were expected to minister had in some ways prepared me for this understanding. But Ray Stedman, a wonderful pastor in Palo Alto, California, who had become a close friend had written a book that caused quite a stir. It was called *Body Life*, and it spelled out what Paul taught about gifts of the Spirit and life in the body of Christ in a number of his epistles and showed how Ray was encouraging the people of the church in Palo Alto to put Paul's teaching into practice.

Most of this teaching was not new to me, although it was presented in a much fuller, broader manner than I had been accustomed to in the Brethren Assemblies, but the shock waves that ran through the church in America were quite extraordinary. In fact, people's reactions to Ray's book suggested that he had discovered something radical or maybe even heretical! So I teased him one day and said, "Ray, a lot of people think the apostle Paul wrote Romans, Ephesians, and Corinthians after someone gave him a copy of *Body Life*."

He nodded and grinned and drawled in his laid back style. "Yep, I just told them what the Bible says, and it caught a lot of people by surprise."

So I went on to my next engagement, having agreed to move the family to America and accept the call to pastor Elmbrook Church as soon as the necessary immigration formalities could be fulfilled. Meanwhile, back at the church, my call was proposed and seconded, a vote was taken, and everybody with the exception of one voted in favor. On hearing this I was delighted to have such a strong vote, but Jill was not at all pleased that anyone would vote against her favorite preacher! When we arrived in Milwaukee, she asked if the identity of the solitary naysayer was known, and the chairman said with a laugh, "Oh yes."

"But wasn't it a secret vote?" I asked.

"It was," he replied. "But when I announced the one nay vote, a man in the audience glared at his wife, and she tried to avoid his gaze. It was obvious that he expected at least two nay votes, as he presumably had instructed her to vote no with him and she had disobeyed." The chairman never told Jill his identity!

On arriving back in England and announcing our intentions to family, friends, and colleagues, we encountered mixed reactions. By this time Jill's father had passed away, so our move meant we were leaving two widowed mothers in England. That was the hardest part. Moving away from Capernwray, which had been our home and base of operations for eleven years and the scene of much of our spiritual development over a much longer period, was also a huge wrench. And then all kinds of messages came our way. "Leaving the sinking ship, are you?" said one eminent ecclesiastic who should have known better.

"Milwaukee?" said another. "You know Dwight L. Moody called it the graveyard of evangelists, don't you?" I didn't.

"You're going to Milwaukee?" asked a member of the Billy Graham team. "You know it's the largest city in the U.S.A. to which Dr. Graham has never been invited, don't you?" I did now!

And my friend and colleague Alan Redpath said, "The worst two weeks of my ministry I spent in Milwaukee. It's a hard place!" (I've met a number of people who were converted during those weeks, so it wasn't as bad as Alan thought.) None of this was particularly encouraging, but we had made a commitment and planned to keep it.

In those days there was a special fast track for ministers applying for visas to enter the United States. We applied, and after a delay our application was turned down because I "wasn't a minister." When I assured them I was and had been for years, I was told, "If you were a minister, you'd have a certificate of ordination to prove it." (I didn't have one.)

On hearing of this problem, my dear friend Hal Brooks, senior pastor of North Richland Hills Baptist Church in Fort Worth, Texas, said, "Come on down here. We'll ordain you, and we'll give you a certificate." I needed to think through what I believed about "ordination," and I concluded that while Scripture takes very seriously the call to ministry and says much about the qualifications for the task, it says little about an official, formal ceremony to install a person in a ministry position.

In my mind I had been ordained to ministry when the Capernwray Missionary Fellowship of Torchbearers identified spiritual gifts in me, affirmed them, and asked me, after prayer, to exercise them in the context of their ministry. They did not formally "lay hands on me," which would have been perfectly appropriate, but they certainly embraced me, and I gladly accepted their invitation to serve with them in the ministry. So for me the ordination in Fort Worth was a formality that confirmed an existing reality, and the certificate was an official record of that formality. Moreover, it made the people in the American embassy in London very happy, and they began to look with favor upon me.

Until, that is, they found out I had never pastored a church. They turned my application down again. I made a quick trip to London and had an interview with embassy officials in which I pointed out that their definition of "minister" was really a definition of "pastor," and by their definition Billy Graham was not a minister. They seemed satisfied.

Until they found I had written books, at which point they said, "You're not a minister; you are an author." A careful explanation that ministers write sermons and sometimes bind about a dozen of them and they become a book was all they needed to hear—until they checked my passport and found I had been behind the Iron Curtain and was therefore suspect. "Why would anyone want to go there unless they were sympathizers?" their questions implied. So the delays went on—and on—and on.

In the end the National Association of Evangelicals and Billy Graham himself contacted them and assured the "powers that be" that I was kosher, so they finally agreed! Subsequently, I discovered that what was supposed to be a fast track had slowed down because a flood of people belonging to the

Reverend Sun Myung Moon's Unification Church, more commonly referred to as "Moonies," had been using it to bring in people with shaven heads wearing saffron robes, sandals, and woolly socks who played cymbals and drums in shopping malls and called it "ministry." The American government had seen enough of this and decided to stop the flow, and in doing so, they stopped the Briscoes too. But as they say, "All's well that ends well," and the resultant delay in processing our visas certainly proved beneficial in the end. It gave Jill more time to deal with the busyness of transferring a family from one continent to another; it allowed us more time to prepare the children for a monumental change in their lives; it afforded opportunities to handle efficiently the transfer of responsibilities we were laying down; and it gave the church a breathing space between pastors.

We were finally called as a family to the American embassy in London to be interviewed. The kids had never been to London. They were both excited and nervous because they thought they might be interviewed, and if they didn't know the answers, they might be left behind. So in answer to their questions, "What will they ask us, Daddy?" I said. "They may ask you 'who is the president of the U.S.A.?'"

"That's easy," said my bright little nine-year-old, Judy. "It's Dick Van Dyke!"

Pete, at seven years of age, was sure he knew better. Incredibly he said, "It's Tom and Jerry!"

David, the eleven-year-old, characteristically and wisely held his peace.

The interview was an anticlimax. In fact, the formalities took about two minutes, and then for about half an hour, our interviewer, on noting that we were going to America to be "in the ministry," asked for advice on his failing marriage. Having done our best for the poor man, we emerged into the pale London sunlight clutching our long-delayed visas — and America beckoned. We stood in Parliament Square and said good-bye to Big Ben and turned to salute the statue of Winston Churchill glowering at us from his pedestal. We checked to see that Old Father Thames was still rolling along and passed Buckingham Palace and wondered if the queen might see us and invite us for a farewell cup of tea. She didn't. So we headed back to the north, sad and excited at the same time, and packed what was left of our belongings, as we had sold or given away everything that would not fit into the two suitcases each we had been asked to bring with us.

Flowing streams cut their own channels. Sometimes the channel sweeps round a bend, and what lies ahead is hidden from view and even imagination. I knew something, Jill knew less, and the children knew nothing of what lay ahead. All we knew was that we were convinced it was the way to go and God had promised to go before us. So we went.

CHAPTER 10

THE STREAM THAT MAKES GLAD

There is a river whose streams make glad the city of God,
the holy place where the Most High dwells.
God is within her, she will not fall;
God will help her at break of day.

—Psalm 46:4–5

"Knowing you as I do, Stuart, I'll give you twelve months in the pastorate!" Thus spake no less an authority than Alan Redpath, former pastor of the historic Moody Memorial Church in Chicago. "Assuming, that is, you avoid a constitutional revision and building programs," he added.

As I had never seen a church constitution, I had no intention of revising one; and having never been involved in a church that needed to do anything about its building except stop it from falling down, I knew little and cared less and had no intention of learning about a building program — whatever that was. So I took heart, smiled confidently, and said to Alan, "I think we'll be okay!" But I walked away wondering.

We left rainy England one Tuesday morning, arriving in Chicago's O'Hare International Airport later that day, where we were met by a welcoming committee from Elmbrook Church and whisked away to our new home one hundred miles north of Chicago in Brookfield, a suburb of Milwaukee. The dear people of the church had bought and personally decorated a house for us, stocked its cupboards, hung specially painted artwork on the walls, and even built a special pen for Prince, our golden retriever.

We had decided that the kids should have a quiet week to help them settle into their new surroundings, but after two days they asked to start school. Before the end of the week, they had developed authentic American accents. I wondered idly how long it would take Jill and me to lose what our new friends called our British accents but which we had been brought up to believe was just English as it is supposed to sound.

Experienced pastors had told me, "You'll have a honeymoon period for a while, and then things will get normal." I inquired about the exact duration of "a while" without any definitive answers, and I received no clarification when I asked what "normal" would look like and how I would recognize it. Anyway, I didn't have time to think much about this as the next night was "Wednesday night prayer meeting" and I was due to lead it. I don't remember anything about the service, but what happened after it is deeply etched in my memory.

I was talking to a group of people who were telling me, "We just love your accent," when a voice behind me said, "Pastor." As I had never been so addressed in my life before, I paid no attention, even when it was repeated. It was only when I felt a gentle nudge in the ribs and turned around that I realized the woman standing there was talking to me in my official capacity. I apologized. She smiled graciously and said, "Pastor, what does the Bible say about so and so?" (I've long forgotten the subject.) As I had no idea, I said, "I'm sorry. I've no idea." She looked hopefully at me and said, "Well, would you find out for me, please?"

I replied, "Don't you know how to find out yourself?" to which she replied rather tentatively and plaintively, "No. I've no idea how to find out." There was a kind of loud hush in the group who had overheard the exchange, and that, plus the look on the woman's face, showed me that I had opened my mouth and put my foot in it. Great start, Pastor!

I didn't know that pastors were supposed to, at least, convey the impression that they know everything—and I was not as yet aware that "straightforwardness" to the British is "putting down" to Americans. So scrambling desperately to recover some pastoral credibility, I said, "Then come with me, and I'll show you how to find out." I took her into my office. It was the first time I had entered it, and it was empty apart from boxes of books that we had shipped over. I ripped open a few until I found a concordance. Sitting down besides the nervous looking woman, I asked her, "Now what was it you wanted to know?" She whispered the topic that she was interested in, and I said, "What is the key word in that topic?" She ventured a guess, and I smiled encouragingly and said, "Good. Now let's look in this book called a concordance. It lists alphabetically the key words in the Bible and then gives references to show you where the word occurs in the Bible."

We found the word—I've forgotten what it was—and then we painstakingly looked up each reference to the word in its context. I asked her to write down in her own words what she had read, and probably about half an hour sped by. We amassed quite a pile of information, and together we were able to talk about what we had discovered. I encouraged her by saying, "You see, I didn't know any of this a few minutes ago, but now both of us have learned. Isn't that a lot better than me finding out and just telling you?" She agreed, with some reservation I think, that this was a much better way of doing things than simply having the pastor do it all, and I went on to tell her how Jesus instructed Peter, "Feed my lambs" and "Take care of my sheep" (John 21:15, 17).

Back in England I had been minimally involved in shepherding sheep—the four-legged variety—so I was able to show this woman that feeding sheep and feeding lambs are two entirely different operations. The only time human beings feed lambs is when the lambs are orphaned. Then the lamb is taken in one's arms and a baby's bottle of milk complete with teat is used to suckle the frail little animal. But mature sheep are never tucked under the arm and suckled with a bottle. They are led into green pastures and expected to feed themselves. In the same way, I explained to my newfound friend that pastors, who are really shepherds, need to bottle-feed new believers but encourage mature believers to feed themselves—and that is what I had been trying to show her. She seemed relatively satisfied and went her way, and I went home realizing that my pastoral skills were at best barely embryonic.

A couple of days later, however, the woman called me and said, "Pastor! You won't believe what happened today. My friend called and asked me, 'What does the Bible say about so and so?' I replied, 'I've no idea.' She then asked me if I would find out for her, and I declined but told her I would show her how to find out for herself. And we've just spent an hour study-ing the Bible for ourselves!" I must admit that I was highly relieved to hear this, but she went on, "I was so angry with you on Wednesday night, Pastor, when you answered me the way you did. But I'm so glad you showed this old sheep how to feed herself. And now I've shown another how to do it. So now you've got two sheep busy feeding." Incidentally, more than thirty years later, "this old sheep," while considerably older, is a competent volunteer counselor, an ardent student of the Word and skillful exponent of it, and an effective evangelist.

Two Sunday evenings later, promptly on starting time, I went into the sanctuary, sat down, and surveyed the assembling people while waiting for the choir, organist, and song leader to enter. I waited. And waited and waited some more. Nothing happened. So I said, "Has anyone seen the song leader?" Someone called out, "He just quit, and the choir isn't singing without him, and the organist is his wife! She quit too." So I responded, "Oh, really," which is the British way of filling in an awkward silence and responding to an awkward situation without saying anything at all. Then having thereby bought myself a couple of seconds for reflection, I added, "Well, I'm really just a frustrated song leader, so let's sing. Can anyone play the piano?"

"Sure, I can," volunteered a woman — none other than "the old sheep" — and off we went. We had a good sing, I preached my message, and then I went home to be greeted by Jill, who said, "Now what're you going to do?" I replied, "I've no idea!" A response that in the following days developed into quite a refrain.

A few days later I attended the first deacons' meeting of my life. I was genuinely excited about the opportunity to see firsthand the inner workings of a church. The first item on the agenda puzzled me deeply. It was a long discussion on the song leader's action on the previous Sunday evening. I listened intently and then opened my mouth for the first time in the inner sanctum of a church and asked, "Excuse my asking, but what are we doing?"

"We're discussing whether to accept the song leader's resignation," I was told.

"But what is there to discuss?" I inquired. "He quit, didn't he?"

"Well, yes, he did," someone explained. "But he was asking for a vote of confidence from the new pastor."

I was dumbstruck and blurted out, "Well tell him he hasn't got it. I have no confidence whatsoever in a man who would do what he did on Sunday night." The meeting quickly deteriorated from that point on, and I was treated to a rather straightforward lesson on the way Americans rather than "Brits" look at things, what it means to be a pastor, and what my role would be in the future in relation to the board. To my amazement it ended with the chairman tearfully explaining that while the church had voted unanimously (minus one!) to call me as pastor, some of the people had changed their minds in the intervening months, and they really didn't want me there.

I went home to discover my little wife in a puddle of tears. As she had no experience of church life, she had innocently asked the women in the church to tell her what they expected of her. So they had leapt at the opportunity and told her. Hence the puddles. Between sniffles she stammered, "There's not one thing on this list I can do!" Demonstrating once again her flair for the dramatic, she continued. "And nothing I know I can do is on the list. I'm going to die, and God will give you an American wife who can be a proper pastor's wife."

I set about damage control. The best I could do was to tell her, "Well, if you can't do it well, do it badly!" Incidentally, "If a thing's worth doing, it's worth doing badly" became something of a mantra in our ministry. Imagine my delight when I discovered that G. K. Chesterton had said it first. There the similarity between G. K. and yours truly ends abruptly.

We soon discovered that Americans are so gifted and so resource rich that they expect things to be done well. And they do things well. However, there's a down side to this pursuit of excellence. So many people see the "experts" performing and producing in the church that they know they cannot possibly work at that level. They are afraid they would fail if they attempted to do anything, so they refuse to try. "If I can't do it well, I won't do it at all!" We believed—and still do—that people should be encouraged to recognize that those who do something well do so because someone allowed them to start by doing it badly. This is not a plea for mediocrity, but rather a cry for people to be allowed to "learn by making mistakes." We believe that "he who never made a mistake never made anything." But if mistakes are going to be made, they must be done at a time and in a place where damage control minimizes destructive possibilities and the mistake maker is supported and encouraged to learn from the mistake and not to make it again. It is all part of flowing streams cutting their own channels—and their teeth!

To her great credit, Jill dried her eyes, made a cup of tea, and set about being a pastor's wife. Fences were mended on the deacons' board, and after about three months, something like normality settled in. Our ministry had gotten off to a difficult start, but soon the leadership steered me through the rough patches, explained to me how hard it is for people to lose a pastor they love and show devotion to another, and suggested that I listen a little more carefully in the future before coming up with one of my "forthright" responses. Learning curve!

Soon three things happened in Jill's life. She discovered abilities she did not know she had. Other people saw her floundering, trying to use gifts she didn't have, and out of pity volunteered to help. And the church began to see her unique gifts that lay outside the box and encouraged her in the development of them. Win! Win! Win! In a very short time, women by the hundreds clamored around to listen to her teaching the Word. There was no further mention of a premature death or a new wife for me, and life in the parsonage began to settle down.

I had announced to the congregation on my arrival that I thought they were either the most courageous or the most misguided congregation on the North American continent in that they had called me, a totally ill-equipped, untrained, inexperienced person as their pastor. I told them, "I don't know much, but I do know an excellent Book on the subject, and I promise you I will read, mark, learn, and inwardly digest it. Then I will come to you and teach it. All I ask of you is 'Will you please join me in making a genuine attempt to do what it says?'" They said yes!

Within six months the congregation doubled in size, and the lovely church sanctuary that recently had been completed became redundant. Nearby the Ruby Isle Cinema stood invitingly empty on a Sunday morning. Its interior showed all the signs of a late Saturday night showing—chewing gum on the seats, sticky Coke on the floor, popcorn in the aisles. In other words, it was an ideal place to invite people who wouldn't go to church to hear the Word of God. The fact that there was little lighting, the roof leaked, and in springtime when the snow melted the front of the cinema was underwater was not a problem. We moved in, I took off my shoes and socks and waded to the temporary pulpit, and the people flooded in.

Milwaukee, settled by Germans and Poles, is a predominantly Catholic and Lutheran city—84 percent of the population claim membership in one or the other of these major denominations. We knew that, unfortunately, for many of them, "confirmation" at age thirteen meant "graduation" from church altogether. So the city had quite a dense population of lapsed Catholics and Lutherans who nevertheless retained a residual respect for the things of God even if they did not respect them enough to do anything about them. But just a few years previously, in 1965, Vatican II announced that Catholics should become better acquainted with God's Word. This instruction coincided with the arrival in Milwaukee of a guy with a "strange" accent who preached for an hour in a cinema instead of a church. You didn't have to dress up, and it was dark so no one could see you were there. So they came—as the hymn says, "Just as I am." Some pastors asked me one day, "What does it feel like to be the biggest sheep stealer in Milwaukee?" But the Catholic archbishop took a more gracious line and said, "Thank you, Stuart, for feeding so many of my hungry sheep."

There was another reason for the rapid numerical growth of the fellowship. On my initial visit to Elmbrook, I visited the home of a couple named Bob and Win Couchman. It was winter, the snow was deep, and as I approached the address I had been given, I noticed the streets already piled with snow were further blocked by parked cars of the "rust bucket" variety. Easing my way through them, I eventually found my destination but was puzzled to find furniture stacked in the snow! The door was opened a crack in response to my knock, and a rather woolly looking young man looked at me, smiled, and shouted, "It's brother Stuart! Just a minute." After a few minutes of scuffling, the door was opened enough for me to squeeze through, and I saw the reason not only for the delay in opening the door, but also for the furniture being deposited in the snow. There was not a stick of furniture left in the room—nothing but wall to wall kids sitting crossed-legged on the floor—about a hundred of them. I recognized them immediately. They were the American counterparts of the British kids we had worked with "back home"—the kids who said, "Tell us about Jesus, just don't drag us into church!"

When Bob and Win's kids got into the '60s drug scene, instead of sending them away, they had invited them to bring their friends home. The hundred kids sitting contentedly on the floor listening intently to my teaching of

God's Word were the result. These kids had made the leap from drugs to discipleship. They loved Jesus.

My experience of these young people in the U.K. had taught me two things. First, if kids like this did not get into a healthy church fellowship, they would drift into more and more exotic and esoteric mystical experiences that would lead eventually to outright heresy. Second, if they were not integrated into the church, the churches that tended to look down on them would miss out on what I believed was the most exciting movement of the Spirit on both sides of the Atlantic. No wins here. Lose! Lose!

So that night after the kids dispersed, I sat with Bob and Win and talked about the necessity, for the sake of the kids and the healthy growth of Elmbrook, for the youngsters to be integrated into the church's life. They agreed, but knowing the fellowship better than I did, they were unsure. And of course at that point I was talking theory. I had no idea I would be the pastor who would be called to preside over such an experiment.

Upon arriving as "pastor," I immediately went looking for Bob and Win and their flock and reminded them of my conviction that the young people needed the church's experience and the church needed their enthusiasm. Experience without enthusiasm can lead to dead orthodoxy, while enthusiasm without experience leads to lively chaos. We didn't need either.

It took quite a while, but after a few months the hundred young people trooped into the church sanctuary one glorious Sunday morning. Late of course! In those days we had one service in the church building and one in the cinema. The first service in the sanctuary was frequented by people who "couldn't worship in a cinema," and the second in Ruby Isle by people who "wouldn't darken the door of a church." Unfortunately, as it seemed at first, the unchurched kids arrived among the more conservative members of the congregation. To say that they caused a stir—clad in blue jeans and sweatshirts bearing a wild variety of slogans, with crosses dangling round their necks that would have graced an archbishop—would be the ultimate understatement. Consternation spread from face to face. The well-dressed and well-heeled people moved uneasily in their pews, and mothers clasped their children to their bosoms. The new arrivals pushed into pews where little room was made available to them, and when the pews were full, they sat on the floor. Some sat on the platform. They had arrived, and I was delighted.

The service was concluded without major incident, but there was plenty of buzz as the people left—and it wasn't about the sermon.

The buzz came to a crescendo a couple of days later when one of the young businessmen in the church, Don Westerhoff, whose father-in-law was a well-known Baptist denominational leader, arrived at my home. He didn't waste any time telling me that he and many other people were very disturbed about what had happened on Sunday morning. He went on to explain that many in the congregation had worked very hard to keep their own young people away from the kind of people whom, he said, "you have brought into our church." He wanted to know if I understood their concerns and asked what I was going to do about them.

I told him that I understood their concerns. But unwisely I compared them to the attitudes in South Africa where I had visited recently. There the blacks and the whites were segregated in the churches—a policy that was given a respectable sheen by the quoting of dubious biblical references but was really based on prejudice and fear. I think what I said on that day many years ago was probably right, but its delivery left much to be desired. I was after all a blunt north of England man with little or no pastoral skills. But Don Westerhoff was wonderful. He looked at me, swallowed hard, and said, "All right, I see your point. So what can we do about it?" He showed more grace than I possessed at that moment.

We immediately sat down and brainstormed how we might integrate the conservative regulars, the "cinema-only" attendees, and our new friends from the counterculture. The starting point on which Don and I agreed was that the church is supposed to model what it means to be "all one in Christ Jesus." You cannot preach, "Whosoever will may come," and then add in the small print, "provided you dress like us, look like us, vote as we vote, and come from a similar socioeconomic background as the rest of us." I knew a lot of theory about "unity in diversity" as modeled in physical bodies that have a lot of members, all different, each with a special function, who must cooperate with and complement the other members. And in my own studies I had learned that God, who is a trinity—three in one and one in three—loves to make things that reflect the unity in diversity he manifests. Hence the church and its members. But theory is one thing—putting feet to it is entirely different.

Fortunately, Don knew what to suggest. Before he left we had devised a new class by invitation only that would incorporate people from all strata of the Elmbrook Church community. They would be asked to commit to a twelve-week study of the epistle of James, and we would call it "Generation Bridge." Both Don and I were tired of hearing about generation gaps. After teaching the class through twice, we were partway through the third time when participants told us that all the issues had been solved. They were enjoying great friendships with one another and now were asking if we could please teach something else. The answer of course was a resounding yes.

Sometime later a university student named Tom Perucci, who had been contacted by Bob and Win, came to faith and eventually indicated that he would like to become a member of Elmbrook. He went through the requisite class, and then on the day he and others were to be received, he asked if he could address the congregation. I agreed. When his turn came, he stood up dressed in tattered blue jeans and a T-shirt, with his long hair gently resting on his shoulders, and said, "A few months ago I would never have thought of coming to a place like this, but some friends met me on the campus, introduced me to Jesus, encouraged me in my faith, and told me about the wonderful church they attended. So I looked forward to coming. But when I did I experienced a great disappointment because I was given the impression that I was not very welcome. Now, I have to tell you that I resented that, but as I want to become a member of this fellowship, I need to confess my resentment and ask you please to forgive me, please try to understand me, and please welcome me." He went on. "I don't know if I'll ever look or think like you, but one thing I know — if we are to be a true fellowship of believers, you need to repent of your prejudice just as I need to repent of my resentment."

With that he sat down to be greeted by silence and then discreet applause that slowly gained momentum. More important, at the end of the service, Tom was surrounded by well wishers, and in other parts of the auditorium, we saw reconciliations taking place. We were seeing a church being born! Tom did start to look and think a little like some of us — only a little — and eventually became a Presbyterian minister.

On another occasion, at the end of a service I was urgently requested to go to the foyer as an argument had broken out. On arrival I discovered that the two protagonists, both good friends and brothers of mine, were a diminutive Jewish gentleman named Harry Sirkman and a huge Polish ex-cop, boxer, and professional wrestler named Andy Andryzsak. Racial epithets were being hurled across the intervening space between the two men. Political correctness had not yet been mooted in the seventies, and if it had, I doubt if Harry or Andy would have been introduced to it. I never did find out what had triggered the interlude, but I managed to pour oil on troubled waters, and everybody went home relieved that Harry had survived the encounter.

During the following week, I had a little pastoral counseling time individually with both men and hoped all would be well. The next Sunday, as I concluded the service, Andy marched purposefully down the aisle to the front row where Harry was sitting in his regular place. With everyone holding their breath, he reached down, put his huge hands under Harry's armpits, and with a great heave, lifted a very frightened Harry in the air, marched across the front of the church with the little man's wild eyes staring and his little legs flailing, and sat him down on top of the organ. Then, putting Harry in a bear hug that must have threatened his very existence, Andy kissed him on both cheeks and, turning to me, said, "Is that all right, Preach (his favorite name for me)—is that what I should do?"

"That's fine, Andy" I replied, hurrying down from the pulpit to rescue the frightened gentleman who, once he recovered from the shock, embarked on becoming Andy's best friend. Odd couple! True. But they were a couple of trophies of God's grace. We were seeing lots of evidence that God was at work in the hearts of people.

As the congregation grew, we ran into traffic problems, seating problems, people problems—lots of problems. When my friends heard that all these problems were related to rapid growth, they insisted on saying, "But they're good problems to have, aren't they?"

Things came to a head one day in a supermarket. Walking the aisles minding my own business and trying to remember what I had been sent for, I encountered a woman pushing a cart full of groceries. She seemed intent on running me down, so I took evasive action in the cereals but still did not manage to get away. Appearing over the cart and groceries parked under my midriff and wagging her finger at me, she said, "We've left your church, you know. We've left your church."

I mumbled something about I didn't know and it really wasn't my church. Undaunted, she went on. "Well, don't you want to know why we left?"

Actually I didn't, but she wanted me to know, so she said, "It's grown too big."

"How big do you think is too big?" I asked, interested.

She replied dogmatically, "Six hundred."

I told her that I hadn't understood that, even though she said it was "an understood thing." I added that I had been reading a book on church growth titled the Acts of the Apostles, and the only statistics it gave on the size of churches as far as I knew was about five thousand in the church at Jerusalem. I readily conceded that now that Elmbrook was getting bigger, we were losing some intimacy compared to the days when it was a smaller group. She agreed and said that that was what she had said, so I didn't argue. Off she went and home I went—straight to my study and the Acts of the Apostles. I wanted to take another look at the church in Jerusalem. (You need to remember that there was no such thing then as the "Willow Creek model" or the "Saddleback model.") Anyway, I was a firm believer in the fact that the Bible was "an excellent book on the subject"—all manner of subjects, including church growth and loss of intimacy.

It did not take me many minutes to see what I was hoping to find. The big question raised in my mind inadvertently by the woman in the supermarket was, "How did the church at Jerusalem handle numerical growth?"

They had grown to three thousand in one day—I figured that counted as church growth—and then had progressed to five thousand, and the Lord kept adding new believers on a daily basis. At the same time, we are told, "all the believers were one in heart and mind" (Acts 4:32). They even shared their material resources—that was intimacy! But how did they do it? Then I saw it: "Day after day, in the temple courts and from house to house, they never stopped teaching and proclaiming the good news that Jesus is the Christ." (Acts 5:42). Apparently the apostles continued the practice of the Master who regularly taught the people in the temple courts. But the growing church also met regularly in the homes of believers. That was it—we needed to organise the large congregation into smaller groups where people could be encouraged and nurtured, cared for, and ministered to. That was how the church in Jerusalem did it, and that was good enough for us. Persuading the deacons that we should do this was another matter!

At first I naively assumed that the people would gladly add another week-night gathering to the regular Wednesday evening prayer service. If I had stopped to think for a minute, I would have noticed that most of the people were conspicuous by their absence on Wednesday evening, so they probably would not commit another evening of their busy lives to church activities. Therefore, the only thing to do was to persuade the leadership that as the Wednesday evening service was not what it was billed to be anyway—a prayer time—and relatively few people showed up—we should do the Christian thing and bury what had expired. A meeting was called, and a grand group gathered—including people I had never seen before on a Wednesday evening. They were presented with a large map of Milwaukee festooned with colourful pins indicating the location of families who were part of the fellowship. These pins were encircled by rubber bands indicating the proposed small groups to which the people had been assigned in their neighbourhoods—it was tidy and made an awful lot of sense to me. To many hearers of this grand plan, however, it was just plain awful.

The depth of feeling on the part of some of the people took me aback. I quickly learned that what some of the people were objecting to was the fact that changes were being thrust upon them from on high—they were not necessarily upset about the actual proposed change. How could they be upset about losing something they didn't value? As some others voiced their "concerns," it became clear to me that they were frankly not ready for the kind of personal sharing—intimacy—that the proposed groups might engender. Some didn't like the Wednesday night service being abandoned; others didn't like what we proposed to put in its place. There was a lot not to like. All this taught me a huge lesson—be very careful how, when, and why you introduce change in the church. Not for nothing do we intone in our worship, "As it was in the beginning, is now, and ever shall be, world without end. Amen."

The proposed change really was major. This, you must remember, was long before small groups became big. When asked for "models," I knew of none. I suggested the church in Jerusalem, but that didn't seem to count. Eventually, after considerable listening and answering, convincing and soothing, Elmbrook did what it has consistently done. It proved willing to try. Not everybody participated, but then not everybody had participated on Wednesday nights. Some started out and fell by the wayside. That often happens in a church program. Others joined belatedly when they heard it wasn't as bad as they had been told. And the result: far more people became involved than previously, more people were cared for at a deeper level, and—surprise, surprise—more people were given the opportunity to discover and exercise their gifts instead of watching me do my thing.

Oh, and we benefited from an event that came from a most unexpected source—the Arabs! They declared an oil embargo, and America panicked. We, however, were able to encourage our people to see how they could help by cutting back on their gas consumption by meeting at home rather than traveling to Elmbrook. I suspect that might have carried the day, but I didn't want to delve too deeply into that possibility.

The early days at Elmbrook were filled with challenges—some avoidable, some unavoidable. One thing we knew: the church is where God dwells by his Spirit, and his Spirit is like streams of water flowing within, among, and through the people, bringing spiritual health and help, spiritual bounty and blessing. We saw it happening, and the streams made glad the house of God.

CHAPTER 11

STILL GLIDES THE STREAM

Still glides the Stream, and shall for ever glide;
The Form remains, the Function never dies.

—William Wordsworth, "Sonnets from the
River Duddon: After-Thought"

William Wordsworth, the Lakeland poet, had a particular love for lakes and rivers, including the river Duddon, about which he wrote a series of his sonnets. This was the river that flowed past my hometown on its way to the boisterous Irish Sea. As a boy I had spent many carefree hours playing along its banks and scouring its marshes for eggs and nests and berries and daffodils. During the war we boys gathered moss for emergency dressings and "hips and haws" (fruit from the wild rose bushes and hawthorn that filled the hedgerows) for medicines, all of which we were told contributed to the war effort. Less nobly we took a ghoulish delight in searching for gruesome relics of a wide variety of planes that had crashed on its banks and in its waters.

Although Wordsworth roamed the same region, he didn't strike me as being particularly carefree. Among the splendor of a "host of golden daffodils," he "wandered lonely as a cloud," and even looking at the Duddon led to somber thoughts about a loved one who had passed away.

I thought of Thee, my partner and my guide,
As being past away.—Vain sympathies!
For, backward, Duddon! as I cast my eyes,
I see what was, and is, and will abide;
Still glides the Stream, and shall for ever glide;
The Form remains, the Function never dies.

As Jill and I went about our work in the congregation of Elmbrook Church, we became increasingly aware that, as Jesus had promised, streams of living water would flow from us. It was happening. The Lord was building his church. And my thoughts went to Wordsworth's view of the Duddon again: "What was, and is, and will abide." In my mind this was a reminder of the work of the Spirit. I knew enough church history to remind myself of what was—as God had birthed the church and established it throughout the Roman Empire and on through the ages until it had reached far away to the shores of Lake Michigan and the old city of Milwaukee. And I could look around me and see changed lives on every hand, crowds of people hungry for spiritual reality, marriages and families restored, relationships healed—and all the time a joyous sense of delight in daily life strengthened by rich worship and fellowship. What was is!

I also took comfort in the fact that if the Spirit was cutting his own channel—and I knew of no other explanation for what was happening—then I was sure that his work would abide. We were aware that what we saw him do was a continuation of what was, and evidence of what is, and a promise of what will abide.

The "Form" of the church as the medium of his activity remained, and the "Function"—the relentless working of the Holy Spirit through ordinary lives—had not died. Some wise person—I forget who—has pointed out that if you step into a river as a boy and return as a man, it's the same river but totally different. The river is still there, the waters still flow, but over time the course has altered, the waters have only recently sprung from the earth or dropped from the sky.

The church is the church, and nothing will change that. The Spirit at work in the church is still the sine qua non of its life and growth. But change is inevitable. And in our case, the big change we had to confront was the rapid growth of the congregation, which I have already mentioned.

When I arrived at Elmbrook, I worked with one assistant pastor who soon moved on, and a part-time secretary who almost forty years later never lets me forget my birthday however hard I try to overlook it.

So it was time to expand the staff. I needed help. But where to start? I knew where I was weak—and everybody else knew too! I had not hidden my weaknesses when I accepted the call. The church leaders knew perfectly well that I had no pastoral experience, and they didn't seem to regard that with concern. Now it was clear that I needed someone who was strong where I was weak. Joe Ballard, an old friend from Alabama, came to mind. Joe had more degrees than I could imagine; he had operated in various capacities in all manner of churches; and he agreed to join me.

Marc Erickson was a physician who had spent time with his wife, Nancy, and five small children doing medical missionary work in Somalia. He was immensely bright and gifted, a creative and attractive teacher of the Word who was tireless in his ministry to college-age people and young adults. Marc had already made himself invaluable, teaching a highly popular and effective weeknight class in a restaurant and another class on a Sunday morning. He offered to cut back on his medical practice in order to join the staff.

Then there was Bob Henley and his wife, Jane, a handsome couple who effortlessly exuded charisma and regularly appeared on Billy Graham's crusades and telecasts. I met Bob on a very early morning show on television in South Carolina. The rapport was instantaneous. Subsequently, we worked together on a number of projects, and it became clear to me that Jane and Bob's experience working through music and drama outside the church with totally unchurched people would be extremely effective in our situation. To my surprise and delight, they agreed to join us too.

There are different ways to build a staff, but the three methods I unwittingly used in the first three appointments proved effective and lasting. I had never built a team of my own, but I had seen enough teams in action to know what I was looking for: godly, happy people with minimal egos and servant spirits who were enthusiastic about ministry in the local church and who exhibited a willingness to learn and adjust and gave evidence of a readiness to work in harmony—and who understood that flowing streams cut their own channels.

In Joe's case, it was a matter of looking at a specific need and finding someone to fill the need. Specific gifting and experience were paramount. In Marc's case, here was a man who, with his wife (who was also raising five kids), was deeply involved and effective in ministry while busily engaged in medical practice. They were already in the fellowship; their ministry was well proven; and in calling them to join us, we were affirming what was perfectly obvious and providing a platform on which their ministry could flourish even more and from which the ministry of the church would be greatly enriched. In Bob and Jane's case, they had only a little church experience, but they showed enough charisma—in the fullest sense of the word in grace, gift, and power—for me to recognise that given the chance they would blossom in ways that they had never dreamed possible. In my view the church's job is to provide people of that caliber that kind of opportunity. In addition, it goes without saying that they would get ahold of our burgeoning youth program and it would take off. They did and it did!

About three or four years later, Drew Trotter completed his Cambridge PhD, and because I had stayed in close contact with him over the years, I knew that he had a vision to take top-flight theological training back into the local church. He had the credentials to teach in any seminary in the world, but he wanted to establish a study center in a local church setting where ordinary believers could study without having to leave their occupations. As I had seen something similar to this in the church Ray Stedman pastored, and as I shared Drew's vision, I asked the church leaders to extend him a call, which they did—and the Elmbrook Church Study Center was established. Nearly thirty years later, it is still turning out well-trained laypeople.

One added benefit of the Study Center became evident over the years as more and more people who would never have gone to seminary completed the training we offered (all the time supporting themselves in their secular jobs and pursuing their ministries in the church). This meant that when we had a vacancy on the staff or an opportunity to develop a new ministry, we didn't have to look very far for a suitable person to give leadership. "Look under your nose first" became a rule of thumb as we built our pastoral team. Added to this, we had a system of internships in which young college students who had shown gifts and aptitudes compatible with ministry were invited to spend a summer working with us at the church. Over the years a number of them found their way into pastoral ministry or missionary activity. Little tributaries were flowing in many directions.

I am not at all enthusiastic about modern methods of "recruiting and hiring" in which resumes of hundreds of people are gathered, endless procedures of vetting and interviewing ensue, various "candidates" are displayed, and eventually one person survives the process. While one church is satisfied and one pastor is happy, many ministries are disrupted, dozens of ministers are distracted, and most of them are disappointed. This issue came to a head early in my ministry when I presented someone as a suitable member of the pastoral staff to the church leaders. One of them asked me, "How many people have you interviewed for this position?"

"One," I replied.

"One?" he questioned, startled. Then he added, "How can you possibly know he's the best person for the job?"

"I don't," I freely admitted. "But I know him, I know his heart, I know what he can do and what he can't do, and I think I know where he can grow. In addition he knows us and he has no illusions about what he's getting into. So why look any further? He may not be the 'best,' but he's one of ours and certainly good enough. And why should we have the best anyway?" I happen to believe good enough is good enough—and in a fallen world, there is no such thing as perfection.

As you can imagine, this started a fascinating debate, but once again the church leaders said, "Okay, it's not how we'd have done it, but let's give it a try." I was blessed to have such a group to work with—not, I hasten to add, that they always went along with my unorthodox ideas. Fortunately!

Alan Redpath, you may remember, had been particularly concerned about my becoming involved in constitutional revisions and building programs when I first told him about my decision to become a pastor. As time went on, both became unavoidable, and Alan had inserted a minor worm of worry in my mind. Without knowing what might lie ahead, I entered both warily.

The constitution of Elmbrook Church had been formulated when the church numbered less than a hundred people and when it was not even called Elmbrook Church. In those days it was the First Baptist Church of Brookfield, in fellowship with the General Association of Regular Baptists (GARB). Later the church had changed association to the Conservative Baptists and become Elmbrook Baptist Church, and still later it had disassociated with all Baptist Associations and become simply Elmbrook Church. All this happened long before Jill and I arrived on the scene. But the original GARB constitution still obtained. Most of the principles and provisions were very close to what Elmbrook had become. But issues related to baptism and church government with reference to the way that the leadership was selected, installed, and operated had to be addressed. It was time to bite the bullet — so bite we did.

The baptism issue arrived first, because the constitution required aspiring members to be baptised — and by that it meant believers' baptism by immersion — while the vast majority of the people who wanted to join the fellowship had already been baptised, to their satisfaction, in either the Catholic or the Lutheran tradition. (Remember, the city was 84 percent Lutheran and Catholic.)

Circumstances had forced me into a situation in which I was sometimes required to baptise people who had previously told me, "Stuart, you can dunk me if you must, but I'm not convinced. Still, I'll do it because I don't want to be left on the outside of Elmbrook looking in! This is where the Lord met me; this is where I want to belong."

I should clarify the situation by pointing out that in the early days our regular baptismal services were totally different from anything I had ever heard of before or since. When they were about to be baptised, people who had recently trusted Christ or been renewed in their faith (I'm glad I didn't have to determine what exactly the Spirit had done in their lives, although it was obvious he had done something life changing!) brought their large families with them to observe this unusual phenomenon. Try as I would to impart an appropriate degree of solemnity to the service, when the baptismal candidate appeared clad in an outfit that made him or her look quite angelic and then emerged from the water dripping wet, he or she was greeted with howls of laughter, cheers, and raucous applause. After the first candidate, no one remained in a seat, as everybody rushed to the platform to get a better view of the proceedings.

Moreover, we were still dealing with the perceptions commonly held in some quarters that Elmbrook was a sect. In 1978 when the deranged "spiritual leader" Jim Jones led his religious followers into a mass suicide in Guyana, one local priest preached a homily in which he said, "If you are having difficulty understanding how somebody like Jones could happen, all you need to do is look at Briscoe over at Elmbrook." This perception of Elmbrook's suspect credentials created enormous problems when young couples who had become part of the Elmbrook fellowship had their first baby, which also happened to be the first grandchild of staunchly committed Lutherans or Catholics. The grandparents, more than anything else, wanted to insure that their precious babies were "safe"—a state they believed was possible only if they were immediately baptised. (Catholic dogma has changed considerably on the subject of Limbo since the accession of Cardinal Ratzinger to "the throne of St. Peter" as Pope Benedict XVI.) From a solid base of long tradition, mixed with genuine concern and not a little fear, they adamantly insisted that the infant should be baptised, while the young parents wanted to follow Elmbrook's practice. I saw too many families fractured on this issue at a time when they should have been rejoicing in the new life and turning their attention to thanksgiving for the gift of a child and committing to the child's spiritual well-being.

While my own convictions leaned toward "believers' baptism," I would have been perfectly at ease baptising the infants without remotely suggesting or implying baptismal regeneration. Rather, the baptism would serve as a demonstration of the fact that believing parents were committing their child—and themselves—to a God of grace in whom they trusted and to whom they entrusted the eternal well-being of their precious little one on the understanding that eventually the child would be able to make an intelligent commitment to Christ. It would be similar in manner to the practice of the children of Israel when they presented their young boys for circumcision on the eighth day. I tried to show how believers' baptism rightly emphasises the fact that the participant had come to *faith*, while the baptism of the child emphasises appropriately the fact that we are dependent on *grace*. Accordingly, my recommendation was to practice both with a careful explanation of what both do and do not signify.

I was taken aback by the vehemence with which some people defended their positions and the way they threatened to "leave the church if we altered one word" of the requirement. In the end the church voted to change the constitution to limit our practice to believers' baptism but not to insist on it for membership, while reminding people that some form of baptism is normative for a disciple of Jesus. This was an awkward compromise that stands to this day—yet some people still left. Most ultimately returned.

The issue of church government arose for essentially pragmatic reasons—the existing procedures didn't work anymore. We had a board of deacons who were elected for three-year terms. Their task essentially was to administer the constitution, which had, of course, been determined by the congregation. So we were a congregational church. I have always maintained, however, that regardless of the form of government, all churches are in the end congregational, for the obvious reasons that if the congregation fails to "show up" and "cough up," there's nothing to govern! There were usually twelve deacons, and as their three-year terms of office were staggered, that meant that each year 33 percent of the board was new. As a result, the first few months of each year were often devoted to going over what had already been decided, and it was not unknown for decisions to be reversed within a few months of having been made. The need for longer "terms" was obvious.

In addition, there was a problem with the way deacons were appointed. Nominations were invited from the congregation and from the floor on the evening of the church meeting at which the voting would take place. When the congregation was relatively small, this was not a problem, because everybody knew everybody, but as time went on, names were presented of people unknown to many. The result was that occasionally when congregants were asked to vote for three of the six listed candidates, we would get votes for only one or two candidates with forlorn little notes, such as, "I only knew two of them." One day I was told, "I only voted for so and so. He was the only one I knew. In fact, I don't know him, but I know his wife. She's a lovely singer." Presumably she reasoned that any man who can capture a wife who sings like an angel must have the qualities necessary to serve like a deacon! I also noted for a number of years that the names placed at the top of the candidates' list always led in the voting. After long discussions by the deacons, which always concluded with "Something needs to be done," I eventually decided to do something. But I was a little sadder and wiser after the former experience of promoting change on the subject of baptism.

First, I wrote a "proposal" and carefully emphasised that it was a proposal and nothing more, nothing less—a starting point for discussion. It proposed:

> The existing board of deacons should be disbanded.
> A council of elders should take its place.
> Elders should be selected by the existing board from names submitted by the congregation or the existing elders.
> All nominated elders should be interviewed by the existing council, and suitable candidates' names presented to the congregation, not for a vote, but with the requirement that congregants carefully check the list. Should they know of any reason why the person presented was unsuitable, they should alert the elders and state their objections. [A minimum of two congregant objectors was required. This was based on the biblical injunction to hear a charge against an elder only if it was brought by two or three witnesses (1 Timothy 5:19). This approach meant that instead of asking people to vote yes for people

they may not know, they were being charged with the responsibility to say "no" or "not sure" about people they did know—very well.]

Nominees whose names were presented by the elders to the congregation who received no "no" votes were then prayerfully considered by the elders, and those who received a unanimous affirmation were invited to join the council.

Elders were invited to serve for six years and were then required to take a minimum of one year off the board, after which they would be eligible to be reconsidered to serve a further term. Reinvitation was not automatic but was predicated on specific needs and abilities recognised by the elders.

Deacons would be recognised and appointed by active participants in the various ministries to assist in the leadership of the ministry and to represent the ministry in a leadership summit once a quarter to which other deacons, elders, and pastors would be invited. Both women and men were eligible. [The board of deacons was equally divided on the subject of women serving on a board of elders, but this was an opportunity for women's gifts to be affirmed and utilised in a way that would probably be acceptable to all. It was.]

This proposal was presented informally to a few men who had previously served as chairmen of the board of deacons. One of them, a great friend of mine named Al Danielson, said, "Only a Brit could have written this—it's positively un-American." Then he thought about it quietly in his customary manner and said, "Go ahead and try it. It might work!"

So "try it" I did, by presenting it to the existing board of deacons who you may remember were being asked to vote themselves into extinction—a rarity for boards of deacons! They understandably objected, some more vociferously than others, and after a "full and frank exchange of views" (if I may use diplomatic language), I pointed out that it was only a proposal and that no other proposal had been offered. I asked them, therefore, if before they tossed it out, they would at least consider it for a month. When I added that I was leaving for India the next morning for a month, they decided to appoint a subcommittee (so what's new?) to consider it. When asked who would like to serve on the subcommittee, all those who were strongest in opposition to it eagerly volunteered. I asked that a very capable young man named Mel Lawrenz, who by this time had joined me on the staff and was showing exceptional leadership abilities, be added to the subcommittee in my absence as we had consulted on the formation of the proposal and he could prove helpful. They agreed.

Off I went to India, and the proposal was left to its fate. In that far-off land, I occasionally wondered what was happening to the proposal without any great hopes for its survival in recognisable form. The only word I received was a note from Mel scribbled on the bottom of one of Jill's airmail letters (this was long before email) saying, "We've decided on an episcopal form of government, and you've been enthroned as archbishop!" That was it!

Meeting together a month later, the subcommittee announced to my surprise that they unanimously supported the proposal and recommended that the full board do the same. Discussion followed as to how the transition from the existing board to the new council would be made, and I proposed that the deacons themselves work on that without my involvement—which they did. The proposal passed intact, and I was commissioned to present it to the congregation with the deacons' endorsement.

Somewhere along the line I had discovered a principle I call "the pebble in the pool." In a group of people, there is a "pool" of thinking, a general consensus that may be born of tradition, long usage, the persuasive influence of a few, or other factors. Like many a pool, it is perfectly tranquil until disturbed. It is not difficult to drop a boulder—a dramatic, radical idea—into such tranquility and immediately cause waves, which at the time suggest dynamic activity, but in the short term do needless damage and in the long term require time for recovery. It was far better, I had concluded, to drop a pebble of an idea into the pool of the thinking process. It was infinitely better to cause ripples than create waves. A new idea, presented simply as an idea for discussion and consideration can be offered, not emphasised, then gently wafted with occasional reminders until eventually the ripples reach the banks of people's opinions. Sooner or later, wonder of wonders, the ripples turn right round and head for the centre again. This means that if we present a new idea to people, give them time to get used to the idea, think and pray about it, help them with it when they ask, and occasionally remind them of it, there is a very good chance they will take ownership; and they may eventually come and suggest it to you. As they say, "You can achieve all manner of things if it doesn't matter who gets the credit."

So we "pebbled"—that is, we told the congregation that we had been considering a proposal to revise the constitution, and I announced that I would teach Paul's letter to Titus in a series of messages to tune our hearts to think of church life and government from a biblical point of view. This series of expositions lasted for about twelve weeks. Three whole months to think at first generally, then more specifically. Weekly opportunities to occasionally "waft" the idea gently across the tranquil pews. Then a special meeting was called at which I summarised what we had learned from the epistle to Titus and presented the proposal.

Emphasising not only that it was just a proposal and that the deacons had endorsed it unanimously, I also pointed out that as it required a congregational vote to change the constitution, only the congregation could decide on it one way or the other. All talk of "ramming it down our throats" and "railroading" or "They're starting an old boys' club" (dark rumbling rumours were already heard in the atmosphere) was countered, because only they could vote. The final decision and responsibility for its consequences would be theirs. Moreover—and this was crucial—we announced that no vote on the issue would be taken for a year to give everyone time to think, study, pray, argue, discuss, question, and decide. Regular small group meetings would facilitate that process.

A year later the vote was taken, with two negative votes by two of my good friends who walked out of the church and returned six months later. The congregation had totally revised their governmental structure and had freshly affirmed the women in their ministry. Significant leaders had voluntarily surrendered positions of influence, and far more people had been introduced to "summit level" leadership involvement. Any of these issues was potentially difficult, but Elmbrook had shown remarkable good sense and maturity with not a little understanding, love, and patience—and I came out of the experience more convinced than ever that there is no substitute for goodwill. We had that in buckets full. In fact, I will go so far as to assert that whatever system of church governance you adopt, it can be problematic without goodwill. Conversely, whatever problems you encounter with goodwill can be handled so as not to be destructive; without it they can ruin the work of the Spirit. Structures are secondary, attitudes are primary, and the flow of the Spirit is paramount.

In the church change is inevitable and is rarely comfortable. It is inevitable because churches are living organisms that grow and decline, that get sick and divide. And to add to the challenge, they endeavour to serve a community that is going through upheavals and developments, booms and busts. They live in and seek to speak to a culture that is subjected to monumental influences that constantly outdo each other in presenting lifestyles that are attractive, seductive, plausible, and carefully crafted to touch people's insecurities and fantasies and fashion shallow thinking. Therefore they need to adapt, but they desire to remain faithful to what cannot and will not change. Accordingly, any change instituted in the church is likely to meet at least reservation and occasionally outright opposition—sometimes for sound biblical and spiritual reasons, other times for less than noble preferences and prejudices that masquerade as principles. So implementers of change should approach the work with care—as Alan Redpath tried to tell me!

I learned a lot from these experiences:

Don't be hasty in introducing change.
Don't knock down a fence until you know why it was put up in the first place.

Do present solid biblical and commonsense reasons for change.
Do present change as a proposal, not as a fait accompli.
Do allow time for reaction, and don't fail to listen to objections.
Do invite suggestions, and don't hesitate to incorporate the best ones.
Do give people a chance to take ownership of the change.
Don't be disappointed by naysayers, and don't forget you're still their
    pastor.

Starting a building program is another issue that has the ability to engender significant congregational tension — and worse — more than just about anything else in church life. The reasons are obvious: a lot of money is involved, people coming from different traditions have different ideas about the kind of facilities that provide a "worshipful" environment, and some don't think the church should spend money on "bricks and mortar" at all. Some object to churches entering into debt, while others doing so in their homes and businesses see no reason not to. This is a veritable minefield where angels often fear to tread.

Much of what I learned about change applied to our (numerous) building programs that were made necessary because of the changes we were experiencing and seeking to respond to. Our numbers had risen dramatically. By the time two or three years had sped by, the original sanctuary was totally inadequate, and the overflow cinema was full as well. So there was little debate about whether we should make facility changes. But there was considerable discussion as to what, where, how much, and when.

At this point, Ray Stedman came to my rescue. He said, "Facilities are designed to facilitate." A truism but helpful nevertheless. He added, "So don't focus on the facility; focus on what you're trying to facilitate. Make sure you have a good rationale for it, can make a solid case for it, can back it up with biblical principles, and can show how it makes perfect sense in the situation in which you find yourselves." This meant an enormous amount of demographic and facility study long before steeples, towers, foyers, seating, washrooms, organs, and drums were mentioned.

I also learned from my friend Hal Brooks down in Texas. He was highly gifted and enormously energetic, and he had led the church he pastored in a large building extension. He functioned as designer, contractor, expediter, fund-raiser, and cheerleader for the project, which was so demanding that he left the church shortly after its completion. Watching Hal, I decided that the pastor should remain in a position to pastor all the opposing forces who will emerge through the process, and that means that while the pastor should be involved in the decision-making and planning process, it is better if he or she is not the lead person. We were blessed with experienced men and women who gladly accepted the enormous burden of overseeing the work, and we successfully completed at least four major building programs, all of which are completely paid for.

During one of the early discussions about buildings, I learned an unexpected but very necessary lesson. The debate was being waged over how large a sanctuary we should build. That would be determined by price and location, planning permission, parking, and a number of other mundane but inevitable factors, so at this time the discussion was mainly philosophical and largely about preferences. Up spoke Burt Keddie, one of the men who had figured largely in our invitation to Elmbrook in the first place. He rarely wasted words, but when he spoke people listened. A man of rare insight and forthright opinion—in addition, I believe he was endued with the spiritual gift of faith, the kind that moves mountains—he said, "It doesn't matter how big you build it. Stuart will fill it—with disgruntled people!" I was too taken aback to parse the statement to determine whether that was a compliment or a criticism. Burt was the kind of friend who would administer both when necessary. So I asked him, in a quiet moment, "What did you mean?"

He said, "It comes down to the fact that you are a wonderful motivator and a hopeless mobiliser. People will come to hear you preach—the bigger the building, the more will come. But if you fire people up but don't give them something to do, they will eventually become disgruntled. So you need to focus not just on preaching, but on putting the people to work. To do that you need to find avenues of service for them." That was some of the wisest, most helpful advice I received in the early years of my ministry in Elmbrook. Of course I knew about the teaching in Ephesians about the saints doing the ministry and the pastor-teacher equipping them, but actually providing things for them to do and getting them to do it were not part of what I did or how I thought. I assumed they would find things to do—and many did—and they would automatically do what they knew—some of them did that too—but by and large, Burt was right! So the motivator began to try his hand at mobilising. It worked.

I think of Fred and Laura Snyder, both professional musicians with the Milwaukee Symphony, who I knew had lots of spare time between rehearsals and concerts. Even though they lived in a small trailer, they agreed to be responsible for duplicating all the messages preached at Elmbrook. We equipped them with about a dozen small tape recorders, which they ingeniously linked to a master tape player in one little corner of their limited space. It was time-consuming and labour intensive, but they did it for years. Because of their efforts, people in the congregation could take message tapes home for additional study or share them with friends. Over time, demand increased to the point that more volunteers had to be mobilised and our basement was commandeered as the new pack-and-ship facility.

Thus began *Telling the Truth*, a media ministry that daily spans the globe, and scores of highly motivated people—particularly retirees—have been mobilised ever since into productive ministry. Without Burt Keddie's initial prodding, it may not have happened; without the Snyders it could not have happened; and without hundreds who followed in their footsteps it would not be happening today. Thirty years later these ministries continue to flourish. "Still glides the stream."

I have seen many dry and parched riverbeds littered with boulders reminiscent of days when rushing waters hurled them along to their resting place. I have walked the shores of former lakes where gaunt skeletal trees reach heavenward like despairing supplicants, relics of the days when rising waters invaded forests and then receded and died. The riverbed is plain to see, the lakeshore is clearly evident. The form remains, but the function has died.

In my native homeland this could be said of numerous churches. The buildings are still there, the steeples rise to the skies, pointing to higher, nobler things, but the doors are closed and the windows are vandalised. Something died.

We tried to pay careful attention to the form—to the structures, the organisations, the methodologies, the strategies, and the systems—of the church. This required change when necessary and adaptation when called for. But we were aware that the focus of church leadership can be so directed to "form" that the "function" of the life-giving Spirit is overlooked. We knew that in imitating "successful" churches that have devised methodology that "works" and techniques that are transferable, we would be in danger of leaning on and trusting in such things at the expense of nurturing a quality of spiritual life and devotion that allows the Spirit of God to do what only he can do. If this were to happen, "success" would become the father of failure.

CHAPTER 12

I CHATTER, CHATTER
AS I FLOW

I chatter, chatter, as I flow
To join the brimming river.

—Alfred Lord Tennyson, "The Brook"

Now that I have arrived at the age where people suspect I am moving rapidly toward my dotage, younger church leaders often ask me for "advice about ministry," usually "in a nutshell." I guess they're so busy that "nutshell advice" has to suffice, and I'm happy to oblige. I tell them, "Preach the Word, love the people, and pray that the Spirit moves."

This tripartite approach to ministry did not appear in the sky in bold, gold letters one bright morning. It was conceived and gestated over the years in my spiritual consciousness as study of the Word, interaction with people, and practical recognition of divine demands and acknowledgment of human insufficiencies made their impact with increasing force.

My recognition of the primacy of *preaching the Word* came first. On arriving at Elmbrook in 1970, I thought I knew a little bit about the subject, but the learning curve was steeper than anticipated. My teachers came from different quarters and arrived at unexpected moments. One such "teachable moment" presented itself at the end of a morning service—zero hour, when a pastor, after delivering his soul on matters of eternal significance, is required in a heartbeat to change a dozen gears. He is called upon to listen to and respond to all and sundry congregants who offer a multitude of more earthbound suggestions than his ethereal thoughts. Complaints, points of agreement and/or disagreement, questions, and words of encouragement follow hard on each other's heels. And always the "preacher portraits" the children draw during the second and third points of the sermon are presented by beaming parents. Everybody takes the chance to "get to the pastor while he's available."

But one woman's question stands out. "When are you going to say something relevant?" she asked at the end, not of a solitary sermon, but of a series of messages preached over a couple of months. Based on the fruit of the Spirit that Paul describes in Galatians 5, the series attempted to explore carefully and meticulously the various characteristics of life in the Spirit. The intense directness of her question took me aback momentarily, so I stammered something like "What exactly did you have in mind?" which is a British way of buying time and regaining equilibrium. So she told me! Precisely.

She said that she came to listen to me every Sunday morning hoping to hear something that would help her during the course of the week, but all I did was talk about the fruit of the Spirit. On inquiry, I discovered that she had a difficult home life, and further questioning showed me where the problem lay.

I asked her, "Is there a lack of love at home?"

"That there is," she replied.

"And a shortage of joy?" I inquired.

"No joy in my home," she responded grimly.

"Are you looking for a little peace?" I asked.

"I'm worried silly," she replied close to tears.

As I worked my way through Paul's famous description of the fruit of the Spirit, I realised that she had made no connection between Paul's teaching to the people in Galatia and the way she was living in Wisconsin. Total disconnect! Perhaps more significantly, I had made no connection for her, so she saw no relevance to my teaching and received no help from my exposition of Scripture. The oft-repeated words of my wife came home with renewed force: "Stuart, you have to make application for the people."

My response had always been, "They are perfectly capable of making application of biblical principles themselves. I don't want to insult their intelligence."

"It's not a matter of intelligence," Jill retorted. "It's a matter of spiritual discernment, and you assume too much." The two women, in different ways, were telling me that the lack of "application" in my preaching was leaving people dangling helplessly over a gap of twenty centuries like parachutists caught in a tree.

In addition to spending time with master preachers like Stephen Olford, John Stott, Alan Redpath, Ian Thomas, and Paul Rees, I had eagerly read many books on preaching by such masters as Charles Haddon Spurgeon and Phillips Brooks. Perhaps the thing that helped me most at that time was a casual remark I overheard a youth worker make to a colleague: "When you teach kids, you need to be aware they will be asking three questions, 'What?' 'So what?' and 'Now what?' So our preparation should enable us to answer those questions." *That*, I thought, *applies!*

"What?" is crucial—what was the text saying? What did the author wish to convey? What timeless truth was there to be learned?

"So what?"—the hump between what Paul told the Galatians and what the Wisconsinites needed to make of it—had to be negotiated. And my listeners would probably need help. It was all about identifying relevance.

"Now what?"—possibly the most neglected part. The takeaway aspect of the message. Presumably the Word of God demands and deserves a response. This should be outlined. At least suggestions if not outright instructions of suitable action should be included. So I consciously factored in these considerations, and my preaching began to take a slightly different course. It was still biblically based—an attempt to give an "exposition of Scripture in its context," as John Stott insists—but I took much more care to identify and illustrate "relevance." And the sermon outlines I prepared for the whole congregation always ended with "Points to ponder," put there in the hope that these points would get a long way past the pondering stage. People noticed the difference, and mercifully it has been quite some time since anyone asked me, "When are you going to say something relevant?" I must admit, however, that a precocious youngster approached me between services one Sunday morning and said, "Good morning, Stuart. Do you have anything significant to say today?" I wonder what the topic of conversation in the car on the way to church had been that morning! *Significance* and *relevance* became important words in my preacher's toolbox.

About that same time, I noted that some of my closest friends in the fellowship who never missed a worship service never made it on time. That, I knew, could be caused by bad management, traffic, or temperamental hair dryers, but the couple in question were very efficient people, and I noted that they were always exactly twenty-five minutes late. I mentioned this to them one day, and they happily replied, "We come for the preaching. We're not interested in the preliminaries!"

Whoa! I thought. *What gives you the idea that the service has two halves? Preliminaries and then the real action?*

It took me all of five minutes to answer my own question: the first part of the services was "thrown together"; the second half was obviously carefully prepared, as the detailed outline available to all clearly indicated. Their perception was that each week we had a few hymns or songs, a prayer, a Scripture reading, and an offering presented by the same people in the same order, and then we got down to business! Repetitive, predictable, disjointed.

Chuck Swindoll had kindly invited me to preach in the church he pastored in California, and while there I had seen Howie Stephenson in action. It was during the era when old-time "song leaders" were morphing into modern "worship leaders." (I asked one old-time song leader, "What's the difference between a song leader and a worship leader?" and he thought for a minute and replied, "Song leaders kept their eyes open!") Back to Howie. He was somewhere in the forefront of the morph. He told me that "predictability in a worship service breeds boredom" and should be avoided. That was food for thought for me. I concluded that if predictability breeds boredom, unpredictability breeds unease. How to avoid both seemed to be an issue deserving attention.

I went home and called together some key people, and we made a list of totally predictable elements of a worship service (we got them from our Bibles). Then we brainstormed four or five different ways of doing all of them. The possibilities of "predictable unpredictability" blossomed before our eyes. How many ways can the congregation pray? How many different people can lead the praying? At what point of the service and from which part of the sanctuary? We explored all of this. Then we turned our attention to the reading of Scripture, to styles of music, to the receiving of offerings, to the place and style of the sermon, and so on until we saw vividly how utterly predictable the services had become. You could tell the time by what was happening each week and who was doing it. That had to be changed. It required work, planning, and prayerful forethought—all the ingredients that had been overlooked. And a little evaluation proved valuable too.

I was delighted when someone told me, "The services now are great. You keep us ever slightly on the front edge of our seats." I hoped that did not mean we were simply being "edgy" or "trendy"—perish the thought. All we wanted was to prepare a setting in which the worshippers were denied an opportunity to settle down to observe and be entertained and were drawn into an exercise that demanded attention, thought, emotional involvement, active participation, and practical outcomes. Ever so slightly on the edge of the pew is exactly where I believe worshippers should be seated.

For a time we even included some drama (Old Testament prophets certainly used it, so we figured it was okay), but with mixed success. I had been introduced to ecclesiastical drama in South Africa. On arrival at Johannesburg after an interminable flight from the States, I was rushed immediately to a youth rally in Pretoria. As I was sitting quietly—partially comatose—on the front row waiting for something to happen, it happened. Suddenly there was a scream, and a huge man dragged a kicking and struggling young woman by the hair into the auditorium. The people froze, and as he drew alongside me, I jumped to my feet like a gallant British gentleman should and grappled with the brute, only to hear him whisper, "It's a drama, let go of me! She's the woman taken in adultery!" I hurriedly resumed my seat while the large man and the unfortunate young woman went their appointed way. But after the experience I was understandably nervous when someone suggested that we should follow Willow Creek Community Church down the path of using drama in church. But follow we did.

One day we transported a huge boulder into the sanctuary on a front-end loader so that when the people gathered for the service, the prominent—and admittedly ominous—rock was the immediate focus of attention. Some people actually came to the front to examine it, including one man who peered up at the ceiling as if to ascertain whether it had made its entrance from the heavens. We ignored the boulder until well into the service when a young man came and sat on it and began to talk aloud about his problems, all the time looking like Rodin's *The Thinker*, except better dressed, of course. He was interrupted by a deep bass voice broadcast over the speaker system. "The voice" engaged him in meaningful conversation. I've forgotten the subject matter, but the people listened intently. The drama group had previously excitedly explained what the skit was about, so I skimmed the script. It seemed relevant, so I agreed to use the dramatic presentation as an introduction to what I wanted to teach. But the transition didn't seem as obvious once it was presented.

On Monday morning at the weekly staff meeting, one of my associate pastors brought up the subject of the drama. He said, "I was surprised to hear 'God' say what he did to the man on the rock."

"That wasn't God," retorted another staff member. "That was the Devil."

"I thought it was his conscience," replied another, while yet another added, "I was sure it was his father!"

And I thought I was the only one who had been confused! We had a problem. If the pastoral staff was confused, I did not want to think about what had happened in the general congregation. So I called our drama team together and told them about the staff's reaction. To my amazement they expressed great satisfaction.

"That's great theatre, Stuart," they exclaimed. "Theatre is all about being provocative. It's designed to make people think. It presents a concept and leaves people to draw their own conclusions."

I was not qualified to say whether or not it was good theatre, and I saw no necessity to decide. It lay well outside my area of expertise and my zone of responsibility. I did know I was not a director of a theatre; I was a pastor of a church. And whatever the merits of provocative theatre might be, I was sure that pastors should not be presenting something that blurred the difference between God, the Devil, conscience, and fatherhood. I had—and have—no doubt there is a rich, bountiful place for the arts in the life of the church, but it is the place of servanthood to the truth, not a position of purveying options or provoking controversy. Unless the arts, like everything else in the church, are carefully managed, they can become masters of the telling rather than tellers of the truth. For when the medium massages the message, mischief can be afoot.

Tennyson's "brook" in its journey admitted it flowed into the shallows at times, and when it did it confessed, "I chatter, chatter as I flow." It's a pleasant, soothing sound, I'll not deny, but it conveys nothing of power, depth, and direction. Film, video, drama, dance, music, literature, image, and parable all rate highly. But they demand time and concentration and skill and finance and practice and can become ends in themselves. Then they chatter, chatter as surely as do thoughtless preaching and regurgitated sermons. If we pastors and preachers drift there, we may forget we are not called to chatter, chatter as we flow. We are called to sound out, to proclaim, to give the certain unmistakable, unequivocal sound of a trumpet call to action. "Preach the Word" is foundational to pastoral ministry.

After preaching the Word, the second foundational principle of my pastoral ministry was *loving the people*. I quickly discovered that this was also something about which I had much to learn.

It is relatively easy to love the people you minister to when you're only among them for a week. They are on their best behaviour, and so are you. So everybody tends to be extremely lovable. In Texas I had met a wizened old preacher named Avery. He was the first — and only — preacher I ever saw who manipulated a toothpick in his mouth, without hands, as he preached. He told me that when he looked over his congregation, they looked like "hootin' owls sittin' on tombstones." With toothpick jutting at an inquisitive angle, he asked me, "How long have you been at the church?" When I answered, he replied, "Oh, you've not been there long enough to make enemies!" Now there was much about this reverend gentleman that I had no desire to emulate, but his words, like his toothpick, were pointed and unavoidable.

I was aware that at first there were some people at Elmbrook who would have preferred that we had stayed in England, but I never thought of them as enemies, and I had no desire to make any. In fact, my idealistic view of the church as the body of Christ left little room for enmity. As I became a little more seasoned, I could see how it could happen, and as I studied 2 Corinthians more carefully, I saw how in Paul's case it really did happen! The passage of time and the accumulation of experience showed me more clearly that unless the pastor and people have a "Spirit-empowered commitment to be primarily concerned with the well-being of the other" — another way of saying "love" — church life in general and pastoring in particular can be fraught with problems. I was fortunate in this regard, as the congregation I served was remarkably loving, forgiving, and open. The kind of pastoral loving I had to learn meant entering more fully into the pain of the people.

Within two days of arriving at the church, I was introduced to a new kind of loving. A young couple had waited for months for my arrival and were very eager to talk to me. Hence the appointment was made before I even arrived in the country. The young man told me his story. On graduating from Wheaton College, he married a young woman in his class and was sent almost immediately to Vietnam. While there she served divorce papers on him. He asked for compassionate leave to return home but was refused, and when he arrived home after completing his service, he found himself divorced. This was his story. I had no reason to disbelieve him, although in my book it was unbelievable.

He had subsequently met the young woman who sat beside him looking at me plaintively. They had fallen in love, and they wanted to marry. They wanted to know if he was biblically free to do so. He placed on my desk a folder about three inches thick filled with articles on the subject and then told me, "We have awaited your arrival because we will take your answer as from the Lord. If you say it is all right, we'll assume God is saying we can go ahead. We've studied all the material. We hope you will too. And we'll await your decision."

You must understand that when I arrived at Elmbrook two days earlier, I had very definite views on the subject, never having studied it in depth and never having sat across a table from someone going through desertion, abandonment, abuse, or a dozen other atrocities associated with "marriage" in its modern manifestation. On the occasions during my traveling ministry that I encountered such problems, I usually replied, "Well, that's a pastoral problem, and you need to talk to a pastor." To use an Americanism I had learned—and perfected—I "punted." Now I was the pastor. And they were talking—and waiting for an answer. Desperately unsure but moved by their obvious hurts and bright-eyed hopes, I decided—as I have subsequently on many occasions—to "err on the side of grace." I married them. Weddings were by and large a joy, funerals and their surrounding circumstances were frequently harrowing experiences. In fact, the first three funerals I conducted were all for people who had taken their own lives. And shortly thereafter I was confronted with another totally unexpected and unwelcome event.

During my first hospital visit, a young mother crippled with arthritis stunned me—there's no other word for it—when she said, "I've been looking forward to meeting you, Stuart. You will bury me. My pain is so unbearable that I'm going to commit suicide when my daughter graduates from high school." Eventually the daughter graduated, and the mother, whom over time I got to know very well, did what she said despite all efforts to thwart her.

Willi Treu, who had shown us extraordinary friendship and commitment in bringing us over to America and helping us settle into our new life, was tragically killed in a blazing crash in his light aircraft. For the first time, I was called upon to bury a dear friend—an emotional experience made even more traumatic by the fact that his elderly parents spoke very little English. I brushed up on my creaking German and conducted some of the service in both languages.

Not long after this, the president of Wheaton College called me one day to tell me that a young student from one of our church families had been killed when he was run over by a train while crossing icy railroad tracks. It was my task to inform the boy's parents. Ironically, I had spent the previous Saturday morning with this earnest, godly young man discussing his future.

We, of course, had no way of knowing that the future we were discussing would be spent almost immediately in unspeakable glory! But for others I was called to serve, their future was nothing short of hellish. For example, the phone rang in the middle of the night and a frantic woman demanded that I go immediately to her home, because her neighbour, a member of Elmbrook, had been attacked and was sheltering in her house. I rushed over and found a young woman barely clad in baby doll pajamas huddled in a corner in a fetal position with half her scalp missing. Her husband, in a drunken rage, had literally dragged her across the room by her hair until it was ripped from her head. Then he threw her out of the house! My pastoral duty, I discovered, included caring for her, confronting him, and dealing with the emergency room attendants and the police.

And on three occasions we at Elmbrook have heard the dreaded news that our missionaries have been martyred. It is the pastor's responsibility—and privilege—to comfort the distraught families and to try to answer the innumerable questions from frightened people who ask, "How could God let this happen? They were our finest people!"

Then there were the endless hours spent hearing stories of broken marriages, family feuds, sibling rivalries, business fraud, wrongful dismissals, addictions, emotional breakdowns, teenage pregnancies, abortions, and miscarriages. John Wesley said that "his heart was strangely warmed" at a pivotal meeting in Aldersgate, London, on May 24, 1738. I can testify that in the early days of my ministry at Elmbrook, "sitting among the people," my heart was "strangely moved." I was learning to love at a new level—a deeper, much deeper, level.

As I was recognising more fully the needs of the people, learning more about loving the people, and recognising more perceptively the relevance of preaching the Word to address the people where they were living, I was being forcefully reminded of the need for gifts of discernment and empowerment. The reality of the spiritual battle we were in had never been so obvious. The total inadequacy of purely human solutions divorced from supernatural intervention had never been so apparent. And the utter imperative of praying that the Spirit would move had never been so clear.

Never had I encountered, genuinely encountered, such pain. Never had I realised so intensely where people really lived. Never had I recognised in such sharply etched detail the awfulness of lostness, hopelessness, and emptiness and seen so vividly the despair and disorientation of heartbreak that the gospel I had preached for years addressed. If I may paraphrase Ezekiel, "I came to the people who lived in Milwaukee, Wisconsin, near Lake Michigan. And there, where they were living, I sat among them ... overwhelmed" (3:15).

It was this sense of being "overwhelmed" that I needed. Years earlier I had been brought up short by the thought that my preaching days might be over — and I had realised that I was perhaps more enamoured with talking about the Lord than I loved the Lord about whom I talked. Now something else was happening. I was been introduced to the pressing need for — in fact, the absolutely imperative necessity of — divine intervention if ministry was to be more than Tennyson's "chatter, chatter."

Gifting was not enough! Practice might make perfect, but it wouldn't address need in its rawest form. Sharpening skills and improving methodology, polishing technique and being innovative and relevant could not effectively counter the presence of evil I was confronting on a daily basis. I was dealing with issues supernaturally conceived and devilishly exacerbated, and only supernatural counteraction would suffice. I needed to put into practice the third foundational principle of my ministry: *Pray that the Spirit moves.*

I freely admit that my prayer life has been deficient and my growth in this area less than stellar. I believe in prayer but don't always do it. I understand that I'm told to pray, but I don't always obey. I am an activist by nature; I am not contemplative by temperament. I am not happy with this state of affairs and have given much thought to what prayer is, what it does, and what I need to be doing about it. Of a few things, however, I am sure; and over the years I have formulated my convictions as follows:

Prayer must be *a declaration of dependence* — a heartfelt cry from a frail human being commissioned to speak in the name of the Almighty and to be the agent of his working among strife-torn people. This agent must be painfully aware of his or her limitations of ability and suitability for such a task and cry out for empowering and enabling that alone will suffice to achieve divine ends.

Prayer must also be *a litany of longing*. The promise of overflowing bless-ing in John 7:37–38 is made to those who are "thirsty"—those who in recognition of their own needs are willing to freely confess them, are eager to address them, and are ready to "Come and drink," to take whatever steps will release the promised provision, because the desire is so strong and the need so pressing. Being thirsty signifies a sense of divine discontent with things as they are, a growing conviction that things could be much closer to what they ought to be, and a willingness to pursue whatever is prescribed.

And finally, prayer must also be *an expression of expectation*—a humble claiming of the immutable promise of blessing made by the Son of God who cannot lie and a settled assurance that the promised Spirit, through whose activity alone the blessing will flow has been given, is resident within and is more than ready to accomplish that for which he has been sent in and through obedient, dependent servants.

This, I am sure, is the kind of praying we need and for which I strive. And in response to this kind of praying, I believe the work will continue to thrive. Thank God that we have many people in our community of faith whose praying is infinitely more effective than mine.

On the relatively rare occasions that Jill and I were able to sit down and take stock of our lives, we sensed that we were growing deeper and stronger, hopefully more sensitive to people, more loving in our response, more aware of our deficiencies, more eager to see our deficiencies redressed, and more anxious that our lives would count for eternity.

Given the chance to live together more than we had previously enjoyed, Jill and I were growing in our relationship too. As I watched her adapt to life in America and saw her embrace her role as pastor's wife—not without its challenges, as she had never belonged to a church until we arrived at Elmbrook—my admiration for her grew. Our experience of mutual encouragement deepened, and the complementarity of our lives and ministries became increasingly obvious. Dr. James Mallory, a Christian psychiatrist and author of the bestselling book *The Kink and I*, was very encouraging after witnessing our maiden voyage into the often turbulent waters of "team teaching." He said, "I've never seen such a classic left brain and right brain on the same platform at the same time. But keep it up. We need this kind of thing!" The terms *right brain* and *left brain* were relatively new at that time—at least to me—so while I was not sure I understood what he meant, I accepted his words as a compliment (a must for pastors) and breathed a silent prayer of thanksgiving that he had not seen us as a classic half-wit and nitwit.

Jill had, over the course of time, developed what she called a "large women's ministry" (I ungallantly asked why she neglected petite women), so she was regularly invited to speak to similar groups around the nation. This afforded me the opportunity to actually stay home and be Dad and Mom in sharp contrast to the years when Jill had played those dual roles in England. When our children were small, I was away so much and felt so clumsy with little ones that my fathering had been somewhat at a distance. But now that they had entered their teenage years with a vengeance, I was in my element and working on the basis "Be firm, be fair, and be fun"—at least that was my theory—and I dived into being more of a dad than I had ever been.

Perhaps the highlights for me in this season were the special times I shared one by one with my three children. When David, our eldest, graduated from high school, my graduation present to him was a trip round the world, in part to allow him to participate in the overseas ministry that was still part of my life. This gave his the chance to see what I had been doing over the years and allowed for some deep bonding that has stood us in good stead ever since. I will never forget his coming to me one night after I had preached to a packed house in the National Theatre in Singapore. With his eyes shining and genuine excitement written all over his face, he said, "Dad, this is great! Now I know what you've been doing all those years you were away!" He approved, and that made my year.

Two years later it was Judy's turn. China had just opened up to the West, and we took a brief break from the ministry itinerary to travel as tourists into the land behind the Great Wall peopled by "inscrutable" millions—as we thought of them and described them in those days. As we left the train station in Canton, we filed through ranks of literally thousands of impassive, silent, staring people all dressed in blue unisex Mao jackets, pants, and hats who undoubtedly wondered about the "big-nosed foreign devils" who were invading their neighbourhoods. They must have been even more perplexed when each morning Judy and I donned our running gear and ran round a tranquil lake near our hotel. The sight of Judy, a tall, slim, long-legged, blue-eyed blond running in shorts was apparently too much for dozens of the locals. They abandoned what they were doing and ran with us chattering, cheering, clapping, and generally behaving in a manner the chairman would probably have found unacceptable. When the ranks of those behind us grew so large that those joining us could not get as close as they wished, they simply formed in front and ran backward to watch our every move—and the carnival spirit intensified as our progress slowed almost to a standstill. The man on the bicycle who lost his concentration on seeing Judy certainly contributed to the festive air as he ran off the road and finished up in a ditch. The downfall of another is apparently funny in any culture—even Mao's unfunny China.

Two more years later, Pete decided he wanted to go to Australia the next time I went Down Under, and we combined that trip with an opportunity he had been given to work for the summer in Hong Kong and then to travel with a team of NBA players throughout China. All these experiences and dozens more solidified our family life and served to crystallise what we had tried to instill in the children from the beginning: "We will serve the Lord." All to this day actively do so. Dave and Pete are pastors, and Judy has taught at Trinity Seminary in Chicago for more than fifteen years.

We have been greatly blessed and encouraged for many years in both family and ministry. However, we have also been challenged by the demands and challenges of being simultaneously ministers, spouses, parents, and grandparents. In fact, wherever we go this is one of the prime issues raised by the people who take seriously their commitment to being disciples of Jesus.

"We belong to two families. The family of God and the family of genes," Ruth Bell Graham once told Jill as they discussed the perennial and daily challenge of balancing family and ministry. My view is that if we use the term *balance* to describe the relationship between family and ministry, we are in danger of setting the two in opposition to each other. According to Webster, balancing requires "estimating the relative force, importance, or value of different things." So the assumption is that family and ministry are fundamentally "different things." I have found it helpful to think of them as mutually complementary aspects of the same thing. If ministry is preaching, teaching, loving, and praying that the Spirit will move, do not all those things figure largely in the family life of the believer? If we see ministry as an extension of what goes on in family, and family as the environment in which ministry is done on a daily basis, then perhaps "blending" rather than "balancing" should be our goal. Involving our children in our ministry when they were young, and involving ourselves in their youth activities was family life for us. Participating in their school activities became an extension of ministry as we met new people and became involved in new families. Now that our children are middle-aged, we are partners with them in their ministries. As our grandchildren move out in life, we have learned the wonders of texting, instant messaging, and emailing to share devotional thoughts with them. We counsel them about girlfriends and boyfriends, and when they can fit us into their busy schedules, we take them with us to the uttermost parts of the earth. Life for us is all about serving, loving, and seeing the Spirit work; and ministry and family are the ideal environments in which these things happen. Thus we are working on blending rather than balancing, and we are having a great time doing it.

Admittedly, we do chatter, chatter as we go. We hope something of substance is heard.

CHAPTER 13

WHEREVER THE RIVER FLOWS

Swarms of living creatures will live wherever the river flows....
Where the river flows everything will live.

—Ezekiel 47:9

In 1977 I wrote and Scripture Press published a small book on the prophecy of Ezekiel titled *All Things Weird and Wonderful.* To my surprise it was reviewed by a seminary professor in a scholarly review of books who said the title was most apt because parts of my treatment of the ancient prophetic book were "wonderful" and other parts were "frankly weird." I instantly liked this guy. My treatment was weird in his eyes because I had used Ezekiel's wonderful vision of the river flowing from the temple as a picture of the Spirit of God flowing out in blessing today from the community of believers that Paul said is "the temple of God" (1 Corinthians 3:16). My new friend and many other believers see the vision as a prediction of life in the millennial kingdom. We will find out who is right one day!

For our purposes, right now, I will retain my original application and tell you about Ezekiel standing on the bank of the river watching what was going on. Obviously, God intended him to be an observer, because he asked him, "Son of man, do you see this?" (Ezekiel 47:6). He most certainly did. In fact, he not only saw it, he experienced it, because on wading into the river, he found at first it came up to his ankles, then his waist, until he was "in over his head" or "out of his depth." Either way, the picture of a mighty torrent boundless in its possibilities is clearly portrayed.

During my thirty years as the senior pastor of Elmbrook Church, I frequently felt that I was standing on the bank of a river of blessing observing what the Spirit was doing through the community of believers. Certainly I waded in regularly, sometimes on the periphery of things, other times more deeply involved, and not infrequently feeling as if I was being swept along by a momentum not of my making, explicable only in terms of the Spirit's activity.

Ezekiel's river was full of fish and flanked by fruit trees, the leaves of which did not wither. Food was in abundance; herbal medicine was readily available. Even saltwater was made fresh, but interestingly the marshy areas were not sweetened, because the people needed salt. Salt for cleansing and healing.

We discovered, as our river was flowing, that healing was necessary—and discovered it in a most unexpected area.

Mel Lawrenz called me when I was in England. At this point in his lengthy career on Elmbrook's staff, Mel, along with another longtime associate, Dick Robinson, had been appointed as my senior associate pastors.

"Stuart," he said, "I've bad news. The police are looking for one of your young associate pastors. He's suspected of inappropriate behaviour with the young people under his care, and he has disappeared."

I caught the first available flight back to the States. On arrival I found Elmbrook in shock, whirling in the midst of vigorous media interest, police investigation, public scrutiny, and of course, congregational confusion and youthful dismay. Then came the news that our young associate's body had been discovered. He had taken his own life. Yet at the core of the congregation there was an air of quiet composure, order, and efficiency. This was directly attributable in my view to the skillful handling of an excruciatingly difficult situation by elders and the pastoral staff led primarily by Dick and Mel. This was undoubtedly their "finest hour," in which they showed their mature, wise leadership capabilities in ministering to the bereaved family, organising congregational prayer, briefing media, cooperating with police, answering parental inquiries, calming traumatised youth, and networking with helpful school counseling authorities. Because much of this activity was well under way when I returned from England, I encouraged my young associates to continue what they were doing. I marveled as I watched them grow and as I stood on the bank and saw the Spirit bring healing in a hundred ways. *"Son of man, do you see this?"* I thought. "Oh yes," I replied.

From the beginning the leadership and congregation of Elmbrook had enthusiastically given me personally and the church for which I was responsible the chance to develop not according to a model or a program, but in an unfettered environment in which individual gifting, vision, passion, and energies (all characteristic evidences of the outflowing work of the Spirit) would be released in possibly unusual, untried, unexpected—and occasionally unwanted—ways. We'd had endless opportunities to see firsthand what Jesus meant when, speaking of the work of the Holy Spirit, he told Nicodemus, "The wind blows wherever it pleases" (John 3:8). Mel, quiet, reserved, witty, and highly intelligent; and Dick, rotund, jovial, philosophical, and passionate about missions and social justice, had been around Elmbrook since college or seminary days. I had seen in them godliness, teachability, team spirit, energy, humour, vision, and a servant spirit. In my view, given freedom and encouragement to develop uniquely, they had all that it takes to cut their own channels and bring a flood of blessing with them. They did—and they still do!

Over the years there have been dozens like them—some with master's degrees or doctorates, and others who served without the benefit of formal theological degrees. Then there were the young guys I invited to work for a few years in youth ministry before they decided if they wanted to spend many years and thousands of dollars in formal theological training for career ministry. I like this approach because I've seen too many graduate from seminaries without any real ministry abilities, and this could have been avoided if they had either done studies before entering and/or, preferably, spent time on a staff before investing in education they would never use. In addition youth ministry doesn't place a premium on Greek and Hebrew but thrives on youthful vigour and acquaintance with youthful thinking and mores, an unending capacity for being let down, and the willingness to wait for years to see lasting fruit. So over the years we have seen many young men and women, including my two sons, Dave and Pete, cut their teeth on youth ministry at Elmbrook before going on to seminary and then on to successful pastorates and missionary leadership. I believe that women, of course, should cut their own channels too—and churches should give them every chance to do so. Without hesitation I endorse the words of grizzly old General William Booth, founder of the Salvation Army, who reputedly said, "Many of my best men were women." There's something specially fragrant about the rivers of blessing that women bring to a pastoral team and a church, not forgetting pastors' wives like Jill, who serves with me now as Elmbrook's minister at large and has been an advocate for and encourager of women in ministry for many years in the United States and around the world. I loved standing on the bank and seeing the fruit grow in all these lives.

Good relations between pastor, elders, and deacons are crucial in all churches and take on unique significance in large churches with multiple staffs. In a small church with a single pastor and a handful of lay leaders, communication need not be a problem—although problems do easily arise unless goodwill is nurtured and insisted upon. But in a larger church with many staff members and a wide variety of ministries, it is neither necessary nor possible for adequate, detailed leadership to be given by people whose major responsibilities lie in their professional careers. At the same time, pastors need proper support and oversight, and it is imperative that amicable, flexible structures of oversight and care be devised for the church and its staff. I found that the key was warm mutual trust between pastors and elders, a clear division of responsibilities and accountability, and regular open communication between elders, pastors, deacons, and congregation.

My own relationship with the pastoral team as it grew along with the burgeoning congregation and church plants was critical. Mel, Dick, and I knew each other well and enjoyed one another's company and recognised and appreciated each other's uniquenesses. While I was responsible for final decisions, we all shared in discussing, praying, and deciding before the final decision was made. Monday morning staff meetings were mandatory and critical to team building and nurturing. I knew from my own experience the importance of ongoing study for pastors, and accordingly we had weekly set readings from a wide variety of books that we discussed together. As the staff grew we took on more people with specialized skills and ministries. I insisted that all of them participate in studies that did not necessarily speak to their specialty and that they all be involved in everyday pastoral activities when called upon—such as marrying, burying, visiting, and counseling. In other words, we were all pastors first and musicians, sports people, counselors, social concerns people, or administrators second. We also prayed in small groups for one another and in a larger group for the church in general. Then we spent time discussing problems, policies, procedures, possibilities—and, of course, people!

Everybody who was invited to join the pastoral team during my tenure as senior pastor had either come through the ranks of the congregation or was well known to me from outside contacts and ministry. This meant that there were very few surprises. I knew pretty well what we were getting, and they knew pretty well what they were getting into. That's how you avoid nasty surprises in what is often called "hiring" and sadly can lead to "firing." I was very aware that Elmbrook took a chance on me and gave me an opportunity to grow into a situation. What they saw in me I never asked and they never said, but I know that nobody, including me, envisaged the possibilities of a flowing stream called Elmbrook when Jill and I, our kids, and golden retriever arrived with two suitcases each to join the "huddled masses." So I was ready and eager to give people a break, to trust them to grow, and to grant them the freedom to make mistakes and learn, which, as far as I know, is the only way people really learn anything anyway. Of course, mistakes should be kept to a minimum and repetition of the same mistake should be strongly discouraged. Mistakes should be made in an environment where maximum damage control is in place, and a safety net should always be in place so that the mistake maker is not totally humiliated while his or her confidence lies smoldering in the ruins.

New staff people were also told their precise area of responsibility. I showed them that my door would always be open to them and my phone off the hook only when someone was talking on it. Likewise, I expected their doors to always be open to me so that they and I could walk in and out of each other's lives and ministry freely and openly for mutual encouragement and help. Colleagues who have gone on to further ministry, when speaking of their time at Elmbrook, tell me they were happy days. As one of them said, "We were never more than fifteen minutes away from a laugh." Not that we were flippant about serving the Lord; we took him very seriously. But we knew that from heaven's perspective there was enough that was ludicrous and comical about our noblest efforts that laughter at our own foibles was perfectly in order. Direction, freedom, encouragement, concern, and love brought together, kept together, and equipped to work together a team through which the Spirit could work. As a result, I was allowed, year after year, to stand on the banks and watch flowing streams cutting their own channels.

Sometimes, I think, too much emphasis is laid on the effectiveness of pastoral leadership in a church at the expense of the lay leadership and the congregational involvement of the fellowship. I wish to redress any imbalance on that score that may have crept into my account. Like Ezekiel's river, a church where the Spirit of God is actively and freely at work will discover that life springs where waters flow. It follows that reproductive life and ministry should be in evidence in a lively church fellowship. I stood on the banks watching this happen, and examples abound.

A young woman who had just come into membership said to me, "All right, I've taken my time becoming a member because I know you expect members to commit to a ministry and I wasn't ready to do that. But now I think I am. So put me to work." That's what a pastor loves to hear. Before I could respond, however, she added, "I don't pour coffee, I can't carry a tune, and I don't change diapers!" Now, in many a church that would mean she was unemployable, because once you've exhausted pouring coffee, singing anthems, and corralling toddlers, what else can the women do in those churches?

I discovered this woman was an accountant by training who practised management consulting.

"Wonderful," I said. "Would you come in and do a thorough study of the pastoral team and show me what we're doing right, what we're doing wrong, and how we can improve?"

She agreed, and we had a win-win situation. Her gifts were mobilised into a fulfilling, valuable ministry, and the church benefited greatly from her willing expertise. A flowing stream emerged.

A young couple approached me after the morning service. Speaking with pronounced Southern accents, they said, "Our parents heard you speak in Carolina some time ago, and when we were transferred to Milwaukee, they said that we must come and visit the church you pastor.

"Put us to work," they said, so we introduced them to senior high ministry. They threw themselves into it, studied in the Study Center, showed great aptitude and enthusiasm for ministry, and generally made themselves indispensable. Two or three years later, the husband joined the pastoral team, completed a master of divinity degree, then planted, and still pastors, a daughter church that in turn has planted a church. He and his wife travel internationally with us, teaching and training pastors in the developing world.

A small card table was erected at the back of the sanctuary when I arrived at Elmbrook in 1970, and a couple of women stood by it selling a very small selection of books. They had seen a need and were trying to meet it, so I immediately got alongside them, loaned them five hundred dollars, and gave them a list of recommended books. We made more space for them in a closet that wasn't used, and our full-time, fully staffed bookstore, the Garden of Readin', was born and established. Thirty-five years later, it annually turns over a million dollars' worth of Christian material, and one of the women went on to become a board member of the influential Christian Booksellers Association.

John Jones, one of nine children born to an African-American couple in Philadelphia, joined the elite 173rd Airborne Brigade and was sent to Vietnam. He said that he wasn't excited about being in the army but decided he would be the best soldier he could be. He volunteered for everything and finished up a paratrooper—a severely wounded paratrooper lying in a hospital bed in Japan for two months before being invalided out of the army with a Purple Heart. He returned immediately to school, completed his studies, and on graduation day was hired by his professor to work in his small electronics company. About that time he was introduced to a group of believers, came to faith, began to attend Elmbrook, and very quickly made himself indispensable. Eventually he was hired as a cameraman by a local network television station. One day he came to me, showed me the mobile TV camera stowed in the trunk of his car, and said, "I'm on call 24/7 for the station to go and film whatever emergency comes up, so I keep my equipment here. I talked to my boss and asked if I could use the camera to shoot in my spare time. He said yes." With his characteristic enthusiasm, John went on, "Stuart, don't you see—we need to do a television program. What you say in church needs to be heard outside the church. We have the media available to do it, and this is state-of-the-art (his favorite expression) equipment. If we buy the film, I can shoot it. Then I can edit it overnight in the station studio, and we can get the Word out!"

Apparently John had not given a lot of thought to the cost of buying airtime. Fortunately, others in congregation, encouraged by Dr. Jim Woods, a surgeon with great medical skills and undying enthusiasm for Christ and his church and those outside it, accepted the challenge. Together we jumped into the flowing stream named John Jones—idea man, artist, tech, and above all, young believer eager to serve. With enthusiasm John worked all day, shot a program in the evening, and edited all night in the deserted TV station studio. Our program was called *In Reality*, and it aired for more than twenty-five years, reaching great numbers of people. John joined our staff, and twenty-five years later, he is still there, working with the eighty volunteers he has trained in audio-visual ministries. His creative videos and DVDs of our teaching are used around the world for instructing small groups, encouraging missionaries, and generally spreading the Word.

Perhaps one of the greatest examples of "the flowing streams cutting their own channels" comes from the unfortunate circumstances of the refugees from Laos who began to find their way to Milwaukee in 1976. Janet Harvey, a young family nurse-practitioner, met a Hmong family in the course of her work. Concerned about their well-being, she went to their home, a very sparsely furnished upper flat on Milwaukee's South Side. They had been in a refugee camp for over a year and had heard about the "wonderful life" in America. But coming to a large city in a foreign land totally unnerved these simple people who knew only subsistence farming, slash and burn agriculture, and ploughing with water buffalo as their forefathers had done for hundreds of years. Their exposure to Western culture was almost nil.

The children, afraid of this American woman, cried and clung to their mother. But the adults were clearly appreciative of Janet's care and concern. They told Janet a harrowing story of being forced to leave their homeland, of their villages being burned, and of the terrifying experience of crossing the mighty Mekong River at night in a small boat under fire.

As more refugees came to Milwaukee, Janet asked her roommate, Kay Bawden, to help her carry the load of caring for them. Janet used her professional skills in advocacy for the refugees with health-care authorities, taking families to the hospital, doctors, clinics, schools, and so on. Kay meanwhile went back to their neighbourhood group and mobilised their forces. They in turn started providing all manner of support, aid, and encouragement—"love," you'd call it—to the latest representatives of the "huddled masses."

Word spread to other small groups from Elmbrook and Elmbrook's first church plant, Eastbrook, and they in turn were mobilised to befriend a family, teach English, train church leaders, teach Sunday school to hundreds of eager children and adults, and pray.

On returning from an overseas tour of ministry one day, I was amazed to find the church's fellowship hall stacked with a huge selection of furniture looking for all the world like a Sears and Roebuck store. On enquiry, I was told breathlessly by a young woman working among the furniture, "It's for our refugee ministry." That was the first I knew about it, but the more I heard, the more excited I became.

Soon Kay had found a school for sale in the neighbourhood where most of the refugees were settling. The elders, led by Dr. Jim Woods and Dick Robinson, got behind the burgeoning ministry and authorised the purchase of the school facility, and Elmbrook's Indo-Chinese Center was established. Kay became Elmbrook's refugee resettlement coordinator. A Hmong church and a Lao congregation were planted, and the Hmong and Lao people were encouraged to share the facility even though their cultures and languages were quite different. While both ethnic groups called Laos home, the former were animistic tribal people from the highlands, and the latter were Buddhist lowlanders. Janet Harvey saw a need, recognized an opportunity, felt a call, and waded in ankle deep. Soon she and dozens of others were in over their heads!

Including John and Shirley Gowdy. They were relative newcomers to Elmbrook who, having gone through a divorce, had been reunited and remarried. During the separation both had come to faith in the Lord Jesus and wanted to reorient their lives on his principles. So John, who had served as vice president of a bank, wanting to make a clean break with his old life, applied for a job at Elmbrook as facilities manager. But on hearing about the refugees, he and Shirley opened their home and took in a family of seven to live with them. The Gowdys knew not one word of Lao. The Laotians knew only *number one*, *okay*, and *cigarette*.

John became increasingly involved with the Indo-Chinese Center and one day told me that he would like to work part-time in the center while continuing his "day job" at Elmbrook. Then he established a cleaning company for the Hmong who needed jobs and asked if we would hire them to clean Elmbrook's facilities, as he explained with great satisfaction, "All your janitorial staff are heading for the mission field." This we did, and all went well until John appeared with another idea. He wanted a month's leave of absence to travel to Laos to see if he could trace family members for worried relatives in Milwaukee. He didn't own a passport and appeared unconcerned or unaware about the restrictions on travel in Laos but set off anyway — after getting a passport. I had grown accustomed to John's regular visits to my office with outlandish ideas that, when he was given permission to pursue them, always seemed to work. He waded in; I watched from the bank.

On arrival in Laos, John found hundreds of Hmong trapped between their country, from which they had escaped and to which they dare not return, and the refugee camps, which they were not allowed to enter. They were living in the forests subsisting on roots and leaves. Returning home, it was clear that John's heart had been broken for these people, and it was no surprise when he asked for a further leave to become an advocate with the United Nations and other nongovernmental organizations for the displaced people. Twenty or more years later, John and Shirley have not come back. These days they spend their time ministering to the oppressed and persecuted peoples of the closed countries of Southeast Asia. The Lao church proliferated literally around the nation. The Hmong church in Milwaukee now has more than a thousand members and has planted churches wherever the Hmong are to be found.

Encouraging the people in the pews to take initiative rather than requiring that everything be directed from the top down is in my view more reflective of church life as it ought to be. At least that is how it appears to be recorded in accounts of the church's early days. It was the ordinary people in the church in Jerusalem who pointed out the problems with the "daily distribution of food" (Acts 6:1). Apparently the apostles had been too busy to notice. When it was drawn to their attention, they addressed the problem promptly and judiciously by handing it right back to the people, who came up with a very good solution. Later, when persecution fell on the same church, the apostles were allowed to remain in Jerusalem, but many of the "ordinary" people fled for their lives. But they did not hide in a corner. In fact, they embarked on initiatives that deeply concerned the leadership—they had not asked for or been given permission—but everything was sorted out, and the church hierarchy recognized a flowing stream in Antioch when they saw one.

In these instances the leaders were leading from behind. In nautical terms they were rear admirals. Not all leadership is "top down" and "up front." There's another kind that takes humility, grace, and wisdom in large doses—wisdom enough to see that all members of the body indwelt by the Spirit have the ability to discern his initiatives when they see them; humility enough to recognise and admit that they may have missed something that others were acute enough to recognise; and grace enough to listen rather than speak, be advised rather than advise, and follow rather than lead. It may be objected that leaders lead—and so they do—but in our case, leadership involvement occasionally came after the fact. Sometimes this took the form of us picking up on an idea that was little more than embryonic and giving it the chance to be born or adding a dash of realism and prudence to a brilliant proposal that was a heady brew of enthusiasm and impatience. What was clear was that the "leaders" and the "followers" were on the same page, they were all active, there was goodwill between them, and the body was functioning like a body because members were discovering and fulfilling their roles in the big drama.

I mentioned earlier that I learned about the refugee ministry on my return from an overseas tour of ministry. Since the church had agreed with me from the beginning that I would continue my overseas work as well as my pastoral responsibilities, it was not unusual for me to be away from Elmbrook and for the work to continue apace during my absence. Sometimes the absence would be brief. For example, one Sunday I preached at Elmbrook multiple times, then caught a plane to Frankfurt, Germany. There I was met early on Monday morning and taken to a nearby Bible school, where I taught during the day before returning to Frankfurt for the overnight flight to Nairobi, Kenya. In Nairobi I taught classes for a few hundred missionaries three times a day from Tuesday through Friday before catching the Friday night flight to Frankfurt and the Saturday morning flight to Chicago to be back in time for the Sunday services at Elmbrook. This was not a regular practice, but at least I proved it could be done!

Occasionally Jill and I were invited to make an extended tour of overseas fields at the invitation of a missions agency in order to learn about their work and bring messages of encouragement to missionaries who rarely had the chance to listen to biblical teaching in their own languages. One such tour took us right across sub-Saharan Africa in the summer of 1979. We started in Liberia, where we worked with missionaries staffing the powerful radio station ELWA, from which we broadcast regularly in those days. This site was later destroyed during the vicious civil war that devastated the nation. From there we were due to visit Ghana, but they had a military coup and the borders were closed, so we were diverted to Ivory Coast—Côte D'Ivoire to the locals. There we ministered to a school full of missionary kids, precious children for whom we had always had a special interest, as they spent long periods separated from their families. The next stop was Ouagadougou, Burkino Faso—yes, there really is a place with that name! There we ministered in cramped quarters to a group of missionaries, all of whom got sick—including Jill and me. On we went to Galmi, Niger, surely one of the most desolate places on earth, where faithful missionaries staff the only hospital in the region and minister to the physical and spiritual needs of large numbers of impoverished people. From there we went down to Nigeria, where we taught in well-established colleges and seminaries, ministered to large groups of missionaries, and had a breather from the dry enervating heat of the desert. Then it was on to Benin. We tried to fly there, but as we were ready to take off, we received a message saying, "Don't try to land, or we'll block the runway with oil drums full of concrete." So choosing discretion over valour, we drove—forever!—across to Sudan, where we were unsure if we would be allowed to enter. We were. And on the banks of the Nile, we watched the "whirling dervishes" and ministered to missionaries of all sorts and shapes, including Egyptologists, Assyriologists, and various other very clever "-ologists." The next stop was Ethiopia, where Marxism ruled and missionaries were watched very carefully. We weren't exactly under house arrest, but some of our number were, and we were all more or less "confined to barracks" but had a great time of ministry nevertheless. Finally, we arrived in Kenya, where at the well-appointed Rift Valley Academy, we not only brought messages of encouragement to missionaries, but also worked among large numbers of lively MKs (missionary kids), whose home away from home we had invaded. To finish off the tour, we were promised time in the famous Masai Mara game park, but extra meetings intervened, so we made a predawn hair-raising, back-breaking dash across the bush to catch the animals waking up, watched them for an hour or two, and rushed back in time for our final meetings.

In our absence Elmbrook thrived. On our return they waited to hear news of what was happening around the world. As time went by, more and more of the people who at first had seen little or no need for "missions" began to recognize—as did the lepers in devastated Samaria, "This is a day of good news and we are keeping it to ourselves" (2 Kings 7:9)—that it wasn't good enough. The people of Elmbrook were lifting up their eyes and looking on the fields—they were white, ready for harvest!

We spent thirty wonderful years serving this buoyant, loving, caring community of faith. Sometimes the waters were smooth and serene; other times they were whipped into a turbulent frenzy. But they never stopped flowing. Sometimes we felt like observers watching the Spirit at work; other times the demands of ministry required us to wade in. Frequently we thought we'd be swept away, but always we could answer the question, "Son of man, have you seen this?" with a resounding affirmative. Yes, we have seen the Spirit move and the waters flow. And we are grateful for the privilege.

PART 3

THE BRIMMING RIVER

On the eastern slopes of the snow- and ice-caked Andes, a thousand streams pour down into the hot and humid valleys where they wind their way through dense forest into the Ucayali River. The Ucayali is one mile wide as it rushes through the Peruvian jungle, yet it is only one of numerous tributaries of the mighty Amazon, thousands of miles distant from the point where the river's freshwater pours with such power and volume into the ocean that the saltwater gives way to freshwater for hundreds of square miles of the Atlantic.

I had seen enough of the Amazonian proportions of the world's needs to recognize that perhaps the time had come for my Ucayali to flow more directly into the affairs of the church worldwide. Or if my life had in any way resembled Tennyson's "brook" so far, perhaps it was time for me more intentionally to "join the brimming river."

CHAPTER 14

TO JOIN THE
BRIMMING RIVER

And out again I curve and flow
To join the brimming river.

—Alfred Lord Tennyson, "The Brook"

My travels had made me painfully aware of the disproportionate distribution of resources between the church of the West and the developing world. Many times I had returned to Elmbrook concerned that we were so resource rich while the brothers and sisters whom I had just left were so relatively impoverished. Not in spirit or in desire, I hasten to insist, but in all the things that we take for granted and on which we lavish so much attention, spend so much money, and come to rely so heavily. Yet it was in so many of those impoverished parts of the world that the church was multiplying rapidly. There was a simplicity and vibrancy to the faith of these believers that always challenged me. I longed to see this faith replicated in the West where more and more the church seemed to be following patterns of predictability and models of management that by comparison left little room for the Spirit of God to work in thrilling and unmistakable, unexpected, unprogrammed ways. Like flowing rivers cutting their own channels! I wanted to bring back home some of the things the church in the developing world was experiencing of which we knew far too little, even as I continued to take to these dear people some of the things that we enjoyed in abundance and that could be beneficial to them in their own unique situations.

Then one day I received a compelling invitation from Dr. Ramesh Richard, a good friend and a professor at Dallas Theological Seminary. He wanted me to attend a conference that his ministry, RREACH, was hosting in Subic Bay in the Philippines during Holy Week—in many churches including Elmbrook, a week full of special activities climaxing in Easter celebrations. This was not a good time for a pastor to be away. I said his invitation was compelling, and so it was—and so I went!

The conference brought together representatives of the Christian church from all over the world—every continent was represented, and every imaginable type of Christian assembly, from Western megachurches to Chinese house churches, had sent delegates. The issue we were required to address was presented by Dr. Richard. He cited U.S. Center for World Mission research concerning the developing world's church leaders. Ninety-five percent of these leaders, that is, approximately two million men and women, have no formal theological training. For many of them none is available, and even if it was, they could not afford it. Furthermore, they could not leave their homes and subsistence farming for three years to take advantage of it. And, he added, it was in many of these areas that the church was growing exponentially but without adequate leadership. As a result, the modern missionary enterprise runs the risk of producing a fast-growing, dysfunctional church. His answer was to suggest that we needed to think of ways of providing informal training for these dear people to whom God had entrusted the well-being of his church. Gradually it dawned on me why Ramesh had been so compelling in his invitation. He knew I had no formal training, and I suspected he had decided that I was a prime candidate to become part of the solution because I would be particularly sensitive to the needs of these church leaders.

I flew back across the Pacific with my head buzzing but had little time to reflect on what I had heard as I plunged straight into multiple Easter services and on Easter Sunday afternoon caught a flight to Europe en route to Zambia in Southern Africa. Way out in the African bush—one of my favorite places—I met with and taught the leaders of a nationwide denomination. But I discovered something that did nothing to alleviate my concerns about disproportionate distribution of resources. Elmbrook had more pastors on staff than the denomination had pastors to lead three hundred churches! And few if any of the Zambian pastors had training up to the level of a bachelor's degree.

From Zambia I traveled to South Africa, where I was to meet Jill. Flying over the parched bush stretching to a horizon hazy from a thousand fires, I remembered the sight encountered by nineteenth-century medical missionary David Livingstone when he arrived in that area—on foot! On seeing the fires of a thousand villages in the distance, Livingstone sensed God's call to reach the people he could not see. I knew that stretching across the vast bush below me were hundreds of villages, many with tiny churches and untrained people trying to lead them, and I experienced something akin to a fresh calling—at seventy years of age! Not specifically to Africa but to the developing world at large to help the leaders of the church to become better equipped for service—informally!

In addition to all this, I was worried about the occupational hazard of a long-term pastorate—staying on too long. I had tried to raise the subject with my elders when I was approaching sixty, but to no avail. They apparently didn't want to address the issue that their pastor was aging and was by no means immortal. Ten years had gone by, and now it was seventy that was the issue. My seventieth birthday coincided with the end of the twentieth century, the conclusion of the second Christian millennium, and the completion of thirty years as Elmbrook's senior pastor. If I had been into horoscopes—which I am not!—I would have seen a convergence of monumental proportions. Being of a more practical turn of mind, I simply thought, *This is a good time to make a change!*

Jill and I shared our thoughts and vision with Dick and Mel and the elders, and we decided I should resign as senior pastor at the end of 2000. The immediate question from all of them was, "What are you going to do?" suggesting that they were all aware of my temperament and my golf game and recognized that I could not survive long on a Florida retirement. I assured them—and later the whole congregation—that I had no plans either to retire or to expire, and it was decided that Mel should assume the role of senior pastor, Dick would continue as senior associate pastor, and Jill and I should be commissioned as ministers at large. The grandiose title—not uncommon in Britain but the cause of American merriment—denoted that we would remain on the pastoral team, travel to minister wherever invited around the world, continue to spearhead the burgeoning *Telling the Truth* media ministries we had started almost thirty years earlier, and when home engage in pastoral work in the church.

Although the United Kingdom was by no one's reckoning part of the developing world, there was no doubt in our minds that the spiritual life of the nation was at low ebb. I was often asked about this, and my response was always, "The church in the United Kingdom is like a forest that has been devastated by a raging fire of liberalism and skepticism, which has consumed much of the undergrowth and many of the trees, leaving a black, barren landscape. But if you wait a few years, you will discover a sheen of green in the blackness—new life in new forms springing out of the ashes." There are numerous illustrations of vigorous new spiritual life appearing in the Isles, but none more so than Premier Radio, based in London and reaching to the far corners of the nation. To the best of my knowledge, there had never been a licensed Christian radio station in the United Kingdom until a group of entrepreneurial leaders, most of whom I knew from earlier days in England, had the audacity to apply for and receive a license and the unheard of possibility of Christian radio in the United Kingdom became reality. *Telling the*

Truth took one of the first broadcast times, and while we are traveling round the world, Jill, Pete, our younger son, and I daily speak to far more people in the United Kingdom by radio than we ever reached when we lived in our homeland. You'll find lots of radio waves in flowing streams.

While in Subic Bay I had bumped into an old friend whom I first met when he was a student in Moody Bible Institute in Chicago. Born in Pucallpa, Peru, where as a boy he became a favorite of missionaries based at Yurina Cocha, a well-known Wycliffe base, Americo Saavedra has grown up to be a key man in the life of the church in South America. He founded a ministry called *Apoyo*—Spanish for "support"—and he asked me if I would be willing to travel with him to various Latin American countries to bring informal training to church leaders. This I gladly agreed to do.

After one such tour of ministry with Americo, I wrote the following on our *Telling the Truth* website (www.tellingthetruth.org):

Our first night in Cuzco we made our way in a taxi that had seen better days up steep streets ill lit and decidedly hazardous to the unwary to what appeared to be a late night market packed with people. We made our way through piles of garbage to a small nondescript building that proclaimed in faded lettering something like "Assemblia de Dios." I was almost decapitated as I entered the low doorway—the Quechua like their Inca forebears are short, stocky people, and they have no need for doors that accommodate six-footers. Rows of hard, empty seats greeted us, and a handful of young people were twanging guitars and banging on a makeshift drum while singing lustily into microphones that seemed excessive given the size of the building. Later I realized the whole worship event was being blasted over speakers to the thronging market outside.

After about an hour's singing, I was asked to speak, and on taking the platform discovered the little church was packed far beyond anything a fire marshal would allow! Some of the audience promptly went to sleep, others listened to the translation with puzzled looks on their faces, and others were obviously in tune with what I was trying to teach. It was the pastor's prayer at the end of the service that made the most impact on Jill and me. He prayed that everybody in the congregation would have enough to eat that week and that none would have to resort to begging!

We invited the pastor and one of his young men to join us for an evening meal in a modest touristy restaurant after the service. And after assuring them that it was okay for them to come inside, they agreed. I noticed them looking furtively at the menu and suggested that they should order anything that took their fancy, which they promptly did, and in no time they packed huge amounts of food into their small brown bodies. These brothers were hungry!

We quizzed them about their lives and ministry. Gavino, the pastor, said that he ministered to about 120 people in the fellowship we had attended that evening, but in addition he was the superintendent of 120 pastors in the region. I asked him about his own theological and pastoral training, and he said it was limited to occasional two- or three-week seminars in Lima and events such as the one we had come to lead. We asked about difficulties he encountered in his ministry, and he listed poverty among the people he was ministering to, discrimination because they are Indians and evangelicals, and occasional stonings and persecution.

I learned a long time ago "If you want something done, ask a busy man," and Gavino was and is a great example of the rule. For it was he who had invested an enormous amount of time and effort in rallying pastors from a large region of the Andes to come for the seminars we were there to teach. In typical Latino fashion, when we started we were a very select number, but by the time we were really under way, other pastors and their wives carrying their bedrolls and few possessions drifted in and took their places on the hard benches of the large Baptist church we were utilizing for the seminar. Whereas we westerners tend to work by the clock and look askance at people who arrive late, these people had come in some instances on rickety buses for days on end, encountering floods and landslides, and it was a marvel to me that they made it at all!

It is sad to see these modern-day descendants of the proud, skilled Incas living in such conditions. But it is wonderful to see that in their poverty and distress so many of them have discovered how to worship the Son rather than the Sun.

These pastors have pitifully few pastoral resources, but we were able to translate and publish one of my books based on Paul's letter to Titus and give them each a copy, to their obvious delight. They were touchingly grateful that we had come to spend a brief time with them, to let them know they are not alone, and to remind them that one day the kingdom will come and all wrongs will be put to right! They believe this, and they work tirelessly to be part of the answer to the crushing needs with which they are surrounded. We came away from the heights of the Andes with our vision expanded and perspectives enlarged.

Soon after the Subic Bay seminar, Jill and I met Diane Thomas. She told us how she and her husband, Bryan, had served as missionaries in the Philippines for a number of years, learned the language, and planted churches there before being asked by their mission to relocate to Russia—Siberia to be exact—and start the ministry there. This they did, learned Russian, and embarked on a ministry of informally training church leaders from various parts of Russia and the former Soviet Union in a school they founded in Krasnodar near the Caucasus. "Would you come and help us teach our church planters in training?" she asked. We gladly agreed.

A year or so later, on arriving in Krasnodar, a pleasant city close to the Black Sea, we found a group of about thirty eager young Russians who had been selected to undergo training in church planting. On Mondays, Wednesdays, and Fridays, they attended classes in the morning and engaged in discussion groups dealing with practical application in the afternoons. On Tuesdays, Thursdays, and Saturdays, each student worked in one of four church plants in the city. Once a year they returned to their home churches with their teachers and shared with church planters there what they had learned. And once a year they returned with a team from partnering churches in the West to teach the same people at home what they had learned since last they met. After a year they were sent to their home areas to multiply themselves. I understood, and liked, the theory of this approach, but it was only when I visited the city of Bryansk on one occasion and the country of Georgia—Stalin's birthplace—on another that I saw firsthand how effective it was in the proliferation of new churches through the ministry of these young people.

Russia and the Russians worked their way into our hearts. They included beautiful and brilliant young interpreters like Katya and Natasha, young men and women suffering from leukemia as a result of the Chernobyl accident, hardy youngsters from Arctic villages, young people who had traveled for days on less than ideal trains across Siberia, and solid, stolid young believers from regions where tensions with Islamic fundamentalists were a daily reality. They were all there ready to be equipped and learning how to equip.

While serving at Capernwray in the '60s, I had been invited to speak to a group of young people in one of the industrial cities that cluster around Manchester in the north of England. The address I was given took me into an area that seemed to be full of derelict factory buildings in a grim, cold town on a dark, wet night. I wandered tentatively into one of them and found an array of beat-up old trucks and a few mattresses, blankets, and seats arranged in a circle that suggested that maybe I had found the right place for a meeting with young people. It was a very strange place indeed. Eventually a wiry young American appeared, thanked me for coming, and rounded up a group of about twenty young people who spoke numerous colourful variations of English. We had our meeting while a small group of children with runny noses ran around us.

After the meeting I enquired about the group. The leader, George Verwer, told me that he had started a ministry called Operation Mobilisation, and the objective was, as the name suggested, to mobilise young people to take the gospel to places that were not easy to reach. When I asked about the trucks, I was told to my amazement that they would be repaired, loaded with Christian literature, and then driven to India.

"India?" I exclaimed.

"India," I was calmly and confidently assured, though I doubted whether they would make it to Manchester.

On arriving home I told Jill about this remarkable young American, his disparate group, and their plans. And I particularly mentioned the young children who looked so cold in the dank warehouse. "Would you pack up and send some warm clothes for the kids?" I asked Jill. She agreed, and the parcel was duly shipped off.

Within a day or two we received a letter from George thanking me for speaking, thanking Jill for the children's clothes, and telling us excitedly that they had sold the clothes and the proceeds had been used to buy books for India. Stuart Briscoe, meet George Verwer!

I soon learned that there was no place on earth too hard to intimidate George, no people too unreached to be beyond his vision, and no task so impossible he would easily abandon it—and apparently no challenge too great to place before himself and his family. For more than forty years, it has been perfectly natural for Jill and me to add Operation Mobilisation and its far-flung ministries to our list of partnerships with whom we travel to help train leaders.

Most places we go around the world, we meet present or former O.M.ers, but one experience with them stands out in our memories. For years O.M. has sent oceangoing vessels into ports large and small, carrying educational books, teams of young Christians, and possibilities for all kinds of ministry. *Logos II*, a 4,804-ton ship with a crew and staff of two hundred young people from forty-five different countries on board was their latest acquisition in 1990 when Jill and I were invited to sail on her "maiden voyage" as an O.M. ship. She had already visited Leningrad, shortly afterward renamed St. Petersburg, and then sailed to Tallinn, the capital city of Estonia, and it was there that we joined her.

In the summer of 1990 the mighty Union of Soviet Socialist Republics and numerous satellite nations across Eastern and Central Europe—such as Romania, Hungary, Poland, and Czechoslovakia, which had come under Soviet control after World War II—were undergoing dramatic change. Many people in the West, when they talked about the U.S.S.R., usually referred to Russia. But the events of 1990 quickly showed that Russia was only part of the U.S.S.R. Far from being a great monolithic nation, the U.S.S.R., as its name clearly explained, was comprised of a large number of republics, and they were demonstrating unmistakably that they were no longer united in spirit—if they ever had been. Nationalistic movements and demands for independence suppressed for decades came to the fore far and wide behind the infamous Iron Curtain.

When we arrived in Estonia, massive protests made it immediately clear that challenging demands were in the air. In fact, two days before *Logos II* sailed into the picturesque port city of Tallinn, the Estonians dared to declare their independence from "Russia." National flags that had remained tucked away in closets for the fifty years of occupation were brought out and proudly displayed from the houses and offices on the narrow, hilly, cobbled streets of the old city. The streets were filled with people experiencing a heady mix of the festivity of a popular uprising and the uncertainty that years of oppression had taught the Estonians was prudent when trying to measure Soviet reaction.

Plans for *Logos II*'s arrival had been placed in the hands of a trio of young people in their twenties, one man and two women from Argentina, Finland, and the United States. It is hard to imagine what they faced when, as the ship's advance party, they arrived in a foreign city and set about dealing with Communist bureaucrats, security officers, harbor authorities, customs and immigration officials, and church and denominational leaders. They worked tirelessly answering questions, allaying suspicions, negotiating berths, purchasing supplies, and handling myriad unexpected issues that would arise before full permission was granted and arrangements were complete.

The effectiveness of their work was evident in the warmth of the reception the ship's crew experienced when the speaker of the Supreme Soviet, in an official welcome address, said, "You and your ship are like messengers of freedom for us." Formalities over the real work began. The book exhibition was opened, and more than thirty-five thousand people flooded in, including some who were unable to purchase books in Leningrad where permission was denied. Incredibly, they traveled nine hours to Tallinn when they heard permission to open the bookstore was granted there. Seminars were held for Christian leaders and church workers, with more than seven thousand in attendance, while aft the "Rock Café" was opened night after night where hundreds of young people congregated to "hang" with friends, listen to music, and engage in earnest questioning about faith in the Lord Jesus. Such was the demand for entrance that young people were limited to stays of half an hour only, and it was heartrending to see them having to leave to make way for others. Other teams went ashore to visit prisons, one that looked like an abandoned building with fourteen- to eighteen-year-olds inside, and two other equally abysmal establishments that held up to a thousand inmates. In these prisons, where only months before men were held captive for their faith, the O.M. teams were invited to go in to proclaim the faith. "The times, they are a changin'."

When it was finally time to sail away, the port and the quay were packed with seven hundred well-wishers. As we cast off and the ship blasted out the deafening signal that she was sailing, I was handed a microphone and invited to give a brief (of necessity!) farewell evangelistic message. Debbie Meroff, the skilled chronicler of the ship's ministries, to whom I am indebted for refreshing my aging memory on many details of the visit, wrote, "Several dozen people responded to the invitation. There were tears both on shore and on board as we realized a number of them were those we had witnessed to at length, and had resisted until this final moment." As we pulled farther away from shore, many young people ran the length of the quay until they ran out of real estate and only the bitterly cold Baltic lay ahead of them, whereupon some intrepid souls leapt into small boats and followed us out to sea as far as they dared. As Jill and I watched the outpouring of love and emotion "on shore and on board," someone whispered in my ear, "When we arrived here there was only a handful to greet us. Now look at the crowd!"

We sailed into the darkening night, and it was decided I should speak to the ship's complement who were not on duty. As I started to teach, the ship began to roll and pitch, and then it seemed to try standing on its bow then its stern, and my audience began one by one to head hastily out of the room while I held on desperately to the podium that was wisely anchored to the deck. Through the portholes on either side of the meeting room, I could see one moment the darkening sky, the next only foaming, threatening rollers. The meeting was summarily abandoned, and I staggered out on deck to watch the pilot boat trying to pull alongside in order to remove the pilot who had steered us unerringly into the wild stormy sea and was now intent on heading for the comfort of home. After a number of unsuccessful attempts and suggestions that he might have to stay on board the *Logos II* for the night, the pilot was able to leap from one heaving, pitching deck to the other and then catch his terrified young son who was traveling with him. They headed for home, and we headed farther out to sea to see how *Logos II*—on her maiden voyage as an O.M. ship—would fare in rough seas. We found out! She weathered the storm, but when we arrived after a long night off Riga, the capital city of Latvia, our destination, we were told that the pilot who needed to board to take us into port may not be able to come aboard because of the weather, and it may be necessary for us to ride out the storm at sea.

Fortunately, the weather abated, the seas calmed enough for the pilot to come aboard, and we made our way into port to be greeted by two young men in their twenties, one from the United Kingdom and the other from the Netherlands—yet another advance party looking very small and lonesome on the deserted docks. Within half an hour of tying up alongside and completing formalities, the trucks that had weathered the storm on deck were swung onto the quay by derricks, teams of young people swarmed aboard, and off they roared to begin outreach in many parts of yet another restive Baltic state eager to hear a message of freedom, hope, and life.

Teams visited hospitals, orphanages, prisons, parks, anywhere where people were gathered. Others came aboard the ship to buy books, attend seminars, and receive prayer and counseling. Volunteers from Leningrad and Tallinn made long journeys to Riga for another day on board. Book sales were so brisk that supplies ran out and the exhibition had to be prematurely closed. All too soon it was time for us to leave the ship for our next engagement, but not before we had a glorious night in the stately, but slightly shopworn opera house. How the advance team did it, I have no idea, but they had not only prevailed upon the authorities to allow the ship's teams to put on an international concert in this historic building, but it was granted rent-free and a meal was provided for all participants equally free.

Moreover, I experienced something in the Riga Opera House that has never been repeated anywhere in the world. After each of my evangelistic talks that concluded the international concerts—one translated into Russian, the other into Latvian, the applause was mingled with enthusiastic shouts of "Bravo," presumably from the opera lovers in the audience. But it must be admitted that to keep me humble, I was admonished by numerous stern Russian believers concerning my beard. I was repeatedly asked why I sported such a hirsute growth—not the exact words in Russian!—and my answer that Jesus had a beard (they did after all pluck the hair from his cheeks) was apparently less than convincing.

Reluctantly, Jill and I left the young people on board with the greatest admiration for them, from the advance team to the professional seamen. The advance team of two worked wonders. They even told me that no one allowed them to pay for anything; even the authorities waived berthing and tug fees and sold them one hundred tonnes of marine diesel fuel at fifteen dollars a tonne and accepted rubles in payment. The professional seamen voluntarily donated time and skills, making it possible for an oceangoing vessel to sail. The dozens of youngsters on board often slept rough, got seasick, ventured onto risk's edge in foreign places, and worked day and night, pushing the limits of their spiritual experience. They showed us unmistakably that while many young people today get—and sometimes deserve—a bad rap, there are hundreds who, given the chance and a challenge, will grab one and rise to the other, show they have character and courage, and if "mobilised," will join the army of those who publish good tidings anywhere on earth. And we will never forget the people of the Baltic states, young and old, who showed by their smiles and their tears, their embraces and their stammered-English requests how greatly they appreciated people who cared about them and their welfare and how desperately they longed for newness of life, which many of them were discovering in Christ.

"Never forget," I suppose, is a recurring theme of my life. It is true that I occasionally go into a room and forget what I went for, I do forget birthdays, and I have been known to forget an appointment. And for a pastor there are few more embarrassing moments than those, such as when you forget a person's name, particularly if it is in the middle of a wedding service! Been there, done that. But there are faces and moments that are so deeply ingrained that it is hard to imagine how they could possibly be forgotten.

I think of the ominously pale, emaciated face of my friend Vlad, a young Russian suffering from serious kidney failure brought on by exposure to radioactivity. He, like many others, had been endangered by the failure of the Soviet authorities to announce the danger and protect the people after a nuclear meltdown. He told me of his need for regular dialysis, of inadequate medical resources, of an interminable wait for a transplant that had already stretched to three or four years, and of how he knew he was running out of time. Despite this he was training to be a church planter. He didn't feel sorry for himself, had no recriminations against a heartless government, and didn't plead or beg for money. Vlad talked quietly to me about his desire to live and love and marry and be a parent. His voice rose as he testified to his quiet conviction that God's will would be done whether in life or death. Determination to make his remaining days count showed in his devotion to study and challenging outreach despite weariness and pain. I laughed out loud in surprise when, in response to my question about how much a transplant would cost, he quoted a ridiculously low figure. I had the amount in pocket at the time. A year or so later, he wrote to ask that as his transplant had still not come through, if it would be all right if he used the money I had given him for dialysis even though it was not given for that purpose. What great integrity this desperately sick young man had despite being raised in a culture where stealing, lying, and cheating are normative and are excused on the basis that the government does it and how else can people survive?

As Vlad expressed deep gratitude for all that he enjoyed in life despite the constant pain and nagging uncertainties, I was deeply moved. I was reminded that the great Victorian preacher Charles Haddon Spurgeon encouraged his Bible school students to spend time at the bedside of the dying. My initial reaction, when I heard this as a young man, was to think that it was a strange suggestion to make to young people preparing for ministry. Now older, sadder, and wiser, having sat at the feet of the Vlads of this world, I agree with Spurgeon, for the sick and the dying have a perspective on life that the healthy seldom gain and a focus on priorities that the distracted rarely achieve. As the sad eyes of Vlad stared at me with a quiet light of deep confidence, I was strengthened in my soul. I'll never forget Vlad.

Nor can I forget a small group of Muslim men I met in Bangladesh almost thirty years ago. They are as fresh in my memory as if I had just drunk Starbuck's coffee with them in my hometown.

Dhaka, the capital city of Bangladesh, like scores of other cities on the Indian subcontinent, is crowded, noisy, and polluted, but out in the villages among the rice paddies where peasants and water buffalo work long hours under an unblinking sun, thigh deep in mud and water, life is much quieter and slower.

It was in one of these villages as I traveled with my daughter that I met Yakob Ali and his friends. Tall, slim, and gaunt, with deep brown eyes set in a face as lean and solemn as an Orthodox icon, he greeted me in traditional fashion. Placing his hands on my biceps and indicating that I should clasp his thin, wiry arms in similar fashion, with his nose practically touching mine, he looked long and earnestly into my eyes as if searching my soul. Then he leaned forward and touched his left cheek stubbly with sparse beard to mine. Drawing back, still holding me, he looked again, expressionless, into my eyes just a little too long for Western comfort, then leaned forward once again and touched right cheek to right. Then he drew back and looked long and deeply before releasing his grip. What he saw I do not know, but he smiled thinly, his stained teeth briefly on display. Apparently satisfied, he indicated I was welcome. I joined him and his friends, similarly clad in long white robes and seated on the hard floor of a small room they apparently used for worship, study, and meditation. So began one of the most fascinating, challenging—and uncomfortable few hours of my life.

The men appeared to be elderly, although my travels have taught me to be careful about guessing age, not least because many people in the developing world live such hard lives that it was not at all unusual to find that men who looked as if they could be my dad were actually younger than me. Through my interpreter I learned that they had studied the teachings of Jesus, whom as Muslims they respected as a prophet born of a virgin, and had concluded that he was more than a prophet. They believed that he was Messiah, Saviour, and Lord, and they had been prepared, in their Muslim village and environs, to say so. Many villagers had believed their testimony, and this had stirred up the wrath of the orthodox leaders of the villages. The little group of men had good reason to believe they would be severely punished if they continued their public witness. They spoke quietly and earnestly about this and invited me and my friend with whom I was traveling to speak to them from the Scriptures.

I looked again into the soulful eyes of these men. Their faces, lined and coarsened by long days spent in the harsh sun, were calm. They were at peace as they discussed possible prosecution for apostasy. I wondered if I would have exhibited such godly equanimity in such circumstances. These humble believers were spiritual giants. Inevitably, I felt diminished in their company. What could my friend and I possibly say to them other than to open the living Word to them and silently pray that the Spirit of God would flow into and from their hearts in power and grace? After long, unhurried discussion and prayer together, we left that simple room, and as I walked into the cool starlit night with the crescent moon shining benignly, I knew once again I had been where the Spirit was working. In a tiny village in one of the remotest impoverished parts of the world, like Barnabas in Antioch, I had seen the grace of God and was glad.

Years later I learned from my friend that the men had indeed been called before an Islamic court and the death penalty for apostasy had been pronounced. As the little group of believers were surrounded by men armed with bamboo poles who were commissioned to carry out the sentence, a mystical "sufi" called out, "Don't touch these men; they are holy and righteous." The villagers agreed, and the imminent execution was delayed. The prosecutor revised his verdict and then, incredibly, asked Jakob to pray with—and for—the crowd before releasing him and his friends! The Spirit was—and is—at work in Bangladesh.

The hard floor of the hut in Bangladesh is not the only one to have left an impression on me. On another occasion I found myself squatting in a similar position of discomfort in a dilapidated building in a rundown quarter of a city on the edge of the Sahara Desert. A friend familiar with the area and the people we were to visit had arranged for us to meet with a sultan who, along with his retinue, had left their traditional oasis far out in the desert during a time of tribal strife. Our jeep bounced along rutted roads devoid of surface other than loose sand and dodged mangy-looking dogs scavenging among the rubbish strewn on the edges of the thoroughfare until we came to a gate guarded by a number of fierce-looking men. They eyed us carefully and asked my friend questions. Apparently satisfied with his answers, they then showed us into a room devoid of furniture save for a well-worn rug on the floor. There, surrounded by about twelve other bearded and turbaned silent men, squatted an ordinary-looking man clad in slightly soiled and worn robes who turned out to be the sultan—a man of considerable standing in the culture of the desert. Greetings were exchanged, tea was served in glasses so hot it was impossible to hold them, and a conversation began. I don't remember details, but as the atmosphere relaxed, I asked the sultan how one became a sultan and whether I could be one. He thought this was funny, and as soon as he laughed, the other men who watched him carefully laughed too. He explained a fascinating ceremony that included the sacrifice of a camel and the ritualistic shedding of blood.

I told the sultan that I represented a community of people who believed in prayer and asked him if he and his people had need for prayer. Immediately he recited a number of issues, mainly related to living conditions, and he clearly showed an interest in prayer. When I told him that people in America would pray for him, he appeared genuinely delighted. Eventually, when it was time to begin our lengthy farewells, the man sitting on the sultan's right, who along with the other men had not uttered a word during the whole conversation, leaned forward, fixed me with a searching gaze, and said, "Tell me exactly what Christians believe."

I learned later that this gentleman was the leading Muslim "holy" man in the sultan's people group who was specially invited to attend for reasons of protocol and prudence. Apparently, as I was regarded as an honoured religious guest, Muslim protocol required the presence of a corresponding religious leader. And on the off chance that the conversation veered into the threatening waters of religion, the sultan wanted him there as a possible counterweight.

I responded by saying, "I believe in God and that there is only one God and that he created the world...." This immediately sparked a response in his eyes. He leaned forward as I went on to talk about Adam, the story of man's fall, the need for redemptive sacrifice, and how Jesus eventually came as the final sacrifice. At this point, I drew an analogy from the shedding of the camel's blood in order to talk about the substitutionary death of Jesus—and his subsequent resurrection, exaltation, and promised return. Our short courtesy call turned into a lengthy visit as we discussed the Christian message, which was precisely what my friend had hoped for in arranging the visit. It is no easy matter to reach the people of the remote reaches of the most desolate regions on earth with the good news.

My friend who arranged this desert visit is a remarkable man who, since resigning a prestigious career in the States, has devoted his life to the people of the desert. He had worked hard behind the scenes prior to my arrival to arrange visits with members of the desert community. He had characterized me as a religious leader in the United States who was visiting the area. I had no idea that he had explored Google, found that my name had received more hits than the president of the country, and had apparently used this information to impress the local dignitaries who were thus willing—perhaps even eager—to welcome me with characteristic Muslim hospitality. As a result, a few days later we visited more leaders of the community, all of whom gladly received pictures of my home church. They were fascinated that seven thousand people attended the services, and they asked questions about this community of people who prayed. They then posed for photos and asked me to send them copies—which I gladly did and which my friend hand-delivered to ensure another personal visit with them.

In totally different circumstances there, we were invited to the home of a wealthy man who was also a leader of a political party challenging the president's party for control of parliament. He arrived in his Mercedes shortly after we arrived, changed immediately from his Western suit to traditional dress, squatted with the group of about twenty men with whom we were gathered, and clapped his hands. Servants promptly served us a magnificent banquet, which we ate sitting on priceless rugs without the benefit or encumbrance of knives and forks. The whole time questions about faith were the main topic of conversation. Reluctantly we said good-bye to this gracious man, never thinking that in less than three months his car would run over a landmine en route to the election headquarters in his hometown in the desert. He was killed on the night of the election because of his faith in a nonexistent democratic process. We now know that he was well aware of the dangers his activities were leading him into, because he had finalized all his affairs, locked the related papers in a briefcase that he entrusted to a friend, kept the key, and given instructions that if he did not return from his electioneering, the lock should be broken and the contents divulged. Perhaps his recognition of impending danger and the uncertainties of life had sharpened his interest in spiritual issues. Maybe that was why he had invited "a religious leader from the West" to eat at his table—or, more accurately, on his floor—and engage in serious spiritual discussions.

The kind of people who, like my friend in the desert, leave their homeland to live in places where the heat, flies, and sand are unbearable, among people who for months or even years remain inscrutable and suspicious, with a view to ministering to their physical, social, and spiritual needs are in my book the salt of the earth. I love them, and I love being with them. It is one of my greatest joys to go to them to encourage and support them and generally strengthen their hands for the task.

Some people tell me they don't like to hear about the "mission field" because it makes them feel guilty. I have no difficulty understanding how that can happen, because my experiences of the "brimming river" of worldwide mission have served to introduce me to men and women who are living lives of radical discipleship that show my lifestyle to be less than stellar. On the other hand, the brimming river has given me a family that reaches every continent—a family of the humble and the mighty, the brilliant and the pedestrian, the wealthy and the excruciatingly impoverished. They all testify to the work of the gracious Spirit in transformation of life. I love hearing, seeing, and recounting the stories of the brimming river, because far from making me hide in guilty shallows, they spur me to enthusiastic plunges into the depths of what the Spirit is doing.

CHAPTER 15

MEN MAY COME AND MEN MAY GO

God buries his workmen but carries on his work.

—Charles Wesley

And out again I curve and flow
To join the brimming river,
For men may come and men may go,
But I go on for ever.

—Alfred Lord Tennyson, "The Brook"

Sitting at my desk writing this morning, I heard two pieces of news that saddened me. I received word that Major Ian Thomas, the British army officer who founded the Capernwray, ministries, had just passed away at the age of ninety-three. And I received a transcript of the final public address of John Stott presented at the Keswick Convention a few days earlier. His health is failing, and he has found it necessary to retire from public ministry. Two great stalwarts of the faith, two men whose ministry made an indelible impression on the lives and ministries of thousands—including me. The world is a poorer place without their voices proclaiming the truth. But as Tennyson said of the "brook," "Men may come and men may go, but I go on for ever." Or perhaps even more appropriately, a commemorative tablet for John and Charles Wesley in Westminster Abbey quotes Charles's saying, "God buries his workmen but carries on his work." There is a timelessness to the work of the Spirit though generations inevitably give way to generations. Men and women may come and go, but what of those who are coming on the scene? I've met them.

My friend Sonny (not his real name) told me his story as we sat down together in the shade of a bamboo shelter, the baking heat assuaged with ice-cold Cokes, the pervasive smell from nearby primitive agriculture moderated if not quite nullified by the fragrance of brilliant tropical blooms. A jovial man in his thirties with a ready grin that regularly and easily lights up his dark face, he is married and has two small children.

His father, a devout Hindu, born into the lowest echelon of Indian society, was a respected leader in his village. He brought up his son strictly, but Sonny's main interests appear to have been playing drums in Hindu festivals and shorting out the electricity supply to the small Christian place of worship in the village. In a rare moment of piety, he shaved his head, made a vow to the goddess Shiva, and asked for help in passing his tenth-grade exams. Shortly afterward he left the village with little interest in furthering whatever Hindu faith he had embraced thus far.

In school Sonny met an old friend who had recently come to faith in Christ and who tried to persuade Sonny to become a Christian too. Sonny responded by orchestrating a gang beating for the young believer. Despite the brutality the friend persisted and persuaded Sonny to read Psalm 115, which talks about the futility of idolatry.

Slowly, over a period of two months, Sonny became convinced and committed his life to Christ. He returned home to tell his father, who responded by slapping him and ordering him to sit outside the house. He gave Sonny three days to reconsider, instructed his wife to give Sonny neither food nor water, and told the villagers to come and persuade the young believer to reject Christ and avoid being disowned. But Sonny stood firm. At the end of three days, he didn't wait to be sent away; he left with nothing but the clothes on his back.

Sonny had no idea where to go, subsisted on rotten bananas begged from fruit stall operators, slept on railway platforms, washed his only clothes in men's toilets while clad in a piece of sacking he found lying on the ground, and eventually found a job that did not pay him for two months. Nevertheless, he survived—all the time eager to find out how he could "know God." Eventually Sonny was befriended by Christians who introduced him to Operation Mobilisation, where he worked and studied. After five years he returned home seeking reconciliation only to be rejected again. But Sonny had been cutting his own channel simply by sharing what he had discovered in Christ.

Living with rejection, Sonny found acceptance in Christ and in the community of faith. Knowing rejection, he understood the desperate circumstances in which the villagers around him were living, so he began to reach out to them with acts of mercy and teaching of God's grace. In a year or two, more than three hundred humble, poverty-stricken people believed, so quite naturally he became their pastor. Soon four more churches were planted from this initial ministry, and in the space of a few years, under the auspices of the "Good Shepherd Community Church" movement in India, Sonny's responsibilities burgeoned into oversight of 160 pastors caring for 240 churches. Eighty percent of the people in these churches are Dalits—formerly known as "Untouchables," some of the most oppressed people in the world. He told me stories of vicious attacks from witch doctors, fatal bites from scorpions, threatened violence from radical Hindus, and through it all the incontrovertible work of the Spirit, like rivers of living water, flowed from this young man's life.

One day I preached in one of the fellowships in which Sonny ministers. The men sat on one side of the room cross-legged on the floor, the women clad in bright-coloured saris on the other. Communion was served, and as we gave thanks for the bread and wine, both men and women leaned forward until their foreheads touched the ground in front of them. They know instinctively that bowing down is the posture of worship. The fragile, thin, emaciated bodies of the women hidden in saris that spilled out on the floor looked like vividly coloured petals of variegated blooms. They had learned about and were remembering the One who for their sake "like a rose trampled on the ground" bled and died for their redemption. As Sonny and I gave them the bread and the wine, I looked into their faces. They were so intent, so thankful, that I could see that they knew that while they too have been trampled on, Christ has raised them up.

I have often heard Western Christians say something to the effect, "Jesus is all I need," but I think it was Mother Teresa who said, "You can only say, 'Jesus is all I need,' when Jesus is all you've got." That may be overstating it somewhat, but the more time I spend with the impoverished of this world and the Sonnys who minister to them, the more convinced I am that they experience depths of spiritual reality to which I, and perhaps many more Westerners like me, am a stranger. When they are sick and no doctors, hospitals, or medical care of any kind is available, they turn to Jesus in ways we seldom do. When famine comes or tsunamis roar or monsoons wash away crops and there is no food in the fridge (in fact, there is no fridge because there is no electricity), they turn to Jesus in ways I have never been called to do. This does not make them any nobler or make you and me any less committed. It simply means that as we are made aware of them, we can learn from them what we may never learn elsewhere, and we can pray and support them with passion and compassion that we may not otherwise exhibit.

In looks, personality, and desire to serve, my friend Pedro reminds me of Sonny. As we waited for a flight in a plane of questionable airworthiness to the Caribbean coast of Nicaragua in the crowded, noisy airport in Managua, he told me his story. Latin American music, which I love, was being played at mega-decibel levels, so at times I had to resort to lipreading, but I got his drift. His father left home when Pedro was five years of age, and his mother left for California a couple of years later. The children were left with an alcoholic grandfather and a loving grandmother who eked out a living bringing in ironing while their mother smuggled in dollars from California as she was able.

The Sandinistas, a leftist group of radicals who with Cuban support had overthrown the government in 1979 and were themselves voted into power in 1984, were ruling the country as Pedro grew up. He told me that as a child he never learned to read and count from books that used fruit, cats, and dogs as illustrations. The only children's books he saw referred to tanks, guns, and bombs to indoctrinate young minds. By the age of ten, he had a leadership position in the Young Communists, and because of his clear soprano voice, he was often asked to sing political songs at various assemblies.

Pedro's evaluation of his formative years was that he and his contemporaries in leadership positions in the party were beyond parental control, anarchic, free to do whatever they wished, and regularly called "spoiled brats of the revolution." This "spoiled brat" knew that at the age of fifteen all kids were required to enlist and at sixteen they were sent to the front where thousands lost their lives. Despite his youth he saw things in the Communist system with which he had the courage to disagree, so he refused to sing for them anymore and was duly threatened and harassed by the authorities. This was to be his dismal future as far as he knew.

But one day, to Pedro's surprise, his mother arrived from California and took him and his siblings to Mexicali. He described in detail how his mother sold her remaining jewelry in order to bribe mysterious men to lead them in the dead of night through the porous border and smuggle them into the United States. The Spanish-speaking population of Southern California made it relatively easy for the young Nicaraguan to fit in, but unfortunately it was the gangs he fit into. Five arrests and a prison sentence followed as he lived out a lifestyle based on the out-of-control behaviours he had learned under the Sandinista regime. However, the court and the prison system allowed him to serve time in a church-based men's home where he not only came to faith, but also grew very rapidly, and his life was so transformed that he became the subdirector.

Because Pedro wanted to continue working in the men's home, he knew he needed to become "legal," so on completing his time, he traveled home to Nicaragua to apply for a visa from the U.S embassy. When asked a routine question, if he had ever been in prison, he knew he could lie and they probably would not check, but he told the truth, knowing full well that ended his hope of gaining legal entrance to the United States. His visa application was turned down.

Taking the setback in stride, Pedro determined that he was needed to serve in his homeland. So he settled down, married, and had three children. Today he is busy pastoring and interpreting and spreading the Word. This young man is "alive in Christ," and the needy land of Nicaragua will flourish as the streams of living water flow through him.

I am often intrigued with the way God works in the lives of people whose circumstances so often are beset with problems. This young man was born in a nation impoverished through earthquakes, hurricanes, political corruption, and violence. With both parents absent, he was raised by grandparents who struggled to make ends meet. He was "educated" under an iniquitous atheistic regime, yet as a boy had insights into what was morally wrong that men far older than he lacked. As a convicted felon, Pedro had grasped the opportunity afforded him in a church-based institution and responded to the message of grace. He had grown so rapidly that latent leadership abilities quickly emerged. Then, as a new believer, he spurned the chance to lie his way into the United States even though he had already lived there for years illegally. I can only interpret these as signs that God had his hand on this young man, and I count it a privilege to call him my friend and brother.

Women, of course, are in the majority in many churches around the world, and while the absence of men must be a cause for concern, the presence of women must be an occasion for celebration. Historically, ever since the days of Jesus, women have been involved in the spread of the gospel, and these days they are caught up in the full flow of the Spirit's activity. They played a major role in the dramatic development of megachurches in Korea and are to be found regularly leading the 5:30 a.m. prayer meetings for which the Korean churches are rightly renowned. In China it was the women—emancipated by Chairman Mao's reforms that unintentionally allowed them to invest their new freedoms, opportunities, and education in traveling and spreading the gospel—who contributed greatly to the phenomenal growth of the church. In India as well, I will never forget seeing groups of lissome, young, sari-clad women barely out of their teens traveling in groups of five or six into Dalit villages and slums, quietly, graciously, and winsomely healing, praying, teaching, and caring—and seeing the gospel take root and flourish in the mire and muck of poverty, oppression, superstition, and disease. "Men may come and men may go," but the women will be right there with them. Or ahead of them!

Take, for instance, Jan Lenz, a quintessential Wisconsin girl. By nature quiet and somewhat shy, this homemaker and mother has made twenty-one bone-jarring journeys into the Sahara Desert. Today Jan goes to 160,000 exiled Muslims who have lived in tents in 125-degree temperatures during the past thirty-two years. Her story begins in her early twenties when Jan and her husband, Bill—a former coastguardsman who had invested his high school years in drugs and alcohol and was a relatively recent convert to Christ—began to reach out to their peers. With a small group of friends, they talked to people about Christ on the sidewalks, started and staffed a "hotline" that people could call to discuss spiritual matters, and eventually built the results of their unorthodox ministry into a thriving church that today numbers more than three thousand people.

Such is the reputation of Christ the Rock Church in Appleton, Wisconsin, that when a local faith-based humanitarian group was unexpectedly asked to host refugee children from the Sahara, they turned to Bill and Jan for help. Incredibly, Jan and another woman responded by setting out for the desert itself, knowing nothing about where they were going or what to expect. They met the heat and the sand. "If you like the beach and don't care about the water, you'll love the desert," Jan cheerfully explains. In the camps they gathered up nine young children who had been assigned to them. They spoke no English, and Jan and her friend spoke no Arabic. Together they set off for the United States without an interpreter.

The journey alone is a better story than most movies! The children who were hosted by church families had no sense of danger and had a fascination with all kinds of electrical and electronic equipment. Anything with a switch, a button, or a key was an irresistible magnet to their prying eyes and itching fingers, and the result was a high-energy, high-octane, often heartrending, sometime hilarious summer. Undaunted, Jan returned to the desert camps, gathered more youngsters, and farmed them out in Wisconsin homes.

As Jan's return visits multiplied, so did her visibility among the elders of the exiled people. Seminars in which Christian leaders and imams discussed spiritual issues from their holy books were arranged, and an English school has been established. Young women are taught of their personal worth, and young adults are taught English and introduced to vistas of life hidden to them in desert exile. Christian concerts are held, and the still desert night air is often filled with the sounds of Jesus praise music, which is captured on cassettes and played constantly and incongruously by Muslim men riding camels or resting in their tents.

Jan has also become an ardent advocate for the forgotten desert people. Her advocacy has taken her three times to make presentations (in the name of Jesus) at the United Nations, the White House, and both houses of Congress. She has spoken with and been hosted by presidents, ambassadors, senators, and diplomats. Quietly and insistently she has told all who will listen about the injustice, the violation of human rights, and the pressing needs of the people who have captured her heart and harnessed her energy. No wonder elders in the desert were heard to remark that "the Christians have done far more to help us than our brother Muslims." This timid yet tough Wisconsin homemaker is cutting her own channel, and a modern-day version of Isaiah's "streams in the desert" (Isaiah 35:6) is flowing for all to see.

As I speak frequently to pastors and other church leaders in situations where matters of church governance are discussed, I am often asked for my views on "women and ministry." I am fully aware that this subject often generates more heat than light, but in an effort to banish some of the former and introduce more of the latter, I have made a simple proposal to the leaders. My suggestion has been that they do not start the discussion where it normally seems to begin — namely, saying "what women cannot do." Instead, I encourage them to ask themselves a more positive series of questions: What, on the basis of their standing in Christ, their experience of the Spirit and his indwelling and gifting, and the example of the women in the New Testament, *can* and *should* women do? If that can be decided, then the second question should be, Are we (usually the male church leaders) allowing them to do it? Then, third, Are they adequately resourced, encouraged, and supported to do what theoretically we agree they can do? My contention is simply this: When women are given their rightful position in church life and ministry, we will see more Jan Lenzes emerge and more rivers flow. If that is true of Jan in Wisconsin, let me tell you about a woman in Peru whom I will call "Mariana."

Mariana is a tiny Quechua Indian woman with weathered skin and tranquil eyes. She wears her thick black hair in a single plait that swings rhythmically as she walks the streets of ancient Cuzco, high in the Andes, selling sweets (candies) to school children and trinkets to the milling crowds of tourists. Mariana attends the seminars for pastors and church leaders that we teach regularly in Latin America — one of the few women among the men. When she speaks, as she does regularly in class, she not only betrays a keen mind and a vital spiritual life, she effortlessly commands the respect of the men. This woman who would pass unnoticed in less crowded places than the packed throngs of Cuzco, while not formally a "pastor," could in my view be said to have earned the titles "bishop" or "impressive woman apostle" more than some who currently bear them.

Born in poverty and raised in deprivation, it was not surprising that when she was introduced as a young adolescent to the Shining Path movement, she threw in her lot with them. This movement, founded by a philosophy professor in 1970, embraced Chairman Mao's radical adaptations of Marxist philosophy with the result that, like so many movements that started out with a view to rectifying wrongs, it finished up violently compounding the wrongs. The adherents were guilty of many atrocities. In Shining Path, Mariana became an advocate for the poor and devoted herself to serving in any capacity she could to alleviate their suffering. Eventually, however, she found herself wanted by the authorities who were coming down with a heavy hand on the movement. They ransacked her humble home and found a Bible that she had been given by a friend and that she had never read. The police nevertheless assumed that she was a Christian and therefore harmless and left her alone. At the same time, some of her Shining Path colleagues disappeared, and others still languish in the jail system.

Mariana had seen enough to recognize that the rebel movement was going wrong, so she made a break from them, much to their displeasure. She also began to read her Bible and eventually found grace and forgiveness, love and purpose in the Lord Jesus. She became an ardent student of the Scriptures, and her life was transformed as she became Christ's devoted follower. Placing herself at the disposal of the Holy Spirit, all her finely developed "revolutionary" energies—you've guessed it!—were transformed into rivers that began to flow in the high plateaus and valleys of the windswept Andes.

Tirelessly traveling any way she can to remote villages, she takes the gospel to the people, encouraging and teaching new believers, organizing small groups of worshipping communities, finding musical instruments and other resources for them, and training the young leaders whose gifts are emerging in the tiny churches. They will never make her a bishop, and I doubt if anyone will ever call her an elder, but titles and status are irrelevant to the Marianas of this world. She will teach and train, encourage by word and deed, and see the Spirit work. She will happily sell her candies on the windswept streets, ride the rickety buses that break down with monotonous regularity, climb the forbidding mountain passes, and keep on keeping on until one day she hears, "Well done, good and faithful servant." I want to be found as faithful.

While the debate on women in leadership continues in the church—and I suspect it will continue until the Lord returns—one thing is inescapable. Whether women are recognized and affirmed as leaders or not, depending on church polity, when a need is obvious and no restrictions are placed before them, all over the world they are taking the lead and meeting the need. Call it what you will—in my book it's leadership!

Consider my friend Lisbeth. I met her along with her Scottish father, her Brazilian mother, and her Swiss husband in Florianopolis on the Atlantic coast of Brazil. She is tall and blond—not what you expect from a Brazilian. She was weary, but the tired lines etched on her face could not hide the quiet intensity in her eyes. At my request she began to talk.

She told me about the smell. Not the pervasive dank, sickly stench from the open sewers. Slum dwellers are used to that. Their olfactory sensitivities appear to be inured to it from birth as their respiratory organs adapt to breathing in the thick smog that lies like a dull yellow blanket over their shantytown. The smell was more penetrating even than the foul, steaming gases that fill the air from mountains of rotting animals and garbage heaped to the sky alongside their homes. Mountains on which during the night hours the people trudge and scrape to find items of "value" that they can salvage and sell. No, it was a different smell—so different the garbage heap dwellers called the police, who were not always their friends, and pointed to a pitiful shack. The door easily yielded to a solid shove, and in the corner of the darkened room huddled two small boys, ages two years and one year, their eyes wide with fright. And on the floor nearby lay the decomposed body of a young woman—presumably their mother. Nobody knew for sure. The mother was nameless; the boys were parentless and homeless. We say of the destitute, "They didn't have a penny to their name." These boys didn't have a penny or a name.

The police took the terrified youngsters to Lisbeth and Balthasar's home—actually to one of three homes they have established for the children of their neighbourhood, those who live on the streets, survive by their wits, drift into crime, and sink inexorably either to prison or an early grave. Unless someone intervenes. Lisbeth and Balthasar are interveners. They went to their church, asked for support, and were told that what they had in mind was not a priority for the congregation at that time. So they opened their home and contacted a judge who, in a matter of days, sent seven homeless children to them. Within a few more days, three more arrived on their doorstep. As I listened I was reminded of the old missionary who advised, "If you have a vision and the board will not support you, bore a hole in the board and do it anyway!" I must hasten to add that I do not advocate that approach, but I do applaud the energy, the conviction, the courage, and the determination of people who are able to press through discouragement, show the way to others who do not or cannot see ahead, and bring about necessary change.

Eventually joined by others whose hearts were touched by the lot of the children, two more homes—not orphanages, I was assured—were opened and staffed. But hordes of kids hung around looking for help, so a "party" was arranged for them—and eighty came. Lisbeth told me, "We wanted to tell them about the love of God, but we knew it would mean nothing to them unless we showed his love to them." Regular Sunday events were arranged, and then parents began to join in. Visits to their homes followed where the young couple learned horror stories about disease, deprivation, destitution, and desperation—all the ills born of and perpetuated by poverty and neglect and a vicious circle of circumstances from which few if any can escape unaided. They found children left alone in squalor while the mother disappeared for the weekend to earn money for the family by engaging in prostitution. They found people, whose ravaged bodies told stories of hunger and malnutrition, suffering from diseases without ever seeing a doctor. In one place they met three children who were alone because their mother was in prison. She had killed her husband and then required the children to bury his body. Everywhere there was endless need and pervasive hopeless darkness.

The Sunday evening gatherings, the bright spot of the dark week for many, were conducted outside until the rains came and then had to be abandoned. Until, that is, a local businessman on hearing of the ministry among the poor built them a simple church. Before walls were erected and floors were in place, the building was crowded. A daycare center was opened, and immediately seventy children began to attend daily from eight to five. The children were taught and directed by ten women from the slums, all of whom found Christ through the ministry. But kids cannot enjoy school with empty stomachs. They needed feeding, but where could food be found for them all? Another businessman, on seeing what was happening, sent a van load of food and promised a regular supply—a promise he has kept.

As the years went by, it was obvious that they could look after the children until they were of school age, but then what could they do—put them out on the street? Obviously not. So they started a school for them in a building financed by people in Switzerland who had heard of the need and were moved to address it. There are now 130 pupils studying, taking cooking classes, learning carpentry, and developing skills they did not know they possessed. And for those still caught in the cycle of poverty, whose lives consist of meager rations, filthy homes, and nightly foraging on garbage mountains, there is at least the thought that they know where in the morning they can find food and a warm shower provided by people who welcome them with a smile, tell them God loves them—and show it!

Years earlier Lisbeth had attended Capernwray on the insistence of her Scottish father. She didn't know where her life was heading, but she knew one thing for certain. Her grandmother had lived a hard life as a widow and a pioneer missionary, and Lisbeth knew she was not going to be a missionary. She did, however, learn at Capernwray that flowing streams cut their own channels, and she committed her life to being what the Lord through his Spirit intended it to be. The Spirit then took over, opened her eyes, broke her heart, filled it afresh with compassion, and unearthed abilities and gifting she had never imagined. The rest is history. Another thing that Lisbeth, and I, learned at Capernwray—"God is more interested in your availability than your ability."

Jesus promised to build his church and insisted that even "the gates of hell" would not and could not stop him. I believe it, and though I, at the tender age of seventy-seven, have more history of which to speak than future on which to speculate, I am confident that the work of the Spirit will continue to flood this world like streams of living water. I have seen the future in the set of the jaw, the intensity in the eyes, the devotion to Jesus, and the love for people in the next generation of believers on every continent. And while there is much in the contemporary church to disturb and even alarm, there is enough positive going on to convince me that I have already met the kind of people whose streams will continue to cut their own channels. Until one day as promised, "the earth will be full of the knowledge of the LORD as the waters cover the sea" (Isaiah 11:9).

CHAPTER 16

STONES FROM THE STREAM

(David) took his staff in his hand, chose five smooth stones from
the stream, put them in the pouch of his shepherd's bag and, with
his sling in his hand, approached the Philistine.

—1 Samuel 17:40

My brother, Bernard, who with my father and me made up a trio of preachers in our family, once remarked to me, "Have you noticed that when Dad preaches he sometimes says 'Finally' and other times 'Lastly'?"

"I have noticed that on occasion," I replied.

"Then you've probably also noticed that when he says 'Finally' he finishes, but when he says 'Lastly' he lasts," he responded with a grin.

I have often recalled my brother's words, and my father's example, when I have realized that it was time to stop talking but I had more things I wanted to say and I "lasted."

Authors are not unlike preachers in this regard, although readers always have the recourse of not finishing the book—one of my vices! However, if by any chance you have persevered thus far in reading my stories, allow me, at the risk of going on a little too long, to share a few concluding thoughts.

"Memoirs," I suppose, are written for different reasons. Some titillate by promising to "tell all." Others seek to "set the record straight," presumably because the author feels that he or she has been misrepresented. Then there are those who have had such a rich experience of worlds unknown to most of us that they feel compelled to introduce others to what they need to know. In my case, I know of no hidden ecclesiastical scandals and would have no desire to disseminate them if I did. I do not feel that I have been publicly misrepresented—or even presented!—and therefore have no need to reset any records. "Why then have you written?" you may legitimately ask, and my reply would be, "I see my stories as examples of what God is doing in the world. True, I have traveled extensively on every continent, including Antartica, and most Americans don't even possess a passport, so I may be instructing them about places they will never see, but that is not my objective. I want to encourage followers of Jesus to see what he is doing through ordinary people and how he is doing it. I hope they will be encouraged, excited, enthralled, and enrolled into his great world-changing cause—the building of his eternal kingdom."

In order for that to happen, my readers, of course, will need to get beyond the specific details and uniquenesses of my stories and dig out the underlying eternal principles that have been illustrated by the stories. Digging them out reminds me of one of my favorite Bible stories.

When David, the youngest son of Jesse, embarrassed his king, his family, and Israel's army by insisting on taking on Goliath when no one else would, the king responded by loading him up with armour too big for him and equipment that he couldn't use. But the boy quickly got rid of the impediments, took his sling and his staff, and hunted around in the riverbed for five smooth stones (Goliath had four brothers!). Then he went into battle "in the name of the LORD Almighty, the God of the armies of Israel" (1 Samuel 17:45). And he won!

So now I would like to spend a little time with you hunting around the riverbed of my flowing streams stories to find five smooth stones, five basic principles, that may prove helpful to all of us who long to see the rivers flow in the days to come.

Smooth stone 1. Stay alert to the fact that young people are able to grasp far more spiritual truth than we assume. They are capable of being moulded in early days into what God wants them to be and to discover gifts and develop aspirations much sooner than we often allow. I learned a long time ago that programs based on entertaining young people with a view to reaching them with the gospel certainly attract a crowd and undoubtedly have been used to introduce many to Christ. On the other hand, ministries that reach young people by teaching them discipleship right from the beginning, while they will not initially attract a crowd, will undoubtedly eventually reach far more people, far more deeply, as the young disciples are mobilised into evangelising their peers. If you reach them by entertaining them, you have to continually upgrade your entertainment to keep them. If you enrich them and employ them—and give them an occasional break to entertain them—in years to come you will find them doing the same thing to succeeding generations. If you entertain them, they will go looking for more "fun things" to do.

Smooth stone 2. Jesus told the woman he spoke with in Samaria that if she drank of the water he would give her, she would never thirst again. In fact, she would experience "a spring of water welling up into eternal life" (John 4:13–14). This was a promise that he would meet her needs at the deepest level. He developed this promise much further when he later talked about "streams of living water" flowing out into the world (John 7:37–38). When we combine these similar passages, we can see that Jesus was saying that he had come not only to "meet people's needs," but to turn the needy whose needs he had met into channels of blessing in their turn—a remarkable work of transformation. All this was predicated on people being "thirsty" and willing and eager to "come to [him] and drink." These basic principles still obtain. They are the foundation on which the basic principle "Flowing streams cut their own channels," which I have tried to illustrate, is founded. Jesus did not stipulate what constituted "thirst," but presumably it refers to a passionate longing to find the resources needed to meet life and its inherent problems, find answers, and live well by discovering satisfaction for the deepest, mysterious longings of the human heart that stubbornly refuse to be satiated by all that is available in the world in which we live. This kind of thirst manifests itself in a thousand ways. Sometimes the thirsty don't even know they are thirsty. Others are well aware of a spiritual emptiness, while still others know there is something missing but have no idea that it is fundamentally spiritual. We have to address these people where they are and then do one thing—lead them to Jesus by introducing them to who Jesus is (eternally), what he has done (historically), what he is doing (contemporaneously), and what he plans to do (finally and irrevocably), and then show them how to live in the conscious enjoyment of his work on the cross for them, the reality of his presence within them, and the certainty of their promised future with him in eternity (constantly)! Sometimes I wonder if we in the church today have not become more proficient as practitioners, diagnosing people's ills and prescribing remedies, than as spiritually skilled and equipped disciples who introduce the thirsty to the living, risen Lord in all his life-transforming power. At all costs, whatever developments and innovations come the way of the church, we must stay on message. His message—all of it.

Smooth stone 3. There is an underlying problem in the church if we major on meeting people's needs without showing that in a real sense needs are met most deeply when outflow results from input. When a well springing up within becomes rivers flowing out, the soul finds its deepest satisfaction. In our commendable eagerness to show how the Lord meets our greatest needs, we may be in danger of presenting our message as if it is an offer that is too good to be true rather than a call to discipleship that is too thrilling to pass up. The result is that we become caught up in the consumerist ethos of the day, scrambling to address the latest fads, whims, and caprices of our target audience rather than steadily and consistently articulating and demonstrating the unchanging truth of the work and ministry of Christ in the world today and the part we are called to play in it. We do this best by noting that the promise of streams flowing is based on those who come to Christ "believing." The word translated "believe" in John 7:38 is a present active participle that means the believing is an ongoing characteristic of the one from whom the streams will flow. But believing is notoriously confusing for many people. For some it is nothing more than a thoughtless nod of the head or an acknowledgment of something unexplored that was lodged on a shelf of the mind in formative years and has gathered dust ever since. For others it is an academic exercise that entails addressing certain data and arriving at a rational conclusion without there necessarily being any change in attitude, decisions, or indeed, life itself—an acknowledgment of a fact that is functionally irrelevant. But the biblical sense of believing as an ongoing factor in a life of blessing means much more. It certainly involves coming to a conclusion about data, but it must include commitment to what the data states—a trusting that the data is true and therefore worthy of trust—and accordingly it will be trusted. More than that, simply believing that what God says is true is basically knowledge. Faith requires us to take another step beyond believing that God can do what he promised to do—expecting that he will indeed bring it to pass. I learned a saying a long time ago: "Blessed is he who expecteth nothing. He shall not be disappointed." We must ensure that we are not producing believers who expect nothing!

Smooth stone 4. The promised overflow of "living water" commensurate with the requisite input of life through communion with Christ is the work of the Holy Spirit, as John carefully and helpfully explains in John 7:39. There is nothing hidden or mysterious about the reception of the Holy Spirit. John tells us that it is those who "believe on" Jesus who receive the Holy Spirit. Sadly, I think we should admit that some segments of the church neglected the Holy Spirit, and in a commendable effort to redress this imbalance, other brothers and sisters addressed the person and work of the Spirit but produced an imbalance in the opposite direction. Tensions and temperatures arose, and divisions resulted, but fortunately, in more recent times, wiser heads have prevailed and a much clearer consensus on the person and work of the Holy Spirit has been forged. Having said that, I still believe that particularly in the Western church the Holy Spirit is too often deprived of his proper standing. Let me illustrate.

People where I live love their Harley-Davidson motorcycles, which is not altogether surprising, since they are built in Milwaukee. I know nothing about such vehicles, but I do know that my friends take great interest in the mechanical workings of their machines and lavish infinite care over the appearance of their expensive toys. I also know that all the oiling and polishing, fine-tuning and decorating are of no avail if they run out of gas. Even the mechanical masterpieces we call Harley-Davidsons are useless without the dynamic to drive them. They need mechanics and dynamics—and so do we! And so does the church. The Holy Spirit provides the dynamic—he *is* the dynamic.

So great is our commitment to the thought patterns of the modern world that assume every effect has a traceable, measurable, and understandable cause, that we assume that if we get the causes right or fix them when they are not right, we can guarantee the effects. So we have seven steps to this and five principles of that. We have five-year plans full of goals and measurable goals and intermediate goals, all of which we believe can be reached if we take the right steps and organise sufficient resources. Then if we can keep the program running smoothly—*presto!*—the kingdom will be built. But what of the mysterious, unmanageable, uncontrollable, unpredictable, irresistible, indefinable, unmistakable work of the Spirit? He is the dynamic factor without whom our latest state-of-the-art, cutting-edge technology and know-how and our most sophisticated management principles are useless to penetrate the closed minds, to open the blind eyes, to demolish the spiritual strongholds, and to work the miracle of regeneration. The Holy Spirit's dynamic working in the hearts of individual believers and the soul of the community of faith must not be lost in the gloss of our sophistication and the polish of our performance. He works as he chooses, not as we plan. If we overlook this, the more likely it is that we will finish with a manmade system of canals and locks rather than a free network of brooks, streams, and rivers flowing into the brimming river of the relentless life-transforming work of the Spirit of God. True, we will be able to keep control, and undoubtedly we can regulate the depth of the water, organise the times when the locks are open and shut, and manage the order in which the boats pass through. But canals don't flow; they stagnate.

Smooth stone 5. The vision of John recorded in Revelation 5:9 tells of the throne of the Lamb being surrounded by people from "every tribe and language and people and nation." This is a fulfillment of the promise to Abraham in Genesis 12:3: "All peoples on earth will be blessed through you." In between these "bookend" statements, there is ample evidence that right from the beginning the church was both local and global—some now call it *glocal*! Call it what you will, there is no doubt that the resource-laden church in the West and the comparatively impoverished church in the developing world are all part of one body, the church of Christ. They belong to each other. Parochialism is a scourge; a worldview is imperative. Both must learn to share and encourage, to instruct and support—the West from their abundant resources while carefully avoiding loading David with Saul's armour; the developing world from their rich store of experience of fundamental spiritual dynamics and brave commitment, which the West all too often lacks. This requires much more than a casual interest in international affairs on the part of many believers. International affairs are happening where our brothers and sisters live—and many die. It demands more than a ten-day mission trip, however worthwhile that may be to the participants. It demands a careful intentional education of individuals and congregations concerning the church not only across the street, but literally around the world. And those who take the trouble to look further afield than their own immediate interests will quickly learn that the Spirit is not limited to the way Westerners "do church." In fact, they will be confronted with incontrovertible evidence that the church around the world is thriving, that opposition is increasing, that tensions are mounting, and that opportunities are burgeoning. And I hope they will hear afresh the call of God to join the brimming river!

As my wife and I still have the rest of our lives to live and we are not planning either to retire or expire, we intend to stay available to Christ and his church worldwide for as long as we can be useful. But now I must go, for as I'm writing, I think I can hear the *tap-tap* of an umbrella on the floor and see a tiny little woman dressed in black striding purposefully in my direction. I think she wants to talk to me about how to reach prostitutes when I'm in my eighties.

I value your thoughts about what you've just read.
Please share them with me. You'll find contact information
in the back of this book.

Share Your Thoughts

With the Author: Your comments will be forwarded to the author when you send them to zauthor@zondervan.com.

With Zondervan: Submit your review of this book by writing to zreview@zondervan.com.

Free Online Resources at
www.zondervan.com/hello

 Zondervan AuthorTracker: Be notified whenever your favorite authors publish new books, go on tour, or post an update about what's happening in their lives.

 Daily Bible Verses and Devotions: Enrich your life with daily Bible verses or devotions that help you start every morning focused on God.

 Free Email Publications: Sign up for newsletters on fiction, Christian living, church ministry, parenting, and more.

 Zondervan Bible Search: Find and compare Bible passages in a variety of translations at www.zondervanbiblesearch.com.

 Other Benefits: Register yourself to receive online benefits like coupons and special offers, or to participate in research.

ZONDERVAN®
.com